PRAISE FOR *THE WATERS* ᴗ

"A remarkable fusion of deep scholarship, engaging insights, and potent practices. This book elegantly navigates the rich waters of ancient Greek spirituality, breathing life into practices that have seemingly long lain dormant, while skillfully maintaining their relevance in our modern world. ... A treasure trove for anyone drawn to the ancient Greek religious practices."

—**MAT AURYN**, international bestselling author of *Psychic Witch*

"Reece stands out as a welcomed fresh voice for seekers searching for understanding in our challenging world. Awakening our divine memory, *The Waters of Mnemosyne* is a thoughtful exploration of ancient religion applied to our modern quest for meaning and connection. Reece guides the reader to develop a stronger relationship between themselves and the divine."

—**ANGELO NASIOS**, author and host of the *Hearth of Hellenism* podcast

"There are few books that weave revelation and research seamlessly, letting them inform each other to create a truly vibrant spirituality. *The Waters of Mnemosyne* is such a book. Rather than dry reconstruction, Gwendolyn gives us a Hellenic religion that is dripping with spirit. ... Reece is uniquely qualified to lay down what will surely be the definitive text for Hellenic-inspired practice for years to come."

—**JASON MILLER**, author of *Consorting with Spirits*

"In her groundbreaking work, Reece doesn't just re-create ancient rituals; she ingeniously reinterprets fundamental concepts for today's Pagan practitioner. With unparalleled clarity, she unveils the intricate terminology and symbolic meanings pivotal to Hellenic polytheism, making it accessible through relatable examples and practical exercises in each chapter."

—**CARA SCHULZ**, author and former journalist for *The Wild Hunt*

"Gwendolyn's passion, wit, insight, and commitment to connecting more people to this stream of culture and practice is a wonder to behold. I have no doubt that this book will be a classic that will inspire current and future generations. *The Waters of Mnemosyne* treats its readers with respect as it challenges and encourages them to become their best selves."

—**IVO DOMINGUEZ, JR.**, author of *Keys to Perception*

"Gwendolyn unites a clear historic and philosophical understanding with her own living magickal experience to offer us a valuable text in remembering and renewing our relationship with the gods of Greece.... The teachings on philosophy, healing, community, fate, cleansing, heroes, virtue, the mysteries, and humanity's relationship with the gods are well worth your time."

—CHRISTOPHER PENCZAK, bestselling author of the Temple of Witchcraft series

"This book is much more than a history text—it is a manual of living practice.... The passion of her dedication to our gods shines through every page.... Even more, she brings to life the ideals my ancient Greek ancestors failed to meet, helping us to imagine new age of Athenian reason and Apollonian harmony for our own times."

—SARA MASTROS, author of *Orphic Hymns Grimoire*, *The Sorcery of Solomon*, and other books

"Gwendolyn Reece presents a thorough and compelling tour of ancient Hellenic culture, philosophy, religion, and magickal practice, and she offers tools to adapt these practices into modern-day magickal work. She is deeply knowledgeable and an excellent teacher, and her love for and deep experience with the subject matter shines through in this excellent must-read."

—ENFYS J. BOOK, author of *Queer Qabala* and *Queer Rites*

THE WATERS OF
MNEMOSYNE

ABOUT THE AUTHOR

Gwendolyn Reece is a high priestess in the Assembly of the Sacred Wheel, leading Theophania Temple in Washington, DC. She is devoted to the Hellenic deities, especially Apollon and Athena. She serves as President of the Sacred Space conference and is a national teacher for the Theosophical Society in America. Visit her at GwendolynReece.net.

THE WATERS OF MNEMOSYNE

ANCIENT GREEK
RELIGION FOR
MODERN
PAGANS

GWENDOLYN REECE

LLEWELLYN
WOODBURY, MINNESOTA

FIRST EDITION
First Printing, 2024

Book design by R. Brasington
Cover design by Shannon McKuhen
Interior illustrations by Llewellyn Art Department
Interior art on page 93 by Napolean Vier, reproduced under the GNU Free Documentation
    License https://www.gnu.org/licenses

Llewellyn Publications is a registered trademark of Llewellyn Worldwide Ltd.

Library of Congress Cataloging-in-Publication Data
Names: Reece, Gwendolyn, author.
Title: The waters of Mnemosyne : ancient Greek religion for modern pagans /
    by Gwendolyn Reece.
Description: First edition. | Woodbury, MN : Llewellyn Publications, a
    Division of Llewellyn Worldwide, Ltd., 2024. | Includes bibliographical
    references and index.
Identifiers: LCCN 2024032023 (print) | LCCN 2024032024 (ebook) | ISBN
    9780738778891 (paperback) | ISBN 9780738778969 (ebook)
Subjects: LCSH: Neopaganism. | Greece—Religion.
Classification: LCC BP605.N46 R443 2024 (print) | LCC BP605.N46 (ebook) |
    DDC 299/.94—dc23/eng/20240814
LC record available at https://lccn.loc.gov/2024032023
LC ebook record available at https://lccn.loc.gov/2024032024

Llewellyn Publications
A Division of Llewellyn Worldwide Ltd.
2143 Wooddale Drive
Woodbury, MN 55125-2989
www.llewellyn.com

Printed in the United States of America

CONTENTS

Exercises, Rites, and Prayers

Rituals and Exercises

Pathworkings and Prayers

THE MNEMOSYNE AFFIRMATION

Re-member who you are.

Re-member what you are.

You are the radiance of the Light Eternal.

You are Beauty beholding the beautiful.

You are the Love that is moved by wonder.

Call your Self back to yourself and re-member.

Strike your own true note and then

Feel all within tune and harmonize.

You are a singer in the Cosmic Song.

Tune yourself and sing.

This healing meditation was a gift from Apollon, the Lord of Light. Mnemosyne, Mother of the Muses, is the goddess of memory, and drinking Her waters restores us to wholeness. Memory has a special place in ancient Greek religion. Each of us, according to Plato, is part of the Source of All, and we can access Truth through a special type of memory. The Mnemosyne affirmation reminds us that our individuated selves are unique expressions of that highest nature and that our work here is holy.

The waters of Mnemosyne protect us from Lethe, the waters of forgetting, which is what makes death so fearful. Many inscriptions convey a formula from the Orphic Mysteries to assist initiates in maintaining continuity of consciousness across the bridges of death and rebirth.[1] I believe; I remember. This is my rendering of the formula the newly dead should say during their transition.

> *I am a child of Earth and starry Heaven*
> *But my race is of Heaven alone.*
> *Give to me the waters of Mnemosyne,*
> *Which are mine to drink by right.*

The power of Mnemosyne's waters can heal us individually and culturally by connecting us to the Divine Realm—bringing more of its Light down. We can recover things we collectively lost and create new alternatives that are in greater alignment with the Divine Ideas.

This book is dedicated to re-membering and rebirthing ancient Greek religion for contemporary practitioners as inspiration for contemporary practitioners within the Modern Pagan movement. The Greek Gods are reaching out, making connections with people today—often felt as curiosity or an internal urging that keeps resurfacing. For some, it may be an old relationship reawakening. For others, it could be a beautiful new contact.

WHY REBIRTH ANCIENT GREEK RELIGION WITHIN MODERN PAGANISM?

Modern Paganism, as a new religious movement, has the potential to help create alternative culture. When I look around, I see an insane society, full of deep soul-sickness. Our society claims to have conquered superstition through reason, yet we are well into an ecological crisis and can't seem to muster the collective will to address it. We have record loneliness and disaffection. The world is full of suffering resulting from human-created systems. We pursue technological advances that might destroy all humanity because we fear if we don't, someone else will beat us to it. Many people lack a sense of purpose. Most tellingly, our society treats living beings as things, reducing our value to our

---

1.   Edmonds, *"Orphic" Gold Tablets and Greek Religion.*

productivity. This suffering is rooted in collective cultural and social decisions. We need to create and embrace different alternatives.

Modern Pagans discovered that the Great Ones we collectively left in the conversion to monotheism remain, waiting to be in relationship with us again. We found that if we stop treating living beings as things and begin to see all life—including the Green World of the plants, the rivers, the mountains, the land itself—as having consciousness and as capable of being in friendly relationships with us, the world becomes enchanted again. Modern Pagans realized we exist on many levels of reality and began taking our full selves seriously. We found that the parts of us that walk in dreams can be trained to walk those lands while waking. In those inner planes, we discovered there are lines of power that were abandoned but still present. All we have to do is plug back into them, and we can bring that power back into the world as an act of healing.

When looking at ancient forms, there will be things we don't want to re-create, but we can rebirth them in new ways, appropriate for now. Nothing living is static. The tyranny of common sense may tell us our current circumstances are "just the way things are," but this illusion obscures a myriad of options. I want to do my part in trying to create healthy alternatives for myself, my beloveds, my community, my society, and for this blessed Earth. I believe many of the Great Ones—the Gods, in Greek, "the Theoi"—want the same. They want to be in relationship with us again and help us realign the way things are with the way things should be if we were living in a healthy way. May this book be of service.

Who Am I?

I make no sense to myself without reincarnation. I don't remember a time in which I didn't love the Greek Gods and when They weren't real to me. This connection does not come out of my blood nor from my upbringing. In the deepest and immortal part of my own nature, I feel the intense love for these beings, especially for Apollon (Apollo), Artemis, and Athena. I believe I carry these relationships with me, no matter what form I wear, and that I hold in my soul certain memories from long ago.

My relationships with the Theoi have continued to evolve, change, and grow—as all living things do. My love spurs me to learn as much as I can, including pursuing advanced degrees and striving to live a pious and philosophical life as a priestess of Apollon and Athena. While I have tremendous regard for the Greeks and their endeavors to revive traditional polytheism, my path and practice are more generally embedded in Modern Paganism and address the needs of the Modern Pagan movement. I am not just a Pagan; I am a witch. I practice magic regularly. Magic is not the same thing as spiritual development. It can aid spiritual evolution—and I try to use it for these purposes as well as for living more fully in the world.

I am engaged in rebirthing rather than reconstructing. Little I do is an exact re-creation of ancient rites. My practice is grounded in history, but I use the past to inform, to inspire, and to tap lines of power and connection rather than striving for historical accuracy. While I have a scholarly background, I am not writing as a scholar studying a dead tradition. I am a theologian, writing theology as part of a living Pagan tradition.

My work and service to the Theoi centers on relationships. Building relationships with the nonhuman and spirit world and the invisible and immortal aspects of our own nature is the root of all religions. The functions of religions are relatively stable, but the forms shift to fulfill those functions in changing and varied contexts. The Theoi want us to be full spiritual adults. We are not peers, since we are not the same, but my relationship with the Theoi is characterized by partnership. There are varying levels of intimacy, just as in human relations—my relationship with Apollon being the most intimate. I understand myself to be apprenticed to Him. I am learning from Him, striving to be like Him, and mediating some of His power into this world. There is a kind of guidance and closeness that differs from my relationships with other Theoi.

Purpose and Structure of This Book

My goal is to give, in a single volume, everything you need to build a rich practice—conceptual knowledge, technique and process, and direct introduction to the Theoi. I hope to inspire you to view the world differently by recovering some important concepts from ancient Greece that inform practice. All major domains of ancient Greek religion are addressed with thoughts about how they are or could be rebirthed now.

Working in Vision

Working in vision—working directly in aspects of reality that are not physical, sometimes called the astral—is an important part of my practice. Many ancient sanctuaries continue to exist there, and beings can be encountered in vision. This is not metaphoric. I have seen results manifest in the physical after beginning in vision. This book will help you navigate—I give initial journeys that are maps, getting you to certain locations on the inner planes. I also encourage you to build on the inner planes. Information provided will help you do this effectively.

Practice Design

While sometimes reconstructing an ancient practice is exactly what is needed, the forms of ancient Greek religion are often not appropriate, practical, or meaningful in our current circumstances. Still, using something from the ancient setting or rediscovered on the inner planes will make the work powerful while fulfilling the necessary religious function. Many practices given in this book are designed this way—to be relevant and functional in our context.

Instructions

Work through this book in order. Later chapters assume knowledge provided earlier. Exercises are clearly marked. Pathworkings are guided journeys in the inner planes that will safely take you to locations and introduce you to divine contacts, including the Theoi. Record yourself reading these pathworkings. Listen to them in a quiet place where you will be undisturbed and shift your focus into the aspect of yourself that walks in dream. Once you have used the pathworkings enough to know your way, you can go on your own and have unscripted experiences.

All experiential activities are intended to give you a launchpad to develop your own practices. There are prayers, rituals, spells, and instructions, but real religion is always growing and changing. Once you are well grounded, I hope you use your developing knowledge and contacts to create novel practices that work for you and your community.

CHAPTER ONE
FUNDAMENTALS

This chapter provides foundational information to deepen your understanding of later chapters. Included is a spatial and chronological introduction to ancient Greece and a discussion about information sources. Fundamental concepts that are crucial to an ancient Greek worldview and enrich the perspectives of contemporary practitioners are examined. The exercises will assist you in incorporating the concepts into your thinking.

THE GREEK WORLD: SPACE AND TIME

If you ever have the opportunity to visit Greece, I urge you to seize it. As an American—descended from uprooted and mobile ancestors—prior to my first visit, my perception of Greek mythology was abstract and romantic. What a joyful shock to discover the myths' immediacy when you find yourself standing in Lerna, where Herakles killed the Hydra! Or sitting beside a palm tree in Delos in the exact spot where Leto gave birth to Apollon! Everything from myth is suddenly hyperlocal and immediately present. This experience of immediacy and hyperlocality was soul-healing.

Below the threshold of consciousness, all living beings and cultures are shaped by their landscape. Greece is geologically very new. When dinosaurs roamed the Earth, it was under the Tethys Sea. The entire region is a clash of tectonic plates, pushing up mountain after mountain

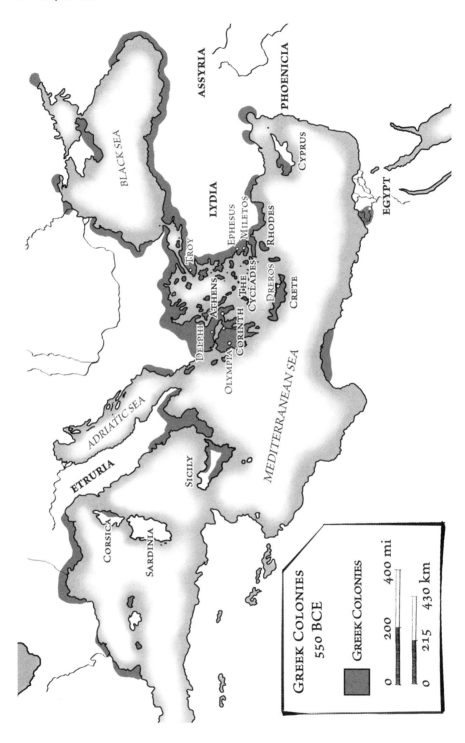

ASSYRIA

PHOENICIA

CYPRUS

BLACK SEA

LYDIA

EGYPT

EPHESUS

MILETOS

TROY

RHODES

ATHENS

DREROS

THE
CYCLADES

CRETE

DELPHI

CORINTH

OLYMPIA

MEDITERRANEAN SEA

ADRIATIC SEA

ETRURIA

SICILY

CORSICA

SARDINIA

GREEK COLONIES
550 BCE

GREEK COLONIES

0   200   400 mi

0   215   430 km

that rise out of the water. To this day, Poseidon, the earthshaker, remains exceptionally active. In the middle of the Cycladic islands in the Aegean Sea is the Ring of Fire, with active volcanoes bringing both periodic destruction and their blessed gift, obsidian—strong enough to cut stone. Obsidian enabled amazing art, technology, and trade all the way back to Neolithic times.

Greece is one of the most mountainous countries in Europe. It may not look large on a map, but its actual surface is greater than it appears since so much is vertical. Olive trees, which can bear fruit for up to two thousand years, thrive everywhere. While there are some fertile planes that are lush and productive, easily cultivated land is limited. From early days, family planning and a low birthrate were essential because the land could only support a limited population. Ancient Greek families concentrated their resources into fewer children.[2] The universal acceptance and even expectation of same-sex sexual behavior was likely related to the moral and practical emphasis on population control. Even with careful family planning, periodically the population would expand beyond what the landscape could support. When that happened, the *polis* (community) would launch an expedition and found a colony. Greeks have been master seafarers since prehistoric times, which is understandable given Greek geography.[3]

There are about 6,000 islands in Greece, which are the tops of undersea mountains. Only 227 are currently inhabited.[4] Between the islands and the mainland, Greece has 13,676 kilometers of coastline.[5] In early days, one could island-hop from one to the next without losing sight of land for long, if at all.

The Greek world was much larger than what we currently think of as Greece. In addition to modern Greece, it included virtually all of western Turkey (Ionia) and parts of Italy, especially Sicily. Scattered Greek colonies ranged all over parts of Africa, Asia, and both Western and Eastern Europe as far as France and all over the Black Sea. Once formed, a colony was independent from its city of origin. Most of the colonies were embedded within non-Greek areas where they lived with and intermarried with their neighbors. As a result, Greek identity was largely rooted in language and certain aspects of culture.

---

2. Feen, "Keeping the Balance," 447–58.
3. Feen, "Keeping the Balance," 447–58.
4. National Greek Tourism Organisation, "Islands."
5. Central Intelligence Agency, "Greece."

When Alexander the Great embarked upon his campaigns in 334 BCE, the Greek world became the Hellenistic world. He was striving to create the *cosmopolis*, embodying the idea we are not just citizens of a particular nation but rather of the cosmos as a whole, and we should bring together what is best in all cultures. The Hellenistic world was one of the greatest cultural mashups of history and included large parts of Europe, all of the Near and Middle East, large sections of northern Africa (including Egypt), sections of Afghanistan, and, for a while, parts of northern India.

When the Greek world came under Roman rule—Rome itself having begun as a colony of another Greek colony (Troy) according to its foundation myths—the Romans maintained many cultural patterns from the Hellenistic world. They continued to use the Greek language for philosophical and intellectual endeavors. When the ancient Pagan world fell to Christianity, the term used by Christians for those who maintained their pre-Christian religion was *Hellene*. They were called Greek, regardless of their actual ethnicity.[6]

Our knowledge of ancient Greece extends into prehistory. There are prehistoric sites on Crete, the mainland, and the Cycladic islands—distinct cultures developing in each. In historical times, the Minoan culture, based on the island of Crete, arose around 2700 BCE. The Mycenean culture, which was partly contemporaneous with the Minoan, was prominent on the mainland and eventually conquered Crete.[7] Both Minoan and Mycenean cultures had written language, and scholars have verified that Mycenean writing, called Linear B, is a form of Greek. The names of almost all the major Gods of Greece are found in Linear B, attesting to their archaic origin.[8]

Mycenean culture vanished suddenly around 1050 BCE and the Greek world entered a dark age. They even forgot how to write.[9] In Greek mythology, the disastrously long war with Troy and all the devastating "homecoming" stories in which hero after hero returned home to experience tragedy is set in the Mycenean world's final days and gives a good picture of what the people believed and how they lived. Archaeologists studying the ruins of Troy have

---

6. Alexiou, *Ritual Lament in Greek Tradition*.
7. Alexiou, *Ritual Lament in Greek Tradition*.
8. Graf, *Apollo*.
9. Morris and Powell, *Greeks*.

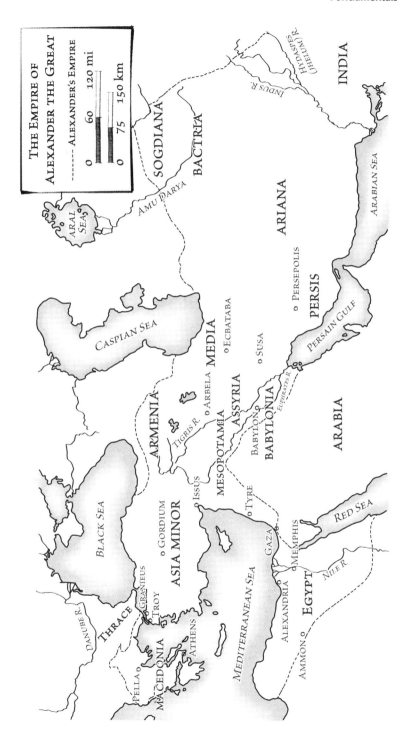

THE EMPIRE OF
ALEXANDER THE GREAT

----- ALEXANDER'S EMPIRE

0   60   120 mi

0   75   150 km

ARAL
SEA

AMU DARYA

SOGDIANA

BACTRIA

INDUS R.

HYDASPES
(JHELUM) R.

INDIA

ARIANA

ARABIAN SEA

CASPIAN SEA

MEDIA

ECBATABA

SUSA

PERSIS

PERSEPOLIS

PERSAIN GULF

ARMENIA

ARBELA

ASSYRIA

MESOPOTAMIA

TIGRIS R.

BABYLONIA

BABYLON

EUPHRATES R.

ARABIA

BLACK SEA

ISSUS

GORDIUM

ASIA MINOR

TYRE

MEDITERRANEAN SEA

GAZA

MEMPHIS

RED SEA

DANUBE R.

THRACE

GRANICUS

TROY

GRANIEUS

ATHENS

PELLA

MACEDONIA

ALEXANDRIA

EGYPT

AMMON

NILE R.

dated a great war from about the same time as the collapse of Mycenean culture. The mythology of Homer was rooted in this history.

During the dark ages, the stories continued to be told until writing was reinvented using a modified alphabet from Phoenicia. Our earliest extant writings qualifying as literature are the epics of Homer and the writings of Hesiod, both from the eighth century BCE. From that point on, ancient Greece is a literate culture, persisting until violently disrupted by the Christians. From 381 to 395 CE, under Theodosius, the Christian Church waged war against the Pagans, forcibly closing and often destroying temples, persecuting priests, and making it illegal to even practice personal piety.[10] Justinian I delivered the final death blow to Paganism in the ancient Greek world, forcing the last philosophical schools to close in 529 CE.[11]

CHRONOLOGY OF ANCIENT GREECE

Neolithic Greece	11,000 – 2700 BCE
Minoan Civilization	2700 – 1050 BCE (from approximately 1450 to 1050 under Mycenean rule)
Mycenean Civilization	1750 – 1050 BCE
Greek Dark Ages	1050 – 750 BCE
Archaic Greece	750 – 480 BCE
Classical Greece	480 – 323 BCE (Death of Alexander the Great)
Hellenistic Age	323 BCE – 31 BCE (Battle of Actium)

10.   Lipsey, *Have You Been to Delphi?*
11.   Edmonds, *Drawing Down the Moon.*

Chronology of Ancient Greece

Roman Empire	31 BCE – 330 CE (Movement of the capital from Rome to Constantinople by Constantine)
Christian ascendency	529 CE the last Pagan philosophical school is closed.

Beginning with the Minoan and Mycenean cultures, the timespan of what we know as ancient Greece is longer than the time from the fall of ancient Greek Paganism to now. In that expanse of time, ancient Greek religion developed and changed. No singular point in time is the "true" moment of ancient Greek culture. Nothing living is static. Therefore, we should feel no hesitation in designing our practice for our current context. We are a living tradition.

Ancient Hellenic culture can give us relevant and interesting models for a global society. Because ancient Greece sent out colonies that were embedded in the midst of other people, they developed an understanding that someone could be culturally Greek if they spoke a Greek language. In most contexts, cultural identity shifted from blood into something that could be learned. This paved the way for the ideal of the *cosmopolis*—the ideal that embraces the abundance of diversity but stands on a foundation of the Rule of Law, the ideal of friendship, and emphasizing the duty we have as citizens of the world. The Greek Gods were worshipped by many people who had no Greek blood, and the Greeks adopted many gods that came from elsewhere. Additionally, the Jews, who did not worship any god but their own, were welcomed and incorporated into Greek society. Any attempt to use ancient Greek (or Roman) society to justify white supremacy is utterly noxious and ahistorical. The concept of "white people" was created about a thousand years after the fall of Paganism and does not map at all onto ancient concepts.

Furthermore, these models can inspire us to look more deeply into our own landscapes and connect with them in a sacred way, even if we are mobile. The Greeks were always connected to the spirits of the waters, the rivers, and the land no matter where they roamed.

Exercise
THREE-MINUTE PAPER ON YOUR LANDSCAPE

This exercise will help you uncover ways your landscape impacts your consciousness.

What You'll Need

Paper/journal, a pen, and a timer.

Directions

Set a timer for three minutes. Write stream of consciousness, answering the question: How does your landscape shape the way you experience reality?

SOURCES OF INFORMATION

Ancient Greece was literate and, although we have lost a great deal, we have literature, histories, philosophical texts, biographies, records of oracular utterances, and letters. Through inscriptions we have state records, hymns and musical notation, and all sorts of fascinating information, like the salary of the Priestess of Athena Nike in Athens. Art and archaeological evidence abound. We have historical texts from other contemporary cultures.

While I hope you will be inspired to study more, I want to give a few warnings. Be wary of the lenses of later scholars. I read many authors, especially nineteenth- and early twentieth-century scholars, who bring significant bias to their study and read their own values backward into the ancient world, sometimes relying on polemical Christian sources.

For example, these prurient intellectuals had a fascination with the Pythia of Delphi, whom they sexualized and discounted as a frenzied young woman, writhing in ecstasy and spewing nonsense that the intelligent male priests then gave meaning.[12] This interpretation distanced them from the idea that there might be anything real happening in oracular possession that would conflict with their (usually) Protestant scientific worldview and placed all the power in the hands of the male priests—reducing the female to a subservient, irrational, and sexual role. This is factually wrong.

---

12.   Graf, *Apollo*.

The Pythias were past the age of menopause, spoke clearly, and were known for their modesty, piety, and firmness of mind and character. We have this on such good authority as Plutarch, who was not only a respected philosopher but also the High Priest of Delphi. He wrote essays about how the oracle functioned. Plutarch told a story that one time the omen that tested if it was safe for the Pythia to prophesy said the ritual should be cancelled—but the omen was ignored. During that one occasion, the Pythia went into a frenzy—a sign that everything was going wrong.[13] Plutarch told that story as a warning not to disobey Apollon's omens, but it was taken out of context by later scholars.[14]

Another challenge relates to taking normative (the way things "should be") statements from ancient texts as descriptions of the way things actually were. For example, the idea that Athenian women were confined to the household is largely rooted in a reading of Xenophon's *Oeconomicus* that takes his statement to that effect literally.[15] I argue he was offering an upper-class ideal rather than describing lived reality.

Let me be clear. If you could transport me back in time, I would not want to live as a woman in ancient Greece. I would find it oppressive and restrictive. I certainly wouldn't want to live as a slave woman. I believe there is tremendous wisdom worth recovering and I believe the Gods are real, but I am not interested in re-creating social forms.

Another challenge is that translations can inhibit understanding. An example is the use of the English word *rape*. Reading English-language translations, the Gods constantly raping mortal women is horrifying. However, looking at the historical evidence, I don't see an ancient Greek concept that means precisely the same thing as our "rape," which emphasizes lack of sexual consent.

In ancient Greece, women's sexual lives were defined by their arranged marriages. Female sexuality was subservient to the *oikos* —the family and household, which was the foundational institution of society. Many situations translated as "rape" involve women who have sexual intercourse outside of marriage but bear no moral blame. This includes sexual violence but also other circumstances we would not think of as rape. It seems to include marriage by elopement

13.   Plutarch and Babbitt, "Obsolescence of Oracles," 348–501.

14.   Graf, *Apollo*.

15.   Pomeroy, *Xenophon Oeconomicus*.

(consensual or not, but not agreed to by the household), and every time a god has sex with a mortal woman (consensual or not). Every child born needed to have a place in a family. As a patrilineal society, a child belonged in the father's family. In cases of extramarital sex where the mother was blameless, the child had a place in her father's family. This includes children of the Gods.

Myths are sacred stories operating at many levels of consciousness. Taking them literally misses most of their power. Be careful with Ovid. Ovid, an accomplished Roman poet, is the primary source of many of our English-language books about Greek mythology. Compilations of mythic stories was not a genre in ancient Greece, but is what Ovid provides in *Metamorphoses*. It is a literary masterpiece exploring the theme of transformation, but is not sacred text and, unlike the myths themselves, has no relationship to religious cult.[16] For mythological sources, I recommend starting with hymns.

UNVERIFIED PERSONAL GNOSIS (UPG)

In recounting Persia's invasion of Greece, Herodotus tells the story of Pheidippides, an Athenian long-distance runner.[17] When the Athenian generals realized they were going to meet the vastly superior Persian force at Marathon, they sent Pheidippides to run about one hundred miles to Sparta and beg for their aid. Pheidippides ran all the way without a break and tried, in vain, to convince the Spartans. When he was unsuccessful, knowing the Athenian strategy hinged on Sparta's decision, he immediately ran back—desperately trying to reach the generals in time. On his return journey, the god Pan appeared and asked why He was not worshipped in Athens. Pan pledged to help the Athenians if they would promise to build Him a temple. Pheidippides told the generals, who promised Pan they would. During the battle, many Persian soldiers were seized by Pan-ic and neutralized.

Unverified Personal Gnosis (UPG) is sometimes looked down on because it doesn't originate from the lore. While important to check oneself for delusions—testing if what is perceived is in alignment with the lore—UPG shouldn't be automatically rejected. The Athenians believed Pheidippides and his experience became the lore—a new cult of Pan was founded. Every tra-

---

16.   Ovid, *Metamorphoses*.
17.   Herodotus and Sélincourt, trans., *Histories*.

ditional cult or practice began as someone's UPG. If the Gods are real, and I believe They are, why would this change? Use discernment but be open.

FOUNDATIONAL CONCEPTS

There are some ancient Greek concepts that are bedrock ways of thinking and can give us new insight. They shake up the way of thinking we have inherited from the dominant culture and can form the basis of practice.

Moira

Moira is often translated as "fate," and the Great Ones who are named Moirai are called the Fates, but what "fate" means is not immediately apparent. *Moira* is not predestination. People and states did not consult oracles to learn their unalterable future. They went to oracles to get advice on how to change their future. That was the whole point.

Moira is better translated as "law," meaning the underlying structure of reality—it is law in the sense of "the law of gravity." *Moira* is the operating code of the cosmos, and a particularly important aspect of this structure is the way in which cause and effect function. Nothing, not even the Theoi, are outside the rule of *moira*.

Moira includes the essential nature of all beings. It is human *moira* that we are beings who die and know we will die. We are social animals who naturally organize ourselves in groups larger than our families. We are not omniscient. Regardless of our intention, we are subject to the law of causation and responsible for the outcomes of our actions. We are, therefore, vulnerable to *hamartia*—the tragic mistake. This is all part of human *moira*.

Although *moira* is not predestination, choice is not unconstrained. Part of *moira* is that everything is interdependent, often in ways incomprehensible to a human psyche. An individual is acting in a context already having countless lines of active causation. Often, using cause against cause, effects can be changed or mitigated—much like how an engineer uses the law of gravity to get planes to fly. Sometimes causation aligns in ways creating a practical experience of inevitability. Simultaneously borrowing language from Indian philosophy and the British television show *Doctor Who*, the ripening of *karma* can result in fixed points in time where the outcome is no longer capable of modification.

One way to read the *Iliad* is as a meditation on the nature of *moira*.[18] From the epic's beginning, it is clear the Achaeans, the "Greeks," are going to win and Troy is going to fall. The most important cause identified is the sacrilege and accompanying *miasma* (spiritual pollution) from two sources. First, Paris, the prince of Troy, broke the sacred laws of hospitality by both seducing and abducting his host's wife and by stealing his treasure. Secondly, knowing full well what had happened, Troy still welcomed Paris into their community instead of casting him out—bringing the *miasma* from these crimes upon them all. So, it is known the Achaeans will win and Troy will fall, but what is not determined is what that would mean. Through the *Iliad*, we learn that although they will win, the Achaeans' behavior during the war is so abominable that they are also destroyed and their entire culture falls—even in their victory.

Now, let's look at Achilles. There are many ways in which Achilles is unusual, but strikingly, he had two distinct possible futures, told to him by his mother, the goddess Thetis. In one of his futures, he earns imperishable glory and is immortal in the minds and hearts of humans—but dies young. In the other, he lives happily to old age and dies in obscurity. It was further known that Hector, the great Trojan hero, could only be killed by Achilles—but it was not known for certain that Hector would actually fall.

Toward the *Iliad*'s beginning, Agamemnon, the high king and leader of the Achaeans, insulted Achilles. Furious, Achilles proclaims he is done with the war. He is choosing his second fate. He is going to take Patroklos—his friend and partner—take their troops, and sail home. Achilles, Patroklos, and their troops withdraw to their ships, waiting for the wind to turn so they can leave. One day, Achilles notices in the distance someone who looks like a friend being carried off the battlefield. He asks Patroklos to find out if it is, indeed, their friend. In that moment, the *moira* of Achilles, Patroklos, and Hector becomes fixed, and all are destined to die young and in glory.

The love Patroklos feels for Achilles would never allow him to refuse Achilles. Therefore, Patroklos goes to check on their friend, which puts him in a tent with Nestor—the ancient and cunning war leader. Nestor plays on the gentleness of Patroklos's character and cajoles him into asking Achilles to let Patroklos wear his armor into battle to raise the spirits of the troops. Achilles

---

18.   Homer, *Iliad of Homer*.

can't refuse Patroklos any more than Patroklos can refuse Achilles. But Patroklos is not Achilles and cannot slay Hector, so he dies by Hector's hand. The utterly bereft Achilles can't rest until his partner is fully avenged. Achilles's natural reactions tend to be dangerously extreme, but Patroklos was a moderating force. Without Patroklos, his grief is so overwhelming he goes far beyond what is acceptable to the Gods or men, creating the conditions for his own demise.

That is an example of *moira*. There are critically important choices that could change everything, but causation is so complex that, as humans, we often only see it in retrospect. Even Achilles, given the foreknowledge of his two paths, did not realize, in the moment he asked Patroklos to check on their friend, that he was making that type of monumental choice.

In our lives, we should always strive to understand *moira*—both as the underlying base-code of reality and the patterns of causation that are in play at any moment, helping us determine which actions can make a difference and which would be wasted effort. Consulting oracles and using divination help. I recommend asking for assistance from the Theoi and then watching for omens. Of course, we must also use our glorious minds and engage in contemplation and analysis.

Apollon and Zeus are the two gods who are given the title *Moiragetes*, leader of the Fates. This has to do with Their oracular function. They have a clear understanding of the base-code of reality and causation. You can approach either of Them or the Fates (Klotho, Lachesis, Atropos) to understand and work with *moira*.

Exercise
THREE-MINUTE PAPER ON MOIRA

This exercise will help you integrate your new understanding of *moira*.

What You'll Need

Paper/journal, a pen, and a timer.

Directions

Set a timer for three minutes. Write stream of consciousness, answering the question: What do you think about the concept of *moira*?

Themistes

Themistes means both "what is" and "what is right." It is what the cosmos looks like in the moment, and what it looks like when it is operating correctly. Along with *moira* these are specializations of Apollon, the oracular and healing god. He understands both the operating code of the cosmos and where things are out of alignment. Things getting out of sync—where "what is" no longer matches "what is right"—is the cause of disease and most social problems.

Miasma

One of the most important reasons "what is" gets out of alignment with "what is right" is *miasma*—spiritual pollution. It can arise from many sources, but, ultimately, I understand it to be about being out of right relationship—out of right relationship with the Gods, with each other, with nature, with our own full essence of self. Human beings are naturally communal, and *miasma* is contagious, such as *miasma* spreading from Paris to Troy. Reaching the collective, it increases, functioning like a toxic, smothering cloud, choking the Light. *Miasma* requires purification, and any withering damage from lack of Light must be healed. The vast majority of historical oracular answers were about purifying and healing *miasma*, avoiding *hamartia* (the tragic mistake), and helping close the gap between "what is" and "what is right."

The ancient Greeks were concerned with avoiding and, if necessary, purifying *miasma*. I recommend functional analysis in this work—lists of "sins" are culturally contingent and not useful. Look for ruptured relationships, including with our own full humanity. When I look at aspects of our cultural context and see the way in which people get swept into baseless conspiracy theories keeping them from being able to exercise appropriate judgment, I see *miasma*. When I see a culture that values profit above human welfare or environmental sustainability, I see *miasma*. When I see criminal justice sentencing disparities that strongly correlate with race, I see *miasma*. Anytime I see living beings reduced to "things," I know I am seeing *miasma* at work. I could give countless examples.

Because we are in collective environments filled with *miasma*—the spiritual equivalent of toxic smog—regular spiritual cleansing is essential. The goal is to cut a clear air passage, but it requires maintenance. Daphne (bay laurel) is both a nymph and a powerful purification ally. Carrying bay branches around an area or burning bay leaves is purifying. Bay laurel tea in a bath can be used as a spiritual cleanser.

Exercise
SPIRITUAL CLEANSING BATH

The following is a basic spiritual purification rite that can be used as part of a regular ritual cleansing regimen or at need. As a regular rite, it is recommended to take the bath on the new moon (Noumenia).

What You'll Need

Three bay leaves (Daphne), a pot of water, a range to heat the water, a bathtub, and a cup or bowl to take into the bath with you to pour the water over your head and back.

Directions

Heat the pot of water until boiling. Turn off the water and steep Daphne until it cools enough to touch the water. Run a ritual bath. Put a finger into the tea, imagining yourself connecting with the spirit of Daphne, and say,

> *Holy Daphne, blessed bay, beloved of Apollon,*
> *I ask you to please cleanse my head, my heart, my hands, my feet.*
> *Purify my mind, my soul, my words, my work,*
> *So I may be clean as a white, unspotted fleece.*

Pour the Daphne water into the bath and step in. Soak in the water and pour the blessed water over you, including over your head, feeling everything that is impure being washed away. Keep pouring the water until you feel deeply cleansed on all levels. See the light in your head become brighter and brighter and keep pouring the water over yourself until your head-light can reach out and connect with the greater Light in the cosmos. When you are done, thank Daphne and let the water drain. You can dispose of the bay leaves by either burning them or leaving them outdoors.

Hamartia

Hamartia is an aspect of human *moira* and a cause of *miasma*. When I was young and studying Greek tragedy, my instructors translated *hamartia* as "tragic flaw" and laid an almost Christian morality on top of the tragic hero. A truer interpretation is "tragic mistake." The term also means to "miss the mark" in archery. It is an error. It is a tragic error. It is one of the scariest realities about being human, because human *moira* is that we are not omniscient—we will always have imperfect information—but we are morally responsible for our choices.

Therefore, our best intentions and most careful study and contemplation are insufficient to ensure we will avoid unexpected and tragic outcomes that are still our fault. The dramatic tragedies of the ancient world are terrifying because they show that even the most privileged, the smartest, the most powerful humans sometimes with the best of all possible intentions can still set causes in motion that utterly destroy them and everything they love.

Those thoughts are so terrifying, we cannot afford to dwell in them for long or we would be crippled by anxiety. Tragedy allows us to experience these dangerous thoughts in a controlled setting, experience the sublime (beauty mixed with terror), and then go back to living. Understanding the threat of *hamartia* is important in relation to ancient Greek religion because getting wise counsel and assistance from the Theoi so we can avoid making tragic mistakes is a large part of practice.

Hamartia creates *miasma* and its result must be purified and healed—even though the harm is unintentional. You have to own it and try to make it right. You must do your utmost to learn from your tragic mistake so you have a better chance of avoiding it in the future. If you make the same mistake over and over again and are not learning, then it can become something different and more difficult to heal. It can become *hubris*.

Exercise
THREE-MINUTE PAPER ON HAMARTIA

This exercise will help you integrate your new understanding of *hamartia* and uncover how it functions in your life.

What You'll Need
Paper/journal, a pen, and a timer.

Directions
Set a timer for three minutes. Write stream of consciousness, answering the question: What kind of tragic mistakes are you prone to make?

Hubris

Unlike *hamartia*, which is part of the human condition, *hubris* is a flaw in one's character causing moral outrage. This is not a mistake made with good intentions. This is something morally wrong with us as individuals (or as a society). For example, the tendency to treat living beings as things is *hubris*. Selfishness is *hubris*. Jealous pride is *hubris*. Cruelty is *hubris*. Chronic overestimation of our power or skill is *hubris*. Willful blindness or carelessness is *hubris*.

The harm coming from *hubris* must also be healed. Like *harmartia*, you must own it, try to rectify the impact of the harm you have created, but you also have to do what is necessary to change your character.

Thankfully, our character is not static and can be changed. As will be discussed in chapter 14, we have good guidance from the ancients—my favorite is Aristotle's *Nicomachaean Ethics*.[19] We become what we do over and over. If you want to change your character, change your habits. Spiritual growth and evolution always involve changing our character.

Exercise
THREE-MINUTE PAPER ON HUBRIS
This exercise will help you integrate your new understanding of *hubris* and uncover how it functions in your life.

What You'll Need
Paper/journal, a pen, and a timer.

Directions
Set a timer for three minutes. Write stream of consciousness, answering the question: What aspect of your character gets in your way most?

---

19.   Aristotle, *Nicomachaean Ethics*.

The Polis

The *polis* means "the community," and when Aristotle famously said that a human being is a "political animal," he meant we naturally organize ourselves into groups larger than the family.[20] We are part of the greater group, and while we have individual rights, our emphasis, from an ancient Greek perspective, should be on duty. A word for someone who looked for their individual gain at the cost of the collective was *idiotes*, or "idiot," from where we derive the Freudian "id."[21]

Ancient Greek citizens vied for the right to spend their money on projects benefitting the entire community. They did not do so with what we recognize as the Christian virtue of humility, but with the virtue of magnanimity—or *megalopsyche* in the Greek—the virtue of being "big souled." It is clear the sense of duty to one's *polis* is paramount and is not incompatible with individual rights. When JFK said, "Ask not what your country can do for you. Ask what you can do for your country," I think every ancient Greek worth their salt would have stood and cheered.[22]

Apollon and Athena called me to service. Part of my work involves magic for the good of the *polis*, which is attempting to rebirth the aims of civic religion into a community of magical practitioners while maintaining strict separation of church and state.

Philia

Philia is the affectionate love that is friendship. My spiritual life and understanding of religion are driven by relationships and relationship building. I embrace the bold vision of the *cosmopolis*. Instead of seeing ourselves as members of a single *polis*, may all humanity unite in *philia*—in friendship—and may we relate to the Theoi as benevolent and shared friends who love us all. May we act with wisdom and from *philia* with all beings. As Aristotle said, there is no need for justice among friends because when you are true friends with someone, your highest wish is for their highest Good. Friendship is, indeed, the highest excellence because no one would forsake having friends even if they could have all other Goods.[23]

20. Aristotle, *Politics*.
21. "Idiot," in *Oxford English Dictionary*.
22. Kennedy, "President John F. Kennedy's Inaugural Address."
23. Aristotle, *Nicomachaean Ethics*.

CHAPTER TWO ☉
WHO ARE THE THEOI?

Theoi is a general term for the Gods, including the Olympians, the Titans, and all those beings called "Minor Gods" in English-language texts. The Theoi want to work with us—not for us, nor we for them. They are looking for partnerships. I am frequently asked how to build a relationship with one of Them. Pagans usually want to know what color candle a deity likes or the incense They enjoy. That is not the way I tend to approach relationship building with the Theoi. In this chapter, I share my method.

GENERAL CHARACTERISTICS

Ancient Greeks understood the Theoi to be real living beings, which accords with my experience. They have existence completely apart from whether humans are in relationship with Them. Our names for the Gods are not Their names for Themselves. There is an aspect of the forms, stories, and names that are co-created with humans. Humans are inspired by the Theoi in a process of creative discovery, generating the human-user interface, allowing us to interact with Them.

Polytheism in Greece coexisted with many other theological beliefs. For example, one can be a monist—believing there is an ultimate reality beyond being and nonbeing, and everything flows from and ultimately is this singular great source—and still be a polytheist. It just means the Gods also flow from this great source as well as everything else. It is possible to be a pantheist or panentheist, believing an impersonal Divine pervades everything—and still be a polytheist, since in that system, the Divine pervades the Gods also. You can believe in panpsychism, believing everything is ultimately a form of consciousness—and still be a polytheist. Many of the great philosophers of ancient Greece were simultaneously monists, panentheists, panpsychics, and polytheists. For example, Socrates held quite abstract ideas about the nature of the cosmos, but he took time before his death to ask for a particular sacrifice to the god Asklepios.[24] These theological positions are not inherently contradictory.

One of the main characteristics of the Theoi is They have the *moira* of the deathless. They may be banished, bound, and harmed, but They do not die. They are, however, in the cosmos and not outside of it. They are subject to the fundamental laws of reality. They have a better understanding of the foundational structures underlying reality than humans and can use this understanding and Their power to alter the world in ways that may seem all powerful from a human perspective, yet They are not omnipotent.

They are individuated, having distinct personalities and histories. Like all living beings, They learn, change, and grow as a result of Their experiences, some of which may be known to humanity, and many, presumably, are not. Each has particular spheres of influence and Their godly powers are related to these domains. For example, Poseidon is principally the god of the sea.

All beings, including the Theoi, have agendas. For example, Poseidon has a strong ecological agenda and is a potent ally in such work. An agenda is just a focus aligning values with actions and desires. If you are striving to develop a personal relationship with any of the Theoi, try to discover Their agendas, uncover your own, and see where there is alignment. From that place, you can best make your approach.

I emphasize consciously developing a personal relationship because the Theoi are already in relationship with humanity as a whole. We may not realize it and we may not be doing what is necessary to maintain healthy relationships with Them, but the world is interdependent and includes beings both seen and unseen.

---

24. Plato, "Phaedo," 193–403.

Epithets

Epithets are specialized titles or names revealing specific aspects of the Theoi and are incredibly useful for uncovering Their agendas. For example, Apollon Alexikakos is "Apollon Averter of Evil." This name simultaneously reveals a lot about Him (He has a protective aspect; He is concerned with promoting and defending the Good) and is important for practice. When you pray to Apollon Alexikakos, the message is going both to this Great One with the additional information that you need His protective presence rather than, say, His power as Apollon Oulios, "Apollon the Healer."

When invoking the Theoi, it is traditional to use numerous epithets, specifying the aspects you are calling as well as making the case your agenda is aligned with Theirs.[25] I have included many epithets in the prayers to the Great Ones in the next chapter, but there are also resources that have compiled lists for exploration.[26]

Onómata Barbariká

In some of the surviving ancient Greek magical texts, magicians used the language of personal friendship with the God, called to many epithets and names of the God, and then ended with "and I call you by your barbarous names (onómata barbariká)."[27] There is an implicit theology here worth unpacking.

Barbariká—from which we get barbarian—is a general word designating all languages that are not one of the Greek languages. When these practitioners, who are claiming a close personal relationship with a deity, use the God's non-Greek names, what is that about? The Theoi answer to names in human languages, but those aren't Their names for Themselves—those are the names we give Them so we can talk to Them. They appear to us wearing particular forms and shapes so we can relate to Them, but those forms aren't what They really look like. The Greeks understood the Great Ones aren't only in relationship with a single culture but would be known by different names in other cultures.

Greek magicians developed an intimate and personal relationship with at least one of the Theoi. This required striving to know the God not just at the

---

25.   Versnel, "Prayers and Curses," 447–61.

26.   Atsma, "Theoi Project."

27.   Graf, *Magic in the Ancient World*.

level of culturally defined form, but to know that Great One at the level of Their true, immortal self. As part of their practice, the magicians looked for their beloved God in other cultures. This is like the fairy tales in which the lover has to recognize the shape-changed beloved by sensing their true essence.

This propensity to recognize the Theoi in the gods of other cultures was not only practiced by magicians. Alexander the Great, whose campaign was at least one-part religious pilgrimage, regularly sacrificed to Greek deities he recognized in other cultures—for example, when he sacrificed to Herakles at Tyre.[28] That was probably Melquart/B'aal. This tendency is a traditional polytheist practice lying behind combining cults, as was common in the cosmopolitan Hellenistic Age. It is important to remember to seek the essence of the Great One, not just Their function. Not all sea gods are Poseidon.

I think this is a potentially useful multicultural model because it grants respect to and defends the spiritual legitimacy of other cultures and their practices while providing a potential bridge for communication, learning, and cooperation. For example, if my goal is to know Apollon as deeply as I can and relate to Him as intimately as possible, if I find Him in India, I would want to learn everything the Indians know about Him. I would defend the integrity of their rites—including knowing when not to participate—not just out of an intellectual commitment to cosmopolitanism, but out of love and respect for Him. At the same time, nobody "owns" the Gods. They, Themselves, aren't anyone's property, and I think we should beware of the *hubris*—the dangerous pride—of using the language of property rights with the Theoi.

GETTING TO KNOW THE THEOI

In the next chapter, I will share details about the most important Theoi and give you pathworkings to actually meet Them. Here I give you a method for beginning a relationship.

If you are approaching one of the Theoi, the first step is to learn what you can about the God. Most of us encounter the Greek myths by the time we are adults. In ancient Greece, myths are always attached to cult, and if you don't know the ways in which the cult works, it is easy to misinterpret the myths. Let me give you an example.

---

28.   Arrian, *Campaigns of Alexander*.

One form of the goddess Artemis is Bear Mother. In the cults of Artemis Bear Mother, like in Brauron, She is responsible for helping girls make the transition into womanhood. She is a protector, a teacher, and, at the end, She drives Her little bears away from maidenhood and into marriage. At the end of their initiation into womanhood, the girls sacrifice their toys and the things of their childhood to Artemis and leave Her.

Consider the myth of Artemis and the nymph Kallisto, recognizing now that Kallisto is a form of Artemis—which would not be apparent if you didn't know about the epithets and cult practices. In the myth, Kallisto is a follower of Artemis, but she has sex with a man and gets pregnant. Furious, Artemis drives Kallisto out of Her band of maidens and transforms her into a bear. Without knowing the cultic information, Artemis seems like a "cold and pitiless" goddess, as the D'Aulaires Greek Myths book of my youth would have it.[29] From this new perspective, both characters are Artemis and it is a story showing a female coming of age process. Also note how utterly unimportant except as inseminator the male is to female identity. This is characteristic of Artemis.

When trying to get to know the Gods, I think it is best to start by looking at cults, religious practice, and epithets and then at the myths. Try to get to know the Theoi one at a time, creating a picture about what a particular deity loves and wants to see happen based on how They were worshipped and what They are called. Learn about Their specific cult centers. Find out about the festivals. Read Their hymns, including the Homeric hymns, Pindar, the Orphic hymns, and any other extant hymns you can find. After you feel like you have a decent grounding in the information about the God you are trying to know, read the myths and stories in narrative form and let them simmer in your deep consciousness. Throughout, try to understand who They are and what They want. Then, if you decide to do so, reach out to Them. Always remember, you are sovereign in your life. If one of the Theoi reaches out to you and you do not want to be in close relationship with Them, say no.

---

29.   D'Aulaire and D'Aulaire, *D'Aulaires' Book of Greek Myths*.

Exercise
MAKING A PLAN

Identify the Great One with whom you wish to build a relationship. This is an ongoing process, but I strongly urge you to keep notes and journal as you are making progress following the steps that are outlined here, including recording notes and reflections from your studies. Here are the steps:

1. Learn about the God; research their cults, epithets, festivals. Read whatever hymns you can find. Read the myths and stories. Ask for dreams while you are studying.

2. Journal about what you think They want to see in the world. Think about how that intersects with what you want to see in the world.

3. Make a sacred space for Them. (See chapter 4.)

4. If it is one of the Great Ones covered in chapter 3, go on the pathworking and use the prayer.

5. Using what you have learned from your research, write your own prayer and begin to use it. (See chapter 6.)

6. Identify a concrete action or set of actions you can take to promote both what you want to see in the world and what the God wants to see in the world. Make that action an offering. (See chapter 6.)

7. Watch for or provoke omens. (See chapter 7.)

THE MAJOR GODS

While there is some variation, there is a traditional order in which the Theoi are listed and often honored. First is Zeus, king of the Gods, and Hera, His queen. Poseidon is god of the sea. Demeter is literally "the mother," and Her daughter, Persephone, is sometimes honored with Her. Persephone is also honored with Her husband, Hades, god of the dead. Hades is usually honored separately from the Olympians. Hestia is the goddess of the hearth and is usually honored first in household practice and is the final of Zeus's siblings. Aphrodite, the goddess of love and beauty, is the first of the next generation of Theoi. Ares, the god of war, and Hephaistos, the smith god, are next, followed by Athena, the goddess of wisdom. The twins, Artemis and Apollon, are often honored with Their mother, Leto, and Zeus as the Holy Family. Hermes, the divine messenger, and

Dionysus, the god of wine (and altered states), are the "youngest" of the Great Gods of Greece.

In the next chapter, you will be introduced to these Theoi in depth and in this order.

OTHER THEOI

There are numerous deities who are not Olympians but are Panhellenic—worshipped throughout Greece.

Hekate

Hekate is the goddess of the crossroads and magic, especially *pharmakon*—the type of magic using herbs and substances.[30] She is especially important to modern witches. Hekate is the goddess of the liminal, in which things are in-between. Finding the liminal moment in any causal chain is where you can best influence causation. Every new moon, which is the night before the beginning of the month in Greek calendars, is Her monthly festival.

Crossroads, doorways, and any type of activity leveraging the power of the liminal is in Her sphere of influence. She stands at the crossroads of birth, death, and the entrance into both the Heavens and the Underworld. Like Hermes, She can move freely in all the realms of reality. She has a particular role in protecting beings who are in liminal social situations, like people seeking sanctuary, refugees, the destitute, and ghosts. She is often depicted carrying two torches, which are symbols of the Eleusinian Mysteries. Black dogs are Her sacred animal.

From an ancient Greek perspective, She always appears as a young woman, but in later cultures She is sometimes seen as an old woman. Remembering the theology behind *onómata barbariká*, if someone in our culture who identifies as a witch tells me they have a relationship with Hekate and their description of Her personality and agenda align, who am I to tell them their experience of Her wearing the form of an old woman is wrong? It is not how the ancient Greeks would have seen Her, but I believe in the reality of these Great Ones, and They are not restricted by our notions of historical accuracy.

---

30.   Dickie, *Magic and Magicians in the Greco-Roman World.*

Pan

The satyr god Pan is important in Modern Paganism. He is a god of the beasts, including the animal part of human nature. There is tremendous wisdom in the animal nature, and a distinction needs to be drawn between what is nonrational and what is irrational. Pan influences both the non- and irrational. Pan's importance to many Pagans arises from how badly we need Him as a corrective after centuries of equating animal nature with evil and trying to suppress and deny it.

Leto

The Holy Family, often depicted together, includes Zeus, Leto, and the twins, Artemis and Apollon. Leto is not considered an Olympian, but the twins are. Leto does sometimes have Her own temples, usually in sanctuaries dedicated to Apollon or Artemis. Leto was an important deity in Anatolia and Crete. When I was in Ephesus looking at a famous statue of Artemis with the many breasts, I turned around and looked right into the eyes of another, less famous statue of the same type. I went stiff and almost fell over backward from the power of it. It felt like Leto. In my experience, the love and connection Artemis and Apollon have with Leto is accurate, and one of the best ways to build a relationship with Them is to honor Their mother.

Leto is known for Her kindness, Her gentleness, and Her modesty—which brings out a fierce protectiveness in Her children. She is the epitome of the sweet, nurturing mother. She has a strong connection with wolves, which are social animals. She is Den Mother. She is honored any place either of Her children are worshipped.

Asklepios

Asklepios, the son of Apollon, was born mortal and became a god of healing. Widely worshipped in the ancient Greek world, He gradually took over many of the healing cults from Apollon. I will address the healing cults in chapter 11.

Others

I encourage modern practitioners to consider many other Theoi. Helios, the god of the sun, as well as Apollon, is typically invoked in the courts and in any situation in which one might need the Truth to come to Light. Aeolus is god of the wind, and the various directional winds can be important when it comes to working with the weather. The Eumenides/Erinyes/Furies are invoked sparingly and carefully, but at times for justice. Chiron, the wise centaur and stepson of Apollon, is the teacher of heroes *par excellence* and can help us understand how to use the wounds each of us bears so we may heal others.

NATURAL AND LOCAL THEOI

The world is full of spirits and Theoi. There are countless sacred beings that are different than humans and are usually invisible to us. Many of Them are related to nature and inhabit natural places. Nymphs are classified according to where They live. Every natural area of fresh water has an inhabiting spirit—a kind of nymph called a naiad. Every grove, forest, meadow, stream, or well has a nymph. There are tree nymphs; star, cloud, and breeze nymphs; and nymphs living in the Underworld. All of nature is filled with nymphs. In some of the traditions, They are long lived but are not necessarily immortal.

Typically, nymphs are directly related to a specific land-base and are inherently local. However, there are occasions in which particular nymphs expand Their scope and power. Two I met and work with are Daphne and Kastalia. Daphne, the spirit of the laurel, is sacred to Apollon and is one of the most purifying substances in all of ancient Greek lore. We met Her before in the purifying bath. Kastalia is the spirit of the sacred Kastalian spring, which still flows at Delphi. Somehow, perhaps resulting from the praise and attention She received over millennia, including from Romantic poets in the eighteenth and nineteenth centuries, Kastallia's reach has expanded far beyond Her immediate locale. She has the power to interact with people from quite a distance, especially if they ever drank Her water. I think She is on the threshold of becoming a bigger goddess and have introduced Her water to other locations to help enable Her expanding reach.

Once you consciously live in a world filled with gods and spirits and realize you are in relationship with Them, then it is important to focus on the health of those relationships. If you have a strong mental and emotional picture of various kinds of nature spirits, They will often adopt and adapt those forms in order to communicate. Iconic forms provide effective and necessary human-user interfaces. Whatever these beings are, They never really looked like any of our culturally created forms, but They choose the costumes that "fit." Sculptural friezes in many Greek temples represent nearby river spirits, because it is important to be in good relationship with your watershed, and having the iconic forms makes clearer communication possible. In my daily prayers, I thank and acknowledge the waters where I live, using the names of the rivers but acknowledging Them as living beings with spirit.

Exercise
MEET YOUR LOCAL NYMPH

To begin building a healthy relationship with one of the Theoi who has a direct impact on your life and to learn how to consciously co-create a human-user interface with a divine being. Most of us cannot rely on lore to help build a relationship with the nymph who is the spirit of our local water source.

What You'll Need

A trash bag and a journal and pen or a recording device. Optional: A sketch-book and art supplies.

Directions

Find a local natural water source—a river, creek, steam, or spring—and visit, bringing a trash bag. Make your approach with the mindset that you want to build a relationship with your local water spirit. When you arrive, introduce yourself and greet the nymph, using the name of the water. (For example, "Greetings, Rock Creek, beautiful nymph! I am Gwendolyn. I come to you in friendship and want to know you.")

Begin picking up trash while reaching out in your mind. With every piece, say, "I honor your beloved spirit, gracious nymph." This is your offer-ing to the nymph.

When either your bag is full or the area is clean, find a comfortable place and sit to commune with the nymph. Be open. You are co-creating a form to be an interface. Verify if it likes the name it has or ask for a new name. Write down or record what you are perceiving and know that the nymph will be using your imagination as the tool of communication. Notice if something seems easy, like it is fitting, or if there is resistance. If you are artistically inclined, begin sketching and see what forms are coming and how the nymph is responding. If you are verbally inclined, begin writing descriptions or speaking and recording the descriptions and test the responsiveness. Imagine yourself talking to the nymph like you are talking to a friend in your head. See what you receive. When you feel that you have received as much as is profitable for the day, thank the nymph by Her name. Be sure that you take all trash out and dispose of it properly.

By the end of your visit, you should have the beginning of a human-user interface. Depending on the nymph's condition, it may take several visits to establish clear communication. If the nymph is a water source for your drinking water, you can give thanks whenever you drink, strengthening the bond.

In the beginning it may seem as though you are really talking to yourself, but over time, you will sense when you are "forcing" something and when it is flowing naturally. Eventually, if you build a strong relationship with the nymph, you will begin receiving information during your imaginative communication that sometimes runs counter to your expectations. This is a good sign your interface is strong enough to be used clearly by the nymph.

Creating artistic representations, if you are able, and including the name in your prayers and devotions strengthen your relationship and the nymph's ability to communicate with humans. If you have a local group, sharing your human-user interface further strengthens its power.

CHAPTER THREE

MEET THE THEOI

In this chapter, I introduce you to the most important Greek Gods, including the Dodeka Theoi—the twelve Olympians. For each, I give information about Them and a prayer and pathworking to a place on the inner planes sacred to Them. Some are intact astral forms of places you can physically visit. Some are on the astral without physical equivalents. Review the instructions for pathworkings in the introduction. You can speak the prayer prior to beginning the pathworking or use it on its own whenever you want to pray to the God. Only do one rite a day. If you are interested in getting to know a particular god, repeat the rite over the course of multiple days. Take notes on your experiences. Be open and trust yourself.

ZEUS

Zeus, who overthrew His father, Kronos (the god of time), is the king of the Gods, and His sister and wife, Hera, is His queen. Zeus is a sky god but has chthonic (of the Underworld) aspects, like Zeus Melichios, in which He appears as a serpent. Eagles and bulls are sacred to Him, but He is also attended by doves. His oracle at Dodona is more chthonic than empyrean (highest Heaven). He is the god of sovereignty and of all rulers. Zeus upholds the Rule of Law—both divine and human—including the fundamental laws of civilization. He protects the sanctity of oaths and promises, the laws of hospitality (which is the duty of strangers toward each other), and protects bonds of friendship, marriage, and the assemblies constituting society.

Zeus is one of the Theoi most involved in what I call the "demigod breeding project." He fathers a tremendous number of children on mortal women, introducing His divinity into human bloodlines, which established many of the royal households. This process changed something fundamental in the human constitution that gradually spread throughout the world. Ancient Greeks did not see this as a bawdy joke. It is a high form of grace. Virtually every family in Greece traced its ancestry back to at least one divine ancestor, and that ancestor was often Zeus, the father of gods and men. In vision, He told me all humanity has His lightning spark in our blood, and this power can be awakened. Lightning, or spiritual electricity, is a type of fire energy that is a conduit for both consciousness and life-force and links the planes together.

Zeus's primary areas of interest are with the nature of Power itself and both *moira* and *themistes*—the base-code of reality and the pattern of the way things should be. Zeus's focus on upholding Divine Order is not inherently anthropocentric.

In general, Zeus is interested in seeing us re-vision our understanding and relationship to Power—rooted in mind and in alignment with and in service to Divine Order. Appropriate restraint in relation to power is essential. Similarly, He is interested in the conceptual evolution of sovereignty within systems of deep interconnection.

PRAYER TO ZEUS

Olympian Zeus, father of gods and men, thunderer, lightning wielder, who fertilizes the fields with Your nourishing rain—I honor You, whose gifts aid all growth and evolution. Zeus Moiragetes, leader of the Fates, help me grasp the big picture and see what should change, my role in the change, and when I should accept things as they are. Zeus Nomos, upholder of Divine Law, help me unite what is with what should be. Zeus Soter, Elethuereus, You are a savior and deliverer who cares about our struggles and helps us live consciously in our highest selves. Great Father, who gifted humanity with Your lightning spark running through our blood, help me awaken the power and potential within. Awaken in me a vision of healthy power and guide me to understand how to harness it in ways serving Themis. I honor You, Zeus, and ask for Your blessing.

Pathworking to the Sanctuary of Zeus at Dodona

With your eyes closed, see the room in which you are sitting begin to fill with mists that get thicker and thicker until you can no longer see your hand in front of you. As the mists fade, find yourself on a path across a flat plain surrounded by mountains. Feel the wind moving across your skin as you walk, seeing in the distance a gate in the wall marking the *temenos* of the sanctuary of Dodona, sacred to Zeus. Approaching the gate, your attention is suddenly pulled upward to a soaring golden eagle. You know this is a sign you are welcome.

Reaching the open gate, you find what looks like a giant birdbath standing to the side, filled with fresh water. Cleanse your hands, your face, and your head in the water, washing away all that does not serve. In this sanctuary, you must enter barefoot and walk upon the hallowed ground with your skin. Remove your shoes and sprinkle water on your feet. When you feel ready, enter the sanctuary. [Pause.]

You are now walking in a grove of ancient oak trees. Brass and bronze implements hang from their branches. As the wind blows through the leaves and instruments, it feels like murmuring voices. You walk, feeling the ground under your feet and knowing the roots of these sacred beings, the Oaks of Zeus, spread beneath you—every bit as large as the mighty trees above the Earth. Wandering in the grove, you are drawn to a tree. Stop and touch its bole. Place your forehead on it and listen. [Pause.]

Hearing the cooing of doves, your attention is directed to the middle of the grove where there is a clearing. In the center is a plain altar. Walk to it. Ask Zeus for an audience. Looking down into your hand, you find an offering for Zeus. Place it on the altar, telling Zeus you hope your gift is pleasing. Somewhere, He is there. Your attention is drawn to Him. Spend some time getting to know Him. Ask Him what you should know about Him. [Long pause.] Ask Him for guidance. [Long pause.]

Ask Zeus if there is anything you should know if you want to work more closely with Him. [Pause.]

Thank Zeus and look around His sacred grove once more. You can return anytime and sit with your back against the bole of a mighty oak of Zeus, allowing the sounds to wash over you and wisdom to arise.

Express gratitude for the intelligence of the sacred grove. Walk back through to the gate, feeling the Earth beneath your feet. Passing through the gateway, pick up your shoes and continue walking the path away from the sanctuary. Mists begin rising from the ground, growing thicker and thicker until the fog is so dense you cannot see your hand before you. The mists dissipate. Find yourself back in your room.

Hera

Hera is the main goddess of the fertile Argolid plain on the Peloponnese peninsula, the birthplace of Mycenean culture. The oldest temple in Olympia is Hera's temple, which She used to share with Zeus.

She is the goddess of marriage and the kind of alliances marriage creates. In the archaic past, these alliances were the glue holding society together. Marriage created a system by which legitimacy of rule could pass from one generation to the next, enabling the peaceful transfer of power. In ancient Greece, allotments of agricultural land were held by a lineage, not by an individual. Marriage ensured the lineage continued and land-custodianship was distributed.[31] Hera is the defender of this social order—which is important to remember when one is ready to condemn Her for being jealous and cruel in the myths. She cares deeply about the female role in sovereignty and part of Her agenda has to do with ensuring people maintain rule and agreement-based approaches to collective power—be it in the context of the state or the household.

Chapter 13 discusses in more detail the reasons why Hera is often antagonistic to heroes. The synopsis is that Hera is the goddess of the natural cycles of time, including the natural cycles of a mortal life. A would-be hero is trying to transcend those cycles. Hera is often the initiatory challenger, creating the ordeals requiring heroic action and, thereby, enabling a mortal to become a hero.

Hera cares deeply about healthy relationships and continuity across generations. Her domain has to do with the way in which life itself continues for mortal beings. Fundamentally, She is concerned with intergenerational relationships of care and the Ethics of Care—including what the generations owe each other. Parents owe care to their children and children owe obedience (which is really accepting care) to their parents. As children become adults, they owe respect to their parents and elders for their greater experience. The older adults owe younger adults mentorship and opportunities for growth. As the

---

31. Cole, *Landscapes, Gender, and Ritual Space.*

parents become truly aged, the adult children owe them care and the parents owe their children the acceptance of that care. Traditionally, the institution of the family was both the locus and support structure for these networks of care. Each generation has responsibility to always make decisions based on the welfare of all the generations, not just itself.

Hera told me She is distressed by the way our society is focused on productivity to the point where we utterly devalue care—which makes our society sick. It also makes us lonely. We cannot thrive unless we are embedded in deep networks of care. The way in which generations think horizontally (of their peers) rather than vertically (where they are caring about the Good of other generations) may well destroy us. Hoarding wealth and power in the hands of any generation is a serious soul-sickness.

The decline of the family is not about the nuclear family. The nuclear family is a very new social form that fell apart quickly for good reasons. The traditional family form that functioned for millennia is the extended family. It is unlikely we will return to a lineage-based form in the near future. She said we need to understand that if whatever new social forms we create in our Families of Choice are not multigenerational, they will fail. We must integrate the generations. Anyone interested and willing to do the desperately needed work of building networks of care, including new multigenerational social forms, and re-envisioning the Ethics of Care will have a powerful ally in Hera.

Prayer to Hera

Hail Hera, beloved and majestic queen of Heaven! Hera Antheia, blooming goddess, may I be ever present to the beauty of the current moment and align myself with the sacred cycles of nature. Hera Alexandros, protector of humanity, Hypercheria, may You hold Your protective hand over me and over all my near and dear. Hera Gamelia, Zygia, protector of marriage and the family, bring sanctity to my closest relationships. Great queen, wife and mother, help me see the impact of my actions and inactions on all the generations and choose wisely from care. Beautiful and beloved divine bride, open my heart to both give and receive love in its fullest sense. Help me become truly, deeply loving and build a community based on love. I honor You, Hera, and ask for Your blessing.

Pathworking to Hera's Garden

With your eyes closed, see the room in which you are sitting begin to fill with mists that get thicker and thicker until you can no longer see your hand in front of you. As the mists fade, find yourself walking on a meandering path inside the most beautiful garden you have ever seen. Everywhere you look there are brightly colored flowers and the air is thick with their perfume. Fruit trees abound, laden with their ripe bounty, and the song of birds fills the air, including the distinctive call of the cuckoo. You pause, taking in the extraordinary beauty. [Pause.]

You hear water and walk toward it, finding a natural freshwater spring flowing into a fountain. As you wander, you may glimpse other beings who frequent these gardens—Iris the goddess of the rainbow, Hebe the goddess of youth, the Graces, the Horai—goddesses of the seasons and natural time. [Pause.]

Your attention is drawn to a peacock strutting through the garden with its feathers on full display, and you marvel at its beauty. Behind the peacock, in the center of the garden, is a beautiful open-air pavilion full of rich and elegant but comfortable furnishings, including a golden throne. Approach the edge and await an invitation to enter. This is one of Hera's favorite places, and She may choose to meet with you here. Ask what you should know about Her. [Long pause.] Ask Her for guidance. [Long pause.]

Ask Hera if there is anything you should know if you want to work more closely with Her. Ask if you have permission to return to Her garden. [Pause.]

Look into your hand and find a gift for Hera and give it to Her. Thank Hera and look around the garden one more time. Begin walking back down one of the paths. Mists begin rising from the ground, growing thicker and thicker until the fog is so dense you cannot see your hand before you. The mists dissipate. Find yourself back in your room.

Poseidon

Poseidon is the god of the seas and brother of Zeus. His wife, Amphitrite, is not an Olympian, but is often portrayed with Poseidon and in the company of the Olympians. His primary care, as far as this Earth is concerned, is not directly related to humans—the cosmos is not anthropocentric. He is predominantly interested in ensuring the health and well-being of the seas. His connection with humans is mostly related to times in which humanity interacts with the seas, including patronage of sailors, shipwrights, and fishers—and also marine conservationists.

He is upset about plastic and humans poisoning the oceans. He could be one of our greatest allies in fighting climate change—phytoplankton make more oxygen than all the world's forests—but the seas are sick and struggling, made worse by the climate crisis. I regularly encounter Him when doing any kind of environmental activism, not just marine conservation. Almost everything has some tie to water, which eventually flows to the oceans. His powers include modifying storms, working with the life of the seas, and He has power over the liquid aspect of the Earth—magma—which is involved in tectonic shifts and earthquakes.

His power and domain is related to all water. Water itself is the blood of the planet, and He is willing and, frankly, eager to work with humans on any of the ecological challenges our world is facing.

Part of the strength of my relationship with Poseidon stems from how I make offerings to Him. As I walk through life, I pick up plastic trash and throw it away. You can do the same. Every time you throw something in the trash can, you keep it from getting washed into sewers leading to the sea. When you do this, say, "Hail Poseidon, Lord of the Seas, I honor you!" It will definitely catch His attention and put you on His radar. Those small acts mean more to Him than traditional offerings.

Prayer to Poseidon

Hail Poseidon Basileus, mighty and blessed King of the Seas! Enno-sigaio, Hippokourios, trident-wielding, earthshaking protector and tender of horses, I call to You and honor You. Poseidon Pelagaios who protects the seas, Great Lord of Water, of magma, of the blood of the Earth, I ask You to aid us in our efforts to heal the damage we have wrought on our planet. Help me see what I can do in this healing quest. Strengthen our resolve, individually and collectively. Great Lord Poseidon, please help humanity stop seeing ourselves as the center of all things and start truly holding the life and health of the planet as sacred. Poseidon Asphalios, You who secure safe voyages, I ask for Your blessing on this voyage of my life and on our collective voyage into a new age. Mighty Poseidon, I honor You and ask for Your blessing.

Pathworking to the Sea Altar of Poseidon

With your eyes closed, see the room in which you are sitting begin to fill with mists that get thicker and thicker until you can no longer see your hand in front of you. As the mists fade, find yourself walking on a beach of soft sand shimmering with silver bits of mica. The beach is a beautiful natural harbor, sheltered from the winds and tides and leading to the vast sea. Breathing the salty air, you gaze at the stunningly clear and beautiful water—turquoise with blue and green. Further up the beach planted in the sand is an ancient ship's mast with a small altar behind it. Walking to the altar, you notice it is decorated with images of various creatures and plants of the sea. Look closely at the altar. [Pause.]

The desire to meet with Poseidon wells up in your heart, and you reach out with your mind toward Him. Open your hand and find a gift for the Lord of the Seas and lay it on the altar. [Pause.]

Your attention is drawn to where you find Poseidon. You may ask Him what you should know about Him. [Long pause.] Ask if He has any guidance for you. [Long pause.]

Ask Poseidon if there is anything you should know should you want to work more closely with Him. [Pause.]

Thank Poseidon and look around one more time. Begin walking back down the beach. Mists begin rising from the ground, growing thicker and thicker until the fog is so dense you cannot see your hand before you. The mists dissipate; find yourself back in your room.

Demeter and Persephone

Demeter is the sister of Zeus, Hera, Poseidon, Hades, and Hestia. She is known for two things: the gift of agriculture, especially of grain, and the Eleusinian Mysteries She shares with Persephone and Hades. The Mysteries give humans knowledge about death and will be discussed in chapter 12. Her symbols include the cornucopia, sheaves of wheat, the sickle, and Her chariot pulled by winged serpents. In addition to sheaves of grain, other things sacred to Her are poppies, pigs, snakes, geckos, and mint.

Demeter is the queen of the Earth and Her powers are related to the health and fecundity of the soil and the Green World. She has power over the process of birth, growth, and death and over the spiritual mysteries of food itself. All life grows by taking in other life and transforming it.

Demeter sent her apostle, Triptolemos, to teach agriculture to humans. This allowed permanent settlements to arise in Neolithic times. Along with Poseidon, Demeter is an amazing ally in working on environmental issues. She cares deeply about sustainable food production that is good for the health of the soil, the plants, and those who consume the plants. Sustainable food security is a pressing issue that will become more critical as the climate crisis deepens.

Demeter, sometimes just called *Deo* (the Goddess), is very close to Her daughter, Persephone, who was often just called *Kore*, meaning "maiden." Together They presided over the festival of Thesmophoria, celebrated at the time of seed sowing throughout the Greek-speaking world. Thesmophoria, exclusively attended by adult women, promoted fertility and is likely the most ancient festival.

An important myth is the abduction of Persephone by Hades, the Lord of the Dead and Underworld. There are obvious meanings having to do with plants where Persephone, who embodies much of the power of the Green World, goes underground and then returns to the surface in full flower before going back to the Underworld again. In the myth, Demeter is utterly bereft and enraged by this abduction and threatens to prevent the Green World from coming back to life until Kore is released. This close connection between mother and daughter and the mother's rage is significant. Demeter Brimos, the terrifying Demeter, frightened all the other Theoi. The power of the Mother's rage is scarier than any battle deity.

PRAYER TO DEMETER AND PERSEPHONE

Hail Deo and Kore, Great Queen of the Earth and Her lovely daughter.

Thank You for Your bounty, Demeter and Persephone Karpophoroi, fruit-bearing ones, Demeter Chloe, of the blooming, Aglakarpos, Agladoros, all-nourishing giver of splendid gifts. Demeter Ploutodoteria, who provides all wealth, may I be attentive to and grateful for all the many blessings of this life. Megala Meter, Great Mother, You are Horephoros, the bringer of the seasons, including birth, growth, and death. Thesmophoros, You help us understand the Divine Law expressed in Nature. Demeter Eleusinia, Persephone Soteria, through

Your Grace we may experience Your Mysteries and be freed from fear of death. I honor You, Divine Mother and Daughter, and ask for Your blessing on my life and death. May I always grow and thrive.

PATHWORKING TO THE TEMPLE OF DEMETER ON NAXOS

With your eyes closed, see the room in which you are sitting begin to fill with mists that get thicker and thicker until you can no longer see your hand in front of you. As the mists fade, find yourself on a beautiful fertile plain with mountains to your right. High up in the mountains, you glimpse a cave sacred to Zeus looking down on the plain. Before you is a pathway to an elegant yet simple temple standing alone, surrounded by fields of verdant green young wheat and bright red poppies. Walking to the temple, a winged-serpent guardian approaches. Stop and greet it. [Pause.]

Approaching the temple, you see an altar with a fire lit on top and a pit dug deep into the Earth beside it. Look into your hand, finding either a liquid or a solid object. Feel in your heart the desire to commune with Demeter and get to know Her. As you are so moved, place it either in the fire or give it to the pit. Demeter has both empyrean and chthonic aspects.

Feeling Her presence, face Her. Ask Her what you should know about Her. [Long pause.] Ask Her if she has any guidance for you. [Long pause.]

Know you may visit this place any time to commune with Demeter. Thank Her and look around once more. Start walking away from the temple. Mists begin rising from the ground, growing thicker and thicker until the fog is so dense you cannot see your hand before you. The mists dissipate. Find yourself back in your room.

HADES AND PERSEPHONE

Hades is not counted among the Olympians nor given offerings at altars dedicated to the Dodeka Theoi, although He is considered the same status. Hades is king of the chthonic realms—of the deep Earth and Underworld. He is god of the dead and of all that is deep under the Earth. Greek ritual practice makes strict divisions between rituals involving chthonic powers and those involving the empyrean (heavenly) powers, considering mixing the two to be a source of *miasma*. Persephone, the wife of Hades and daughter of Demeter, is queen of the Underworld and is usually worshipped in that form. Hades is clearly devoted to His wife and queen.

Hades, as Aidoneus, is the enthroned Lord of the Dead, known for being absolutely impartial and fair to all souls. I experience Him as deeply compassionate, and He was called the savior of the dead. He takes in the dead and, in His realm, they consolidate and integrate their experiences into their immortal souls, which are the seeds from which their new life will grow. This is like a bulb being nurtured deep in the underworld until it can grow again. Reincarnation is a common part of many ancient Greek traditions.

Hades (as Plouton), Persephone, and Demeter are givers of wealth. Some of this wealth is related to the plants growing with their roots in the Underworld, some is from the metals and gems mined from the Underworld, but Hades understands and bestows wealth more generally. Hades's power is more related to actual material wealth—real estate, business ownership, material objects, etc.—than symbolic wealth like money.

Regularly invoked in funerary rites, both Hades and Persephone are interested in the work of death doulas, hospice, and any efforts helping people pass through the transition into death with as little fear and pain as possible. Hades facilitates communication with the dead, especially ancestors. He sends dreams allowing ancestors to interact with us and had an oracle that allowed the dead to speak to the living. He is known for giving wise counsel Himself and for enabling the dead to give advice so we can live well.

These Great Ones want to heal us from our fear of death. That is a tall order given our human *moira* as beings who die yet cannot see all things—but if this feat could be managed, it would radically transform us and our *moira*. The Mysteries, discussed in chapter 12, were striving to accomplish this objective.

Prayer to Hades and Persephone

Lord Hades, Aidoneus, I hail You, great king of the Underworld, and Your queen, Persephone Despoina, who receive the dead into Your grace. Hades Isodetes, Persephone Praxidike, You impartially uphold and carry out justice. Hades Euboulous, You send dreams from our ancestors to guide us. I ask for Your blessing so I may live wisely and well. Ploutous, giver of wealth, I ask for the blessing of Your bounty so I may live without unnecessary struggle and anxiety. Neikron Soter, savior of the dead, and Persephone Soteria, bless my ancestors and those I love who have passed before me. When it is my time, may I pass easily, fearlessly, and painlessly into Your embrace, fully integrating all lessons and growth from this incarnation into my immortal soul. Thank You, holy and compassionate king and queen of the Underworld. I honor You and ask for Your blessing.

PATHWORKING TO THE PLOUTONIAN CAVE AT ELEUSIS

With your eyes closed, see the room in which you are sitting begin to fill with mists that get thicker and thicker until you can no longer see your hand in front of you. As the mists fade, find yourself in a large courtyard inside a walled sanctuary. This is the Outer Court of the Sanctuary of Eleusis. You smell burning offerings at various altars, honoring the Gods of the Mysteries.

You are here to meet with Hades and, perhaps, Persephone. A priest approaches you with pure water, brought from the sea, to wash your head, face, and hands, purifying yourself. [Pause.]

The priest hands you a barley cake and you walk to an altar that has a fire on top. Place it in the fire with a prayer in which you state your intention to pay homage to Hades and Persephone. [Pause.]

Turn toward the center of the Outer Court. Up some stairs is a roofed portico serving as a passage to the Inner Court of the Mysteries. Walk up the stairs through the portico. On the left, immediately on the inside, is the sacred Kallichoron Well—the well of beautiful dances—where the young maidens of Eleusis tried to bring cheer to the grieving Demeter. Keep walking straight until you come to a large stone, shaped so you can easily sit on it. This is the Agelastos Petra, the Mourning Stone, on which Demeter rested in Her search for Her stolen daughter. The great heroes who went to the Underworld and returned first sat on this stone. Thinking of Her sorrow and honoring Her lamentation, sit on the Agelastos Petra. [Pause.]

Making a close and sharp turn to the right, walk up a short path to a temple right above the Agelastos Petra. This temple, the Ploutonian, is built into a shallow cave and is an entrance to the Underworld. In front there is a *bothros* pit. Look into your hand and find an offering for Hades. With gratitude for His care for the dead, drop your offering into the *bothros*. [Pause.]

Go into the temple and into the back, into the cave itself. You see the cave is shallow, but with certain small openings, smaller than a human body can go through. You are drawn to one of them, and you feel with your mind that it is deep and goes into the Underworld. You call into yourself the desire to get to know Hades, the host of the dead, the giver of wealth, and the god who enables the ancestors to speak to us. Feel your attention pulled to where He, or possibly Persephone, is.

Ask Hades what He wants you to know about Him. If Persephone is there, ask the same of Her. [Long pause.] Ask if He has any counsel for you. If Persephone is there, ask the same of Her. [Long pause.]

Thank Hades and Persephone and spend a moment more in this liminal space. Turn and go out the temple door. Go back down the path to the Agelastos Petra, realizing the Telesterion, the main temple of the Mysteries, is off to your right, but today is not the day of initiation. Turn to your left, passing the Kallichoron Well, going through the portico, down the steps back into the Outer Court of the Mysteries. Mists begin rising from the ground, growing thicker and thicker until the fog is so dense you cannot see your hand before you. The mists dissipate. Find yourself back in your room.

HESTIA

Hestia the goddess of the hearth flame, fundamentally, is the hearth-fire. In Her Roman form as Vesta, She is completely aniconic. She is sometimes counted among the Olympians, and sometimes not, but is of equal status. Hestia is important in household practice. Having a household shrine and asking Her to ensure all members of the household are safe, healthy, happy, and have stable finances is a good practice. Hestia presides over cooking and meals, which is the site of a tremendous amount of social bonding.

In addition to the household hearth, She is the fire in the hearth of the city, the *prytaneion*, where public oaths were sworn. She presides over the hearth in each of the sanctuaries, including the eternal flames. The fire of the *prytaneion* embodied the unity and vitality of the whole community. The act of claiming asylum happened in front of a hearth-fire—usually at the *prytaneion*, but it could be at any hearth. The asylum seeker was then under the protection of Hestia. Most sanctuaries have a building dedicated to Her where sacrificial food was cooked and the community shared a meal with the Gods.

Hestia is the conscious interface with the aspect of Fire itself that is Tamed Fire—fire that is in relationship with us. We only became human as opposed to animal through this relationship. Originally, this would have happened because of grace. Fire would have decided to be in relationship with us and shown us how to tame part of it. Mythologically, we see this in the myth of Prometheus. Tamed Fire protected us from predators and kept us from freezing. Tamed Fire allowed us to cook food and enabled us to stay up at night and develop the human arts like storytelling and music, which changed our minds and brains. Tamed Fire lies in back of countless advances in technology and culture. This partnership makes us human.

Hestia, as the interface, understands what it means to be human and can teach us about our true nature and purpose. She generally cares about nurturing humanity and humans nurturing each other. The Tamed Fire of the hearth both nurtures and must be nurtured and given attention. It is a fundamentally reciprocal relationship.

The purest forms of taming fire come from capturing sun-fire with a parabolic mirror or fire by friction. When there is *miasma*, the hearth-fire was sometimes extinguished and then relit from one of the temple hearth-fires, which were originally lit from the sun.

Prayer to Hestia

Hail, blessed Hestia, goddess of the hearth and flame that nurtures humanity. Bringer of domestic bliss and of comfort, whenever I cook or eat, may I remember You and Your grace. Whenever I am warm when it is cold, may my heart swell with gratitude. May I see You in the light allowing me to be active after dark. Great Hestia, Your ongoing partnership lies behind all civilizations. I see and know this and am grateful for Your kindness and care. In Your honor, I will strive to be kind, giving, and full of care in the course of my life. Help me hold Your example in my mind. I honor You, Divine Hestia of the hearth-fire, and ask for Your blessing.

Pathworking to the Hearth of Hestia

With your eyes closed, see the room in which you are sitting begin to fill with mists that get thicker and thicker until you can no longer see your hand in front of you. As the mists fade, find yourself in a room with a hearth. There are two empty chairs beside the hearth. This is a space in your own inner landscape. We all have an inner hearth-fire that is an intimate place to go for our own spiritual work. You are standing in your personal archetypal dwelling. Note the room. What is its general shape and décor? What size is it? What furnishings are there? Are there any objects you note? Wander around the room and explore. [Long pause.]

Return to the hearth and note the fire within. Sit in one of the chairs and contemplate the fire, conjuring a desire to meet with Hestia and understand the perspective of Tamed Fire and its partnership with humanity. Reach out with your mind and find yourself in the fire itself. Allow the fire to reveal what it will to you. [Long pause.]

Your mind withdraws. Finding yourself back in the chair by the hearth, You look at the other chair and see Hestia. Ask if She has any further messages or blessings for you. [Pause.]

Look into your hand and find a gift for Her. Thank the Goddess who is the hearth-fire and look around, once more, at this room to which you can return anytime. [Pause.]

Mists begin rising from the ground, growing thicker and thicker until the fog is so dense you cannot see your hand before you. The mists dissipate. Find yourself back in your room.

APHRODITE

Aphrodite is the goddess of erotic love—the power of lust and procreation, which is the creative power of nature. Her parentage varies according to the myths. Sometimes She is a primal force emerging from the sperm and blood of the sky falling into the sea. Occasionally She is a daughter of Zeus by Dione, a goddess worshipped as Zeus's mate in the northern mainland of Greece. Aphrodite is sometimes portrayed as gentle and relatable, and sometimes as an implacable force of nature. She is wife of Hephaistos and lover of Ares.

Cosmically, Aphrodite's power is attraction itself on all levels. Aphrodite guides us toward our spirit's true desire, which can lead you to your correct path. Her power feels like "flow" when you are in alignment but feels negative when you resist your true desire or pursue what is misaligned. Aphrodite's power requires surrender to true desire and allowing yourself to be worked by it. This requires courage.

Being born from the sea, Aphrodite can be called on to ensure safe passage or safe harbor (literally or metaphorically). She had protective relationships with certain cities, including Rome, but any warrior aspect is probably related to particular relationships She had with certain groups of humans rather than characterizing Her power and domain.

As noted in chapter 2, I don't usually focus on "what color candle" each Greek deity likes. But in Aphrodite's case, she really does like almost everything you would expect. Pink, cherry red, seashells, pearls, roses, anything sweet smelling, doves, sparkly things—if it's sold on Valentine's Day, She will like it.

Prayer to Aphrodite

Blessed Aphrodite, goddess of love and of beauty, I invite You into my life. Aphrodite Urania, Aphrodite Pandemos, Aphrodite Doritis, great goddess of Heavenly Love who brings love to all the people, blessing us with bounty, I honor You and ask You to bless all my days with Your gifts. Blooming One, Aphrodite Morpho of lovely form, Aphrodite Symmakhia, may You be my ally in all forms of love. Apostrophia, protect me from unhealthy desires, but help me follow my heart to those that are healthy and generative. Most blessed Aphrodite, above all else, help my human nature hear the call of my own divinity and answer in love. Thank You, mighty Goddess, to whose power all beings, gods and humans, long to surrender. I honor You and ask for Your blessing.

Pathworking to Aphrodite's Garden

With your eyes closed, see the room in which you are sitting begin to fill with mists that get thicker and thicker until you can no longer see your hand in front of you. As the mists fade, find yourself inhaling the scent of roses, reclining on a beautiful and comfortable couch in a large gazebo set in the middle of a garden. Hearing the cooing of doves, you look around. Everything in this place is designed to delight your senses. Pay attention to what you find attractive and what draws your attention. Explore for a while. [Long pause.]

Conjure in your mind a desire to meet Aphrodite, the goddess of love and beauty. Think about Her and wish for a gift She would enjoy. Open your hand and find it. [Pause.] You feel Her smiling presence. Face Her and give Her your offering.

Ask Her what you need to know about Her. [Long pause.] Ask Aphrodite if there are any healthy attractions you are avoiding or unhealthy attractions in whose snare you are caught. Ask if She has any advice or empowerment for you. [Long pause.]

Ask if there is anything else She wants to tell you. [Pause.] Thank the Goddess. If you have wandered, go back to the comfortable couch and lie back on it. Close your inner eyes. Feel the beauty of the place and the Goddess sinking deeply into you.

Mists begin rising from the ground, growing thicker and thicker until the fog is so dense you cannot see your hand before you. The mists dissipate. Find yourself back in your room.

ARES

Ares, son of Zeus and Hera, is the god of war. He is a protector who gives courage and defends civil order. He has many children with Aphrodite and His main rival is His brother Hephaistos. Historically, Ares was regarded ambivalently. He had few temples, but warfare was part of life in ancient Greece, and all Greek societies expected men to participate in military service. Ares was mostly worshipped on the battlefield and training ground. Every warrior culture shares the same problem: the qualities making an individual a good warrior and protector make the same person a menace to their own society in a different context. Therefore, Ares wasn't universally adored.

Years ago, to my surprise, I had a powerful encounter with Ares, who was upset about the conditions of modern warfare. His grievance is that the power of Hephaistos had taken over His domain. Modern warfare is no longer primarily about the courage and skill of warriors—it is about technology. There is no glory for Ares in it. I saw His point.

I would never pretend Ares is sweet—He isn't. There is no denying His capacity for violence. However, He is the warrior, *par excellence*, and embodies a number of positive characteristics. He is a protector, and protectors put a higher level of priority on something other than themselves. This can be motivated by love, honor, duty, loyalty, or commitment. The warrior builds and embodies the virtues of courage, self-discipline, and camaraderie. The warrior focuses on developing the will. We are in a society in which our technology and our social systems undercut our capacity to develop a strong will. Most of us could use some assistance with self-discipline and will development. Ares is a useful ally. He has a long history in helping His warriors "graduate" from humanity. I will discuss this in depth in chapter 13.

Prayer to Ares

Hail Warlike Ares, Enyalius who gives courage. Ares Stratios, Laossoos, who trains and rallies warriors. Ares Enkhespalos, Ares Thoos, Ares Oryx, spear-brandishing Ares who is swift and piercing, I ask You to protect all I love and empower me to be a protector. Help me fortify my will and self-discipline so, like You, I may be mighty and strong. Great Ares, help me strengthen my capacity to maintain focus and my willingness to sacrifice for what is worthy. Thank You, Ares. I honor You.

Pathworking to the Training Ground of Ares

With your eyes closed, see the room in which you are sitting begin to fill with mists that get thicker and thicker until you can no longer see your hand in front of you. As the mists fade, find yourself in a gym under the open sky. All around you, people and other beings are training. They are focused but are also supporting each other. As you observe more closely, you note there are some beings acting as coaches, giving instruction, advice, and encouragement. There are a couple of dragons on the premises as well. They are sacred to Ares.

You feel a presence sizing you up and turn to find yourself looking at Ares. Tell Him you want to learn more about Him and ask if He will speak with you. [Pause.] Ask Him what you should know about Him. [Long pause.]

If you want to increase your self-discipline and train your will, ask if there is any assistance for you here. [Pause.] Knowing you want to give something to Ares to thank Him for His attention, open your hand and find a gift for Him. [Pause.]

If you desire, ask if you can come back to this place to continue any recommended training. Ask if there is anything else you need to know or do at
this time. [Pause.]

Thank Ares and begin to walk out of the open-air gym. Mists begin rising from the ground, growing thicker and thicker until the fog is so dense
you cannot see your hand before you. The mists dissipate. Find yourself
back in your room.

HEPHAISTOS

Hephaistos, the smith god, is sometimes considered the son of both Zeus and
Hera and sometimes of Hera alone. Hephaistos is not just the god of metal-
lurgy, He is the god of *techne*—of technology. There are some forms of *techne*
He shares with Athena, and They can be worshipped together. He is married to
Aphrodite but has no children with Her, although He does have children with
other goddesses. Hephaistos is an inventor, maker, and transformer. Like all
smith gods, He can assist humans in transforming themselves.

Similar to Ares, the power of Hephaistos has dangers associated with it.
Technology's allure is about trying to solve problems by tweaking the cosmos
and it is always possible the desire of the maker to make can overcome clear-
headed restraint. Sometimes inventors are driven by an obsession to invent,
even when they know their invention is dangerous.

Something Aphrodite, Hephaistos, and Ares have in common is the powers
associated with Them (desire, the power of a warrior, and the drive for invention) want to expand and can become unhealthy. Therefore, working with
these three Great Ones to ensure our approach is healthy is important. Technology is a tool—it should not be an end in and of itself. It should make both
the humans that use it and the world better. Hephaistos can help with that.

Many environmental and social challenges have their roots in technologies that also create many wonders. For example, the climate crisis is the direct
result of our fossil fuel technology—and everything in our society since the
industrial revolution has its roots in this technology. The answer to this quag-
mire will require the development and deployment of new technologies that
do not cause this (or equally bad) damage. This lies within the domain of
Hephaistos.

Similarly, information technology transformed our world in almost miraculous ways. Yet the designers used the scientific discoveries of the mechanisms of addiction to make their technology addictive. Hephaistos can help us manage our technology use on an individual level and support us in putting ethical guardrails in place for technology development. He can be called upon to inspire technological advances that can effectively and ethically make the world better.

Hephaistos is often depicted with His hammer and tongs, sometimes riding a donkey. He has a close working relationship with the cyclopes and is attended by golden feminine sentient robots He created who were known for their beautiful singing.

PRAYER TO HEPHAISTOS

Mighty Hephaistos Klytometis, famed for Your knowledge and Your skill, I praise You, Polytechnes, god of technology. Hephaistos Polyphron, Polymetis, You are inventive and possess many knowings. Hephaistos Kyllopodion, I am grateful to You for inspiring the many inventions that make life easier and better. Help me be in right relationship with technology so it serves my Good. Divine Smith, help our society be in right relationship with technology so it serves the Greater Good. Inspire inventors with clear vision so they may creatively and ethically be the makers they are called to be. Holy Hephaistos, may I be melted down in the forges of transformation to become my rarified self. Noble Hephaistos, I honor You and ask for Your blessing.

PATHWORKING TO THE FORGE OF HEPHAISTOS

With your eyes closed, see the room in which you are sitting begin to fill with mists that get thicker and thicker until you can no longer see your hand in front of you. As the mists fade, find yourself inside a forge and workshop, deep within the Earth. You feel intense heat and hear hammers clanging on metal. Three cyclopes are present and working. If you like, you may approach them. [Pause.] You are surprised, given the enclosure, to see a donkey and a crane. Go to the crane and ask if you may seek an audience with Hephaistos. [Pause.]

You have the urge to turn. A bit away from the fire, you see Hephaistos at a table filled with drawings, plans, and models. He waves you over.
Ask Hephaistos to tell you about Himself and what He wants to see in the
world. [Long pause.] Ask Him about your relationship with technology and
if there is anything you should know. [Pause.] Ask Him about your relationship to inventive creativity and if He has any counsel for you. [Pause.]

With your new understanding, build a desire to give Hephaistos something meaningful. Open your hand and find it there. Give it to Him. [Pause.]

Take a final look around. Thank Hephaistos and walk toward the forge's
door. Mists begin rising from the ground, growing thicker and thicker until
the fog is so dense you cannot see your hand before you. The mists dissipate, and you find yourself back in your room.

ATHENA

Pallas Athena, goddess of wisdom and strategy, is the mind-born daughter of
Zeus and Metis. I consider Her to be the goddess of humanity. She is a civic
goddess—the main goddess of the *polis*. She is a common patron and guardian
of heroes and is known for Her nearness to humans. In Her cults, She is usually involved with taking something raw and natural and transforming it into
something useful for humans. Many of Her epithets are abstracted virtues—
some of which get spun off and worshipped as separate goddesses. Themis and
Dike, both goddesses of justice, and Nike, the goddess of victory, are all epithets of Athena.

A few myths are particularly revealing about what She is and cares about.
Before Her birth, Zeus received a prophecy that His child by Metis would have
the power to overthrow Him, as He had overthrown His father, Cronos, and
as Cronos had violently overthrown His own father, Uranus. Zeus swallowed
the pregnant Metis (mythologically, Zeus took Metis/Knowledge inside Himself). Later, Zeus had a headache, and Athena, the mind-born, sprang forth,
fully armed, from Zeus's head. The Heavens and the Earth quaked at the birth
of the most powerful being yet born. As Her first act, Athena laid down Her
weapons. She could have overthrown Zeus and continued the pattern of trans-
ferring power through violence but chose not to do so. In response to this

pattern interruption, Zeus chose to share power.[32] Athena stands as His right hand, but also as His equal. It is not accidental that democracy, literally "rule of the people," was born in Her city of Athens.

Another revealing story is Her role in the trial of Orestes. Agamemnon's family was full of violence, adultery, and revenge—a pattern going back generations. Preparing to sail to Troy, Agamemnon sacrificed his daughter, Iphigenia, earning the wrath of his wife, Clytemnestra. Upon Agamemnon's return, Clytemnestra killed Agamemnon. Agamemnon's son, Orestes, was caught in a web of causation that would doom him. Vendetta required he avenge the murder of his father, but to do so, he had to kill his own mother—also a violation of Divine Law. Orestes, pursued by the Erinyes—spirits of vengeance—went to Athens to plead his case and receive judgment. Athena, as judge, sided with Orestes, ending the cycle of vengeance and establishing Rule of Law. She offered the Erinyes a different cosmic role as the Eumenides, enforcers of the Rule of Law, rather than continuing as the spirits of vendetta.[33]

Athena wants us to become full spiritual adults. She wants us to take responsibility for ourselves and our societies and commit to fully evolve. When we are working in this way, She is a source of amazing help. I find one metope from Zeus's temple at Olympia particularly expressive of how She works. The temple shows scenes from the Twelve Labors of Herakles, and Athena is depicted by His side. During one labor, Herakles must take the place of the Titan, Atlas, and hold up the sky. He is shown using all His might—the strain is evident, and He is giving it everything He has. Behind Him, using one hand, She holds up everything Herakles cannot manage. He has to have the daring and put in all the effort He can, but if He does, She will make sure He does not fail.

) PRAYER TO ATHENA

Bright-eyed Pallas Athena, Athena Boulaia, wise counselor, bless me with Your wisdom and guide me, companion of heroes, on my life's journey. Athena Promachos, great protector, shield me from harm. Athena Ergane, divine weaver and maker, grant me Your skill as I weave the pattern of my life. Athena Polias, great goddess of human civiliza-

---

32. Athanassakis, trans., "Homeric Hymn to Athena," 66.

33. Aeschylus, "The Eumenides," 155–202.

*tion, may Your wisdom guide our society and may I honorably fulfill
my duty as a citizen of this world. Athena Soteria, savior, You lead
us on the path of spiritual evolution to apotheosis—to fully realized
divinity—bless me. May I know You as You walk by my side. Athena
Nike, may I walk through this world with confidence knowing that if I
do my best, striving to evolve, You will support me. Hail Athena, mind-
born maid, I honor You and ask for Your blessing.*

Pathworking to the Temple of Athena Polias

With your eyes closed, see the room in which you are sitting begin to fill
with mists that get thicker and thicker until you can no longer see your hand
in front of you. As the mists fade, find yourself on the Athenian Acropolis.
To your right, you see the Parthenon, resplendent with its painted friezes.
The statues look as though they could get down and begin talking with you.
To your left is a gigantic bronze statue of Athena, and, behind this monumental statue, you see the Erechtheion with its famous caryatid porch.
Walking toward the porch, you pass a courtyard where you see Athena's
gift to Athens, the venerable olive tree. Looking at the porch, you almost
believe the pillars, shaped like glamorous young women, are alive and moving slightly. You may see a sacred serpent there. The caryatids guard the
tomb of Kekrops, the first king of Athens—half man and half serpent—
pulled from the Earth by Athena Herself. [Pause.]

You continue walking past the caryatid porch toward the temple's far
side. Reaching the end, turn left, and see before you the temple of Athena
Polias. It is beautiful and refined. On the right, past the temple's edge, are
steps leading down to the portion of the Erechtheion where Poseidon's
fountain is located, but you stop here, at the temple of Athena. Looking
inside, you see an indescribably ancient statue of Athena enthroned, made
of olive wood. This statue fell from the sky as a gift from the Goddess, and
wherever it and the people of Athens are present, that is Athens. In your
mind, you feel the desire to give a gift to Athena. Open your hand and see
your offering to Her. [Pause.]

You feel Her presence and She beckons you. Give Athena your gift and
ask what you should know about Her. [Long pause.] Ask if She has any wise
counsel to impart to you. [Long pause.] Ask if there is anything else She

wants you to know or do. [Pause.] If you wish to work with Her more regularly, ask how you may do so. [Pause.]

Thank the Goddess and feel the power in Her gaze. Turn, going back toward the front of the Acropolis, feeling the empowerment you have received. Mists begin rising from the ground, growing thicker and thicker until the fog is so dense you cannot see your hand before you. The mists dissipate; find yourself back in your room.

ARTEMIS

Artemis is the goddess of wild animals and animal nature and is the defender of the wilderness—those areas away from humans. She is the protector of all children, but especially girls, and protects women, particularly during childbirth. Artemis is *parthenos*, often translated as "virgin," but really meaning that She holds Her own sovereignty, separate from any male. She is not, originally, the moon goddess—that is Selene—but She does become a lunar goddess.

Artemis is deeply concerned about violence against women and girls and sexual violence, generally. For any work we do to protect people from this type of violence, to help victims heal, to interrupt aspects of our culture enabling sexual and domestic violence, to stop and punish perpetrators, Artemis is a powerful ally. She will support opposing any and all exploitation of girls and women.

One important cult was at Brauron, which I mentioned in the context of the myth of Kallisto. The girls of Athenian citizens were sent to Her sanctuary when they were in their late childhood approaching womanhood. There, under the care of Artemis and Her priestesses, they were known as "little bears." They lived in dormitories and prepared for adulthood, similar to the mandatory military service of the youths spending a couple of years becoming full adults under the care of Apollon. Some women would return to Brauron later in life to thank Artemis for assistance in childbirth—especially those surviving dangerous births.

As goddess of the hunt, Artemis is goddess of the wilds. Hunters honored Her, but knew they had to avoid killing animals incorrectly—like those that were pregnant or too young, or where hunting would upset the balance of nature. Hunted animals should be killed with minimal pain. In our times, humans have decimated the wilds. There are some animals, like deer in the United States, that must be hunted by humans because the apex predators are gone. In general, any efforts toward conserving the wilds are important to Artemis.

She can assist us in reconnecting with our own wild nature. Humans are pack animals, like wolves. We are social—that is part of our animal nature. We are often extremely out of touch with our natural selves, having built a society that treats humans as machines rather than as living beings. Artemis can help us recover our true nature and the beauty of the wilderness within.

PRAYER TO ARTEMIS

Hail to You, Artemis Pheraia, queen of the beasts and the wilds. May I feel Your presence and embrace my own true nature. I pray for the protection of the wilds and the restoration of the wilderness. Help me be aware of the impacts of my actions on the wilds as I go through my day and act rightly. Artemis Philomeirax, friend of young girls, I pray to You to protect all the girls of this world and help them thrive. Protect the young boys of this world from danger and from indoctrination into toxic ideas about masculinity so they, too, may thrive. Protect and walk with the children who feel different, so they don't feel alone. Big Sister, Bear Mother, Bright Daughter of Lovely Leto, protect the women of the world from harm and help them thrive. Thank You, Artemis Soteria, savior of girls, children, women, and all wild things. I honor You and ask for Your blessing.

PATHWORKING TO THE SANCTUARY OF ARTEMIS AT BRAURON

With your eyes closed, see the room in which you are sitting begin to fill with mists that get thicker and thicker until you can no longer see your hand in front of you. As the mists fade, find yourself walking on a road toward a flat stone footbridge over a small river. Stop on the bridge and ask for permission to enter the sanctuary of Artemis Brauronia so you may honor Her and get to know Her.

If you are granted entry, walk across the bridge. Immediately in front of you is a building shaped like the Greek letter Pi with a courtyard in the center. This is the dormitory of the little bears and priestesses. Your attention is drawn to the girls playing in the large courtyard, laughing and running around, under the watchful eye of the priestesses and the Goddess. Turn to your right and see a large spring next to the temple of Artemis, close to a large rock outcropping. Walk to the sacred spring.

Feel your desire to meet Artemis. Look in your hand and find a gift for Her. Pay attention to what it is and ask the spring to take it in honor of Artemis. Throw it in. [Pause.] You feel Her presence and turn to find Her. Ask Her what you should know about Her. [Long pause.] Ask if She has anything She wants you to know or do. [Pause.] Ask if you are permitted to return here or if there is somewhere else you should seek Her in the future. [Pause.] Thank the goddess of the wilds. Walk back to the stone footbridge. Give thanks one more time as you cross the bridge, leaving the sanctuary of Artemis. [Pause.]

Mists begin rising from the ground, growing thicker and thicker until the fog is so dense you cannot see your hand before you. The mists dissipate. Find yourself back in your room.

APOLLON

Apollon is one of the most complex of the Theoi. He is not initially the sun god—that is Helios—although He becomes a solar god by the fifth century BCE, just as Artemis became the lunar goddess.[34] He is the god of Light, which is also Truth. He is a healer and the main oracular god. He and Zeus are the only Theoi who have the title *Moiragetes,* "leader of the Fates." He has a comprehensive understanding of *moira* and sees *themistes*—both "what is" and "what is right"—and His oracles are designed to help close that gap, which is a form of healing.

He is a god of civilization, complementing Artemis as the goddess of the wilds. He is the protector and guide of young men in their process of becoming adults, like Artemis is for young women.

Musagetes, "leader of the Muses," is another of His epithets. The Muses are not only responsible for music, but for all the human intellectual arts and endeavors. Apollon is Their patron and is the Great Musician.

Apollon is the only of the Theoi who periodically becomes temporarily mortal without really giving up His immortality. This happened a couple of times in mythology, and I believe His son, Orpheus, is one of His avatars. He

---

34. Graf, *Apollo.*

is simultaneously a powerful and cosmic Olympian, and yet is deeply intimate with humanity.

Apollon is the god to whom I am closest. He has a profound understanding of humans in all our frailty. His love feels simultaneously cosmic and profoundly personal and I feel His sadness for our suffering. As I will discuss in the chapter on listening to the Gods, Apollon's cults are unusually personal. He invites His worshippers into His house and temporarily takes possession of a human vessel in order to interact directly. In His healing cults and the cults of His son, Asklepios, the patients have deeply personal interactions and intercessions.

Artemis's birth was painless, but Apollon's lasted nine days with Artemis acting as midwife. Apollon was destined to be particularly powerful, and Leto was cursed so She could not give birth on land. Delos was considered to be a floating island in the Cyclades. On this floating island was a lake, and within the lake was another island with a palm tree at the center. Holding on to this palm tree, Leto birthed Light into the world. Delos became an important cult center for Apollon. Artemis and Leto were also honored there. During historical times, because the whole island is so holy, no one was buried there and the dying were transported off Delos. The entire island is now an archaeological site. The power around the lake is the strongest I have ever experienced. I could feel it thrumming from quite some distance.

In the myth about Delphi's founding, the young Apollon found a nymph, Kastalia, who was the captive of the serpent, Python. Kastalia could help humans be capable of divine possession. Apollon slew the serpent so humans could receive His oracles. Because He had killed, Apollon needed to find a way to purify the *miasma* of this act. He spent eight years wandering in exile, investigating ways to purify *miasma*. He found Daphne, the bay laurel, and created purification rituals using the laurel. Delphi is His first oracle, but many others were established. His gifts and counsel had significant historical impacts. Through His oracle at Delphi, many pieces of the social order were created, including the Athenian constitution for the first democracy, various articulations of rights, and the establishment of the Rule of Law. His oracle at Delphi gave Socrates His quest to become a philosopher.

The main characteristic linking all His aspects is that Apollon is the preserver of the Divine Plan. He understands how things should be and is always trying to do what is necessary to heal what has gone awry and prevent things from going off course—all while helping us grow and become fully conscious participants. He takes discord and weaves it back into harmonious patterns. In His most cosmic level, I perceive Him as playing the Music that is creation—yet He is simultaneously intimately loving on a personal level.

PRAYER TO APOLLON

Phoebus Apollon, bright and shining Lord of Light, Apollon Oulious, Apollon Maleatas, Iatros, great physician, healer of souls and societies, I call to You and ask for Your healing. Help me cleanse myself of all that does not serve and to be a healing force in the world. Apollon Nomimos, may I see and understand Divine Law with clarity and align myself with it. Apollon Mousigetes, leader of the Muses, inspire me so I may always continue to learn and grow. Apollon Alexikakos, You are hagnos, You are absolutely pure and no unholy thing can withstand Your holy presence. I ask for Your protection. Apollon Moiragetes, leader of the Fates, may I see and know what change should happen, my role in the change, and when to accept things as they are. Lord Apollon, ever loving to humanity, I thank You for Your grace and for caring so deeply about us. I honor You and ask for Your blessing.

PATHWORKING TO THE SANCTUARY OF APOLLON AT DELOS

With your eyes closed, see the room in which you are sitting begin to fill with mists that get thicker and thicker until you can no longer see your hand in front of you. As the mists fade, find yourself in a small natural harbor on a rocky island, with the stunning blue-green sea behind you. Follow the road up to a square, smelling the clean salty air mixed with sweet incense. To your left, see an ornate column-lined walk with temples on either side. Begin walking down this road and seeing multiple temples to Apollon and a temple for Artemis. At the path's end are steps leading to the sacred lake. Feel power thrumming from that direction.

Approaching the steps, you discover an altar to Leto. Stop and pay your respects to the Holy Mother. [Pause.]

Climb the steps and come to the lake's edge. In the middle of the lake is another smaller island with a palm tree in the center. Pay attention to the rhythm of the thrumming. This is the place where Light was born into the world. Take a moment and focus on your desire to meet Apollon. You feel Him close by and look. Greet Him and ask what you should know about Him. [Long pause.]

Think about what weighs heaviest on your heart and ask if He has any counsel for you. [Long pause.] Ask if there is anything else He wants you to know or advise you to do. [Pause.] If you desire, ask if there is anything you should know if you want to work with Him more closely. [Pause.]

Feeling gratitude for your time with Him and for His counsel, build a desire to give Him something. Look into your hand and find a gift. Offer it to Him. [Pause.]

Thank Apollon one more time and turn, walking down the steps, through the colonnaded walkway past the temples, and then walk back toward the harbor. Mists begin rising from the ground, growing thicker and thicker until the fog is so dense you cannot see your hand before you. The mists dissipate. Find yourself back in your room.

HERMES

Hermes is the son of Zeus and the nymph Maia. As divine messenger, Hermes bridges all the realms, including the Underworld. Originally, He was a pastoral god. He remains a god of shepherds and herds but became the god of things that link and the process of linking.

Hermes is the god of communication; practices using symbols are His domain. He is the god of travel and all forms of transportation. Herm statues, with only a head, a block, and an erect phallus, protected the roads, the travelers on the roads, and the region in which they were erected. He is the god of trade. Currency, money, and finance are all under His purview. Other deities have some responsibilities for wealth, but money is symbolic energy, moving in a system linking people, organizations, goods, and services—which is very Hermes.

He is a psychopompe, guiding souls to their appropriate afterlife. I find Him to be deeply sensitive and compassionate in this role.

Hermes is the god of athletic contests, heralds, and diplomats. In ancient Greece, the great athletic contests in which athletes traveled from one city-state to the next linked the cities to each other and included what we would call state diplomacy. In all areas of His purview He can choose to block or bind as well as help. He is often the greatest enabler or disabler of any human pursuit.

Like Athena, Hermes is frequently directly intercessory in heroic quests. In myth, He is usually acting on behalf of Zeus. The power of Hermes helps make spiritual will manifest in the world. Hermes figures out how, specifically, to operationalize Zeus's will. Hermes is depicted as taking messages from humanity to the Great Ones and advocating on our behalf.

While Apollon, the god of prophecy, speaks directly to humans, Hermes oversees two forms of divination. The first is divination by *kleromancy*, like throwing dice, lots, or knucklebones. The second is astrology. These are systems linking humans with knowledge of the hidden nature of reality. Tarot, though modern, falls under the purview of Hermes since it is a form of *kleromancy* that also uses symbols.

Hermes is often characterized as a trickster—one story involves His theft of Apollon's cattle while still a toddler. He was worshipped by all manner of ne'er-do-wells who relied on trickery—thieves, fraudsters, cattle rustlers, and so on. Many of His epithets have to do with these less-than-noble attributes, like Arkhos Pheleteon (the Leader of Thieves).

Acknowledging this, I trust Hermes and find alliance with Him is critical in magic. Magic involves moving through various levels of reality, using symbols and communicating with nonhuman consciousness. All these activities fall within the purview of Hermes.

In general, Hermes likes activity. He likes it when things are dynamic. One of His ancient epithets is Hermes Poneomenos, (the Busy One). In my experience, He always seems positive, upbeat, and consistently delightful, albeit with an interesting sense of humor.

PRAYER TO HERMES

Lord Hermes, Angelos Athanaton, Great messenger of the Gods, I call to You and give You thanks. Hermes Diaktoros, blessed guide, thank You for Your many gifts and blessings, for You are the giver of good things. Hermes Hermeneutes, divine interpreter, may I always receive, recognize, and correctly interpret messages from the Gods and the cosmos. Help me understand what I must do to thrive financially and ensure all my acts of communication are clear and correct. Hermes Eri-

ounes, luck-bringing ready helper, I am grateful to You. Great Hermes, may I always see, know, and honor Your power. I honor You and ask for Your blessing.

Pathworking to the Market Shrine of Hermes

With your eyes closed, see the room in which you are sitting begin to fill with mists that get thicker and thicker until you can no longer see your hand in front of you. As the mists fade, find yourself on a road walking into a busy market full of outdoor stalls and a number of large buildings with porches and merchants selling wares. Loud and bustling, it feels like the colorful cacophony of a festival. Anything you need, goods or services, can be found in this place. Little shrines and places for people to stop and sit or chat are scattered throughout the market. You feel drawn toward something in the center but can't see it through the crowds. Walk toward it. Wending your way through, you discover it is a small shrine to Hermes Agoraios. Walk to the shrine and stand in front of it. Before you can formulate what to say, there is a sound on your right side, and you feel a quick puff of wind. Turn and see Hermes standing beside you with His winged shoes, short cloak, and caduceus wand.

Take some time to talk with Hermes. Ask Him what you should know about Him. [Long pause.] Ask if He has any messages for you. [Pause.] Ask if there is anything else He wants you to know or do. [Pause.] Ask Hermes to show you something in the market He would like as an offering. Let Him take you there, get the item, and give it to Him. [Pause.] Thank Hermes and turn to leave.

Walk back toward the road. Mists begin rising from the ground, growing thicker and thicker until the fog is so dense you cannot see your hand before you. The mists dissipate. Find yourself back in your room.

Dionysus

Dionysus is the latest addition to the Olympians, replacing Hestia as the twelfth of the Dodeka Theoi. Considered exotic by the Greeks—often depicted as coming from Thrace—He is accompanied by wild beings, including satyrs, panthers or leopards, and serpents. He is often depicted as gender neutral or gender fluid. Dionysus is unique. Born a mortal, He became immortal and was welcomed as an Olympian.

He is the god of altered states of consciousness. Wine can induce one form of an altered state, but so does the theater or any method of invoking trance. He rules over the methods that induce states of consciousness that help us see differently. Such states may or may not lead to wisdom and knowledge. In their highest form, altered states of consciousness can lead us to transcend our mortal limitations and see without meditation. Dionysiac methods for invoking ecstasy include ecstatic music and dance, ecstatic art, and any other known methods for achieving altered states of consciousness. Some are safer than others—music and dance are relatively safe options.

Dionysus is often paired with Apollon and They are seen as complementary. Dionysus ruled over Apollon's sanctuary at Delphi during the winter months when Apollon was with the Hyperboreans. Dionysus is an important deity in some of the Mysteries, including the Orphic Mysteries.

His origin story as twice-born is important. Zeus took Semele, a Theban princess, as a lover, and She conceived Dionysus. Semele became doubtful her lover really could be the king of the Gods and demanded to see Him in His full glory. When He revealed Himself, as demanded, it destroyed Her mortal form. Zeus rescued the unborn Dionysus and sewed Him into His "thigh," probably testes, until He was ready to be born.

In the Orphic version of this myth, Zeus and Persephone became lovers and had the child Dionysus Zagreus. This child was taken to Mount Ida, like Zeus was when He was a baby, and was guarded by the Kouretes. The Titans seized the infant Dionysus and ripped Him limb from limb and ate Him—but Athena intervened at the last moment and managed to rescue the heart of Dionysus. From this heart, Zeus enabled Dionysus to be born again from Semele. In both mythic versions, Dionysus is twice-born, and His Mysteries involve rebirth. The Orphic Mysteries are explicitly about reincarnation.

Dionysus, as the son of Zeus, had certain godly powers, but was initially mortal. Wandering the Earth, as far away as India, He invented wine and was followed by a retinue including satyrs and maenads (divine dancing women). He is depicted with a leopard skin, holding a thyrsus (a pine cone–topped staff), and wearing a wreath of ivy. Together, His band embraces different activities leading to ecstasy, which is from the Greek *ekstasis* and means "to stand outside oneself."[35] Ecstasy is a type of divine mania allowing you to be filled with divinity.

Dionysus achieved full *apotheosis*—becoming a god—after successfully descending to the Underworld, bringing His mother, Semele, back from the dead, and taking Her to Olympus. His queen, Ariadne, was also mortal and achieved *apotheosis*. Ariadne was a priestess and princess of Crete who assisted the hero Theseus in his escape from the minotaur. Theseus took Her from Crete but abandoned Her on the island of Naxos while She slept. Dionysus discovered Her, fell in love with Her, and made Her into a goddess and His queen. In some versions, Ariadne died before They could wed and Dionysus retrieved both Her and Semele from Hades at the same time. Importantly, Dionysus is a twice-born deity who was human, became a god, and rescued other mortals from death, leading them to immortality.

Theater is born from the worship of Dionysus and is a form of ritual purification. The word *katharsis* literally means "to cleanse" and refers to cleansing *miasma*. The people performing have their consciousness transformed and they bring through divine power while reenacting heroic tragedies, summoning the society's *miasma*. The audience allows the collective *miasma* to be invoked in them, and it is cleansed. Theater is an expiatory ritual. It allows the audience, as members of their society, to enter an altered state, see differently, and potentially change. You can find Dionysus on the inner planes at any of the ancient theaters, but He wanted me to take you someplace else in the pathworking.

PRAYER TO DIONYSUS

Dionysus, Bacchas Adoneus, Dionysus Mellichios, Zagreus, Dionysus Akratrophos, bringer of mixed wine, Dionysus Eleutherios, great liberator, o' twice-born god, I pray to You to be with me. Great God who shifts the minds of men, opening us so we may perceive differently, make me receptive to wisdom. Open my mind and heart to receive the messages of the cosmos and understand its mysteries. I ask You to inspire me and let inspiration flow through me into the group mind and soul of humanity as a blessing. Great God of divine ecstasy, help me stand outside myself and allow the Divine to fill me, enabling

---

35. Burkert, *Greek Religion*.

transcendence. My Lord Dionysus, thank You for Your presence and for the gift of communing with You. I honor You and ask for Your blessing.

PATHWORKING TO THE REVELRY OF DIONYSUS

With your eyes closed, see the room in which you are sitting begin to fill with mists that get thicker and thicker until you can no longer see your hand in front of you. As the mists fade, you find you are in a pine forest high on a mountain. You hear music and move toward it. As you get closer, you realize you are seeing a procession dancing through the forest: human revelers, satyrs, and a few leopards. You have discovered the train of Dionysus. A being comes up to you and asks what you want. Stop and ask, with respect, if you may come closer to meet Dionysus. [Pause.]

If you are given permission, allow yourself to be guided into the revelry. Allow yourself to experience this for a bit. [Long pause.]

Suddenly, it feels as though the air is thin and you experience a disorienting sound, like bullroarers. You turn and find yourself facing Dionysus. Look down in your hand and find a gift for Dionysus and offer it. [Pause.]

Tell Dionysus you want to learn about Him. Ask what He would like you to know. [Long pause.] Ask if He has any message for you or anything He would like you to do. [Pause.] Ask if you may return to this place to seek His company again. [Pause.] Thank Dionysus for His grace and generosity. If you desire to stay longer, you may. If not, give your thanks to all the retinue of Dionysus, turn, and walk away. Mists begin rising from the ground, growing thicker and thicker until the fog is so dense you cannot see your hand before you. The mists dissipate. Find yourself back in your room.

CHAPTER FOUR
SACRED SPACE

The Greek word *temenos*, meaning "a space cut off or set aside," is a frequent word in the ancient record referring to sacred space. In essence, sacred space is an area separated from normal human activities and belongs to the Gods. It is holy (*hieron*), and special rules apply because it is qualitatively different from the places where mortal activities and consciousness dominate.[36]

Some hallowed areas—like precincts dedicated to Zeus Katabaites that had been struck by lightning—were completely set apart and humans were forbidden entry.[37] Most sacred sites provide meeting grounds where humans come to interact with the Theoi. This includes sites on the physical plane and on the inner planes where there are inner sanctuaries. Some of these places exist independently on the inner planes, like the places I took you to in order to meet the Theoi, but you can also construct a sacred space by establishing a *temenos* on the inner plane.

This chapter explores ancient Greek understandings of sacred space and practical methods for creating sacred space within your home.

---

36. Kearns, *Ancient Greek Religion*.
37. Kearns, *Ancient Greek Religion*.

Sacred Directional Orientations

Directional and elemental correspondence is one main method of relating to space, not just in Wicca and Western Ceremonial Magick, but also in various Indic traditions. Although the Hellenic Gods of the Winds are related to the directions and you can work with Them in that way, there is an additional set of sacred directional orientations in ancient Hellenic religion—the center, the periphery, the liminal, going up, and going down. In practice, you can use these orientations to create changes in consciousness.

The Center

The center is the place of stability and order. When you are standing at the center, there is balanced assurance. The hearth is the home's center. In many cities, the *acropolis* was built on the site of the Bronze Age palace and was the center of social order. The sacred center of any city usually included temples of the Theoi associated with governing the *polis*. The *agora*—the marketplace—was also the seat of civic government. A *prytaneion* is a building in the *agora* that included the hearth of Hestia for the *polis*.

Apollon's sanctuary at Delphi included the *omphalos*—the naval stone—and was considered both the Earth's center and the ultimate hearth of the Greek world. Through His oracular priestess at Delphi, Apollon was the great lawgiver—establishing order and Rule of Law. All of this is associated with the directional orientation of coming to and being in the sacred center. If you want to enhance order and stability, you can summon the power of the *omphalos* and use it to connect to the sacred center.

Exercise
Creating the Omphalos Stone

This is a spell to create a tool to hold the power of the sacred center. Traditionally, sacred stones were often collected from local rivers or creeks; however, such actions can disturb vulnerable waterways. In this spell, we will link the powers of the land where you live with the local nymph.

What You'll Need

A trash bag, three bay leaves, a stone you will ritually collect, a sink in which to wash the stone, a pot of water and a stove on which to heat it, and olive or bay oil. Optional: Two more bay leaves and a vessel in which to safely burn them. A wool cloth if you do not have a permanent altar.

Directions

Find a reasonably-sized oval stone close to where you live that will serve as your *omphalos*. Take a trash bag and your stone and go to a local river or creek. Greet the nymph and, as an offering, pick up any trash you see. When your bag is full or the area is clean, ask the nymph for permission to wash the stone in Her waters as a blessing. If the nymph agrees, wash the stone while praying to Her. Thank the nymph. Be sure to dispose of all trash properly. Take the stone home and wash it well. Boil the pot of water. Turn off the heat and steep three bay leaves in the water. Let it cool. Put a finger in the tea and say,

> *Holy Daphne, blessed bay, beloved of Apollon, I ask you to cleanse this stone to make it a fit and pure vessel for the power of the omphalos, the naval stone of the world. Thank you, Blessed One.*

Bathe the stone in the tea. If you can have smoke, burn a couple of bay leaves and pass the smoke over the stone. Once it is purified, rub some olive oil or bay oil on the stone and say,

> *You are the omphalos. You are the naval stone of the world, holding the sacred center.*

Place the *omphalos* on or under your altar or, if you don't have a permanent home for it, wrap it in a wool cloth and store it. When you use it, rub more oil on it and tell it again it is the *omphalos*. It will hold the power of the sacred center for you. Dispose of used bay leaves by either burning them or putting them outside.

The Periphery

The periphery is a wilder place of transformation. Every *polis* had both a city center and *khora*—territory outside the city proper—including agricultural land. Sanctuaries of agricultural gods, including Demeter, Persephone, and Dionysus, were usually in the periphery, as were temples of Artemis and often

Apollon (who was in both the center and the periphery).[38] Although the *omphalos* of Delphi was the cosmic center, Apollon's oracular temples tended to be away from cities. In seeking His counsel, we leave behind the daily concerns of the *polis* to go on pilgrimage—moving away from everyday human thoughts and into a rarified state of spiritual seeking.

The periphery is where the mortal aspect of our nature can fall away more easily—for good or bad. In the *eschatia* (the farthest reaches), there are two special beings—monsters and heroes. Humans are social creatures, and we are only fully human in community. Those who live outside of human community cannot remain truly human. However, those seeking *apotheosis*, seeking to become more than human, must temporarily leave human society in order to transcend their mortality. In Greek mythology, the line between monster and hero is blurry and the hero is always in danger of becoming monstrous. The periphery is the place to seek transformation, but it is also a place of peril. Heroes wandering in the *eschatia* require the assistance of the Theoi.[39]

Pilgrimages into the *eschatia* can be powerful. These are times in which you can leave your center and either wander with the mindset of being on pilgrimage or go on retreat someplace away from daily life with the intention of focusing on spiritual things. Silent retreats are especially powerful. If you have the opportunity to make a pilgrimage, even just to break your typical routine or attend a retreat, take it—especially if seeking spiritual transformation.

Any type of initiatory experience is at least a metaphoric journey into the periphery. Such processes can be enhanced by using this imagery and understanding.

The Liminal

The magical power of liminality—the state of being in-between—has been discussed in many treatises and holds true in Hellenic religion. Hekate is the goddess of the crossroads and magic. Liminal spaces, like the periphery, are powerful and perilous.[40] Crossroads, doorways, borders, and thresholds are liminal spaces. The places where you are neither here nor there have liminal power. In the liminal, the potential of transformation can be harnessed. Lim-

38. Ensdiø, "To Lock Up Eleusis," 351–86.

39. Ensdiø, "To Lock Up Eleusis," 351–86.

40. Ensdiø, "To Lock Up Eleusis," 351–86.

inal states are fluid and can tip and change easily, for good or for ill. Liminality is harnessed by magicians and in initiations. Within daily life, liminal spaces require protection. It was common to ward doorways and have protective statues, like Herms, at crossroads and boundaries. In many ways the far periphery functions as liminal space.

Anabasis

Anabasis (ascent) is the name given by Arrian to the stories of Alexander the Great's conquests and is the title of Xenophon's work chronicling the march of Cyrus the Younger. The experience of "going up" is evocative, and the divine geography of Greece utilizes this orientation. Most Hellenic cities put temples to the gods of the *polis* on an *acropolis*—which literally means "the high city." Festivals typically include processions in which the people ascend to the place of the Theoi to make sacrifices, pray, and celebrate. There are numerous shrines and sacred caves on holy mountains. The worshippers must climb to reach the Gods' abode. The spiritual meaning of ascent is similar to its connotations in English. To ascend is to shift into a rarified and "heavenly" state. There is effort associated with ascending in which you leave your usual state behind and approach the Gods. Climbing up to a hallowed site with intent is experientially powerful. You can create an experience of spiritual ascent by choosing a hike requiring you to climb and doing it with conscious intention of climbing up to your most rarified aspect. Spend some time in silence at the top.

Katabasis

Perhaps the most interesting sacred directional orientation is *katabasis*—descent. *Katabasis*, "going down," is also the word used to describe going inward in a building and references the idea of spiritually and psychologically turning inward. *Katabasis* is the word used for descent into sacred caves. Many of the holiest and most dynamic sites in Greece are caves, including temples incorporating caves or chambers created to be artificial grottos. Through *katabasis*, one descends into darkness in order to find the Light that is Truth and Wisdom. *Katabasis* has initiatory and transformative implications. In many cults, the worshipper first goes up in order to go down. For example, first worshippers climbed up holy Mount Parnassus, the Muses' home, to reach Delphi. Once there, they processed up the Sacred Way in the Sanctuary of Apollon before entering His temple and descending into the darkness to the chamber outside the artificial cavern where the Pythia sat on the holy tripod. Only after making this ascent and descent could they ask questions seeking guidance and wisdom from the Lord of Light. The ways in which these directional orientations interact is complex. In fact, in the case of the Oracle at Delphi, not only did they ascend in order to descend, they travelled into the periphery (Delphi was remote and not under the control of any *polis*) in order to reach the *omphalos* at the whole world's center.[41]

Like going into the periphery, you can use "going down" metaphorically to access deep wisdom. In addition to "going down" into sacred caves and grottos in vision, going into any intentionally silent and dark space with the purpose of deep contemplation can function as the equivalent of *katabasis*.

PURIFICATIONS AND PROHIBITIONS

When visiting a sanctuary, we are entering an area "cut off" from human activity and belonging to one of the Theoi. We are asking for some level of communion and are stepping into Their territory. There are usually rites of purification, like sprinkling ourselves with water at the sanctuary's boundary to remove any possible impurity before crossing the threshold into the God's domain. Boundary purification assists worshippers in shifting psychological orientation away from daily life and toward reverence.

Traditional Prohibitions

Humans are composite creatures. We are mortal yet have immortal aspects—the parts of self that survive death. When entering the *temenos* to commune with the Theoi, we should make the approach centered in the immortal parts of ourselves. Humans are both individual and communal. We think of ourselves as fully individual, but we are far more affected by our environments and other humans than we realize. The positive implication is we can have an elevating effect on our fellows and be influenced by people who exhibit excellence in our environment. A negative implication is that when we enter sacred space, if there are other humans in close proximity operating from the mortal aspects of their nature, this can inhibit our capacity to hold attention in our immortal aspects.

In ancient Greece, there were prohibitions against visiting a sanctuary when in the midst of strongly "mortal" experiences. Hallmarks of mortality

---

41.   Ustinova, *Caves and the Ancient Greek Mind*.

are birth, death, and sexuality (especially procreative sex). These parts of life are powerful, deeply emotionally affecting, and quintessentially mortal (not bad, just mortal). Usually for a period of time after having contact with birth, sex, or death, Greeks did not go to a space belonging to the Gods.[42] It is important to honor our mortal experiences, such as grief, by not prematurely forcing ourselves into identification with the immortal aspects of our nature, as is required to commune with the Gods. There were other common prohibitions grounded in morality rather than mortality, like rules against murderers entering certain sanctuaries. Finally, there are a host of specific prohibitions about the preferences of particular Great Ones that are not generalizable to the others.[43] Ultimately, it is the actual process of following special rules that makes and upholds the boundary of sacred space. The *temenos* is sanctified by the fact it is treated differently than the space around it.

Purification of Self

I don't think the traditional prohibitions concerning the mortal aspects of life are normally necessary, yet I think it is good practice to verify it is the right time and way to approach one of the Theoi by asking and paying attention to your intuitive response. While there may be times in which special preparation is needed, like preparing to serve as *mantis*, for most purposes, basic intentional purification is sufficient. Generally, washing one's hands, face, and head with sea water or salt water while identifying with your immortal aspects of self is enough. However, if there is a major event or ritual—like an initiation or a particularly important rite—anything we do to more thoroughly purify ourselves is good. Using the Daphne bath described in chapter 1 over a period of days would be a more intensive form of purification. You can also bathe in the sea.

Boundary Maintenance

In order to keep the *temenos* spiritually clean, sanctuaries performed routine boundary maintenance. These techniques can be used to purify any space. For most purposes, simply taking a bowl of water with sea salt or Daphne tea and circling your space will work. You can carry burning bay leaves around your space.

---

42. Cole, *Landscapes, Gender, and Ritual Space.*
43. Cole, *Landscapes, Gender, and Ritual Space.*

If an area or person has extreme *miasma* or requires what amounts to an exorcism, more extreme measures are required. In ancient Greece when something needed serious purification, they used a piglet expiatory sacrifice. To purify a space, they would cut the throat of a piglet and let the blood drip out while walking the perimeter. To purify a person, they would have them hold the piglet and cut its throat. The blood (close to human and fresh with life) draws the unwholesome thing, which the corpse absorbs. The piglet's corpse was then either burned or buried. I absolutely do not recommend using animal sacrifice. It is utterly inappropriate in our culture and unnecessary. I have created a functional cruelty-free version that I have used effectively.

Exercise
CRUELTY-FREE PIGLET EXPIATORY SACRIFICE

This is a heavy-duty purification rite that can be used for either purifying an area or a person.

What You'll Need

A canning jar, black paint, two two-inch round glass mirrors, glue, and a fresh chicken egg. You'll need either a sacred fire or a shovel and sea salt for disposing of the bane. For the sacred blood (recipe courtesy of Ivo Dominguez, Jr.), you will need the following:

- Red Ochre Powder ¼ ounce
- Fractionated Coconut Oil ½ ounce
- Amber Oil 5 drops
- Dragon's Blood Oil 5 drops
- Myrrh Oil 5 drops
- Ambergris Oil* 5 drops
- Violet Leaf Oil 5 drops

*Note: Ambergris can be a 25 percent real, 75 percent fragrance blend. If you can't get it at all, you can substitute oil of ambrette (*Abelmoschus moschatus*).

Directions

This spell involves two preliminary steps: creating the trap with sufficient time for the paint to dry and creating the blood. You will also want to have planned your method of disposal before actually trapping the bane.

Step 1: Make the trap. This spell combines a void trap with a mirror maze. Take a canning jar and paint the glass black, making sure it is fully covered. Summon the void within yourself (imagine the concept of the void) and tell the black jar it is the void. Inside the bottom and in the center of the lid, glue the mirrors. They create a hall of mirrors. Chant the following spell over it until the trap feels like it knows its job. You are calling on Hermes the Restrainer, which links the trap to binding spells.

> *You are the maze.*
>
> *You are the void.*
>
> *In you I will trap*
>
> *What needs be destroyed.*
>
> *Hermes Restrainer,*
>
> *Protect me from harm.*
>
> *Bind the bane's power.*
>
> *Enliven this charm.*

Step 2: Make the blood. Mix the ingredients for the sacred blood. Enliven and charge it for this purpose using the chant. Repeat until it is shining.

> *You are the blood of Life,*
>
> *Shining, vital essence,*
>
> *Victim's blood upon the knife,*
>
> *The Sacrifice quintessence.*

Step 3: Capture the bane. When you are ready to do the purification, do the trap chant again over the trap to remind it. Place a fresh chicken egg in the trap and see it glowing with vitality. Remind the blood what it is by repeating the blood chant and put some over the egg. See the entire thing glowing with so much vitality that it is very attractive. Either begin walking the boundaries of the area you need to purify or have the person needing purification hold it or pass it over them. Draw the bane by chanting,

Pig blood, human blood

I call to those who feast!

Come, come, come!

Sense the unclean bane come. When you feel something has made its way into the jar, quickly put the lid on tightly so the bane is in the trap. You may repeat the trap chant if it needs strengthening.

Step 4: Dispose of the bane. There are two methods to dispose of the bane. The first is disposing of the bane by fire. Create a sacred fire that will purify all that burns. Consecrate the fire by chanting,

Sacred Fire,

Sacred Flame,

Upon Your pyre

Consume the bane.

Once the fire is burning and consecrated, pour the contents into the fire and see the bane being consumed and purified by flame.

The second is disposing of the bane by burying. Dig a hole someplace away from water or where food will be grown. Pour sea salt in the hole and place the whole jar into the hole. Pour more sea salt on top and bury it. Chant,

Great Blessed Earth,

Within this mound

Of holy ground

Transmute, reweave, rebirth.

Step 5: Giving thanks. Pray to Hermes the Restrainer and to the spirits of either Fire or Earth as well as to all the substances that allowed you to use them in this way and express your gratitude for their support.

CREATE YOUR SACRED SPACE

When we are looking at ruins and historical records, remember we are seeing the most developed versions of sacred spaces that evolved over hundreds of years of continuous use. None of the sanctuaries began their existence in their fully elaborated form. Since we must build everything from scratch, looking at the simplest archaic forms can help us see what is necessary. There are only two essential characteristics. There must be the invisible boundary of the *temenos*, the space is set apart. Within the *temenos*, however large or small, the rules are different from the area outside. Because we are human, we need to mark it in some way so we don't accidently trespass into the Gods' area and break the special rules. It is the actual change in behavior that hallows the space.[44]

If you are creating sacred space outside, the easiest way to mark the border is by using boundary stones (*horos/horoi*). A more elaborate version is to build a boundary wall (*peribolos*). The purpose is to help humans remember to purify themselves and shift their mindset when entering divine territory, thereby upholding the space's sanctity.[45]

In our practice, we can create a *temenos* by giving over part of our home or land (even if it is just a corner) to the Theoi. Create a clear boundary and mark it. Most importantly, we should ensure we only interact with that area when seeking to approach the Gods or do spiritual work.

The second essential component of sacred space is a place where you repeatedly make offerings. Sacrificial rites and offerings will be discussed in detail in chapter 6, but the act of giving pleasing things to the Theoi is central to Hellenic religion. In the fully elaborated versions, like the altar of Zeus at Pergamon or the altar of the Twelve Olympians at Athens, the altars upon which sacrificial offerings were burned could be monumental structures covered in brightly colored sculptural reliefs and other rich decorations. The earliest archaic altars were often just the piles of ash from previous sacrificial fires. Some sanctuaries, like Olympia, maintained the venerable ash altar.[46] Having a place where offerings are repeatedly given or where you go over and over again to interact with the Gods is crucial.

---

44. Pedley, *Sanctuaries and the Sacred in the Ancient Greek World*.
45. Sourvinou-Inwood, "Early Sanctuaries, the Eighth Century and Ritual Space," 1–17.
46. Pedley, *Sanctuaries and the Sacred in the Ancient Greek World*.

For many of us, our sacred space is likely to be an altar, and our *temenos* where we act differently is simply the way we interact with the altar itself. If you have a permanent altar, tell others it is not to be disturbed. Sometimes spaces not used for other purposes, like tops of bookshelves or mantles, are good options. Only interact with your altar when you are doing spiritual work. As an urban apartment dweller, I know many of us lack abundant space. If you cannot have a permanent altar, you can have a *temenos* by having an altar cloth you only use when you are in sacred space. When that cloth is in use, you are in your *temenos* so long as you treat it with reverence. Whenever you are interacting with your household altars, take a few moments to shift focus into your spiritual nature, telling yourself, "I am crossing the boundary into the *temenos*." You can adopt other changes in behavior signaling the shift, like wearing a prayer shawl.

If you have control over a piece of land, having a space set aside to leave offerings, pour libations, or even burn offerings, if you can do so safely, is good. If you are an apartment dweller, your altar is a place set apart where you can burn incense, candles, or paper, or where you can leave offerings before they are taken out. It is a place you come to interact. What is important is the function, not the form. If you pour libations or leave edible offerings, leave them in the same spot each time. The repeated action in the same location is important. For city dwellers, I strongly recommend emphasizing libations rather than food offerings because of urban wildlife.

Potential Altars

Try to have at least one altar that is your main area of communion with the Theoi. If you have particular devotion to one or more of the Theoi, They will ideally be represented on your altar. Knowing altars can be small (a space with a statue used for nothing else), you may want to have multiple if you have repeated functions. Some possibilities could include the following:

- A main personal altar with statues of the Theoi you work with most closely.
- A household altar with a statue of Hestia and a votive candle representing the hearth-flame.
- A healing altar with a statue of Asklepios, Apollon, or Hygeia.

- An altar for the dead with Hermes, Hades, or Persephone.
- An altar for protection with Ares or Athena.

Exercise
SETTING UP AN ALTAR
Create a place that will be your main interface point with the Theoi in your daily practice.

What You'll Need
A space that will only be used for your spiritual work and a dedicated vessel for offerings (like a bowl), frankincense or bay leaves, and a vessel in which to safely burn the frankincense or bay leaves (such as a bowl filled with sand or salt). If using frankincense, you will also need charcoal. Optional: Candles and candleholders, statues, other votives, olive oil, or spring water.

Directions
Choose the location for your altar. Ideally it will be in the east and will be a surface that is used for nothing else and where you can comfortably sit or stand in front of it. Burn frankincense or bay leaves and smudge the area. Pass the vessel through the smoke and say,

Holy Theoi, I dedicate this space to You. This is the temenos, the sacred precinct. When I interact with this altar, it is to honor and commune with You. Hear me and accept this sacrifice.

If you like, you may consecrate and add other items. Pass them through the smoke and say,

Holy Theoi, I dedicate this [name] to You.

Common things to add to an altar:

- A vessel for incense offerings.
- Candles for use as offerings (I recommend votive holders with tealights).
- Consecrated statues offered to the Theoi as vehicles.
- Other votive offerings.

To consecrate statues, smudge them with frankincense or bay. Hold the statue of the Great One and pray. Ask if the statue is acceptable as a vessel and listen. You can anoint the statue with oil or with spring water but see the God's power entering the statue. You can paint the statue to make it lifelike. Interact with the statue as though you are talking with the God. You are offering the statue as a vehicle of communication. Pay attention to how it appears to you. If you make a statue an offering and it is accepted as a vessel, give thanks to the Great One.

You can add additional items to your altar as time goes on, using the basic consecration. When your altar is set up, thank the Theoi. If there is incense still burning, leave it to finish burning out.

CHAPTER FIVE
SHRINES, SANCTUARIES, AND OTHER PUBLIC SACRED SPACES

Public and natural sacred spaces were of paramount importance to ancient Greeks. It is my hope that one day we will be able to rebuild public shrines and temples. Right now, we can visit some that still exist on the inner planes and build new sanctuaries on the astral. This chapter includes pathworkings to sacred places existing on the inner planes. You can use a similar technique to find other sites on the inner planes, like going through archaeological sites but stepping into them in vision as they once were.

NATURAL SACRED SPACES

All the world is holy and the Gods are everywhere. However, some places are particularly important to Them, and we set those areas aside. Often, we know this from an epiphany of one of the Theoi. Some areas in nature that require special rules for humans to interact with them include caves, springs, mountains, and special trees and groves. Many of these natural sacred sites were incorporated into sanctuaries. For example, the sanctuary of Apollon at Delphi includes a sacred spring, a sacred grotto, and sacred Daphne/laurel trees, all of which are on the sacred mountain of Parnassus. You can invite sacred experience by approaching any natural landscape as holy, maintaining a spiritual frame of mind and being open to guidance about what is and is not acceptable there.

Sacred Caves

Caves are related to *katabasis*. Apollon's oracles are typically delivered in caves or artificial grottos, usually in the recesses of His oracular temples. Three other oracles of heroes related to Apollon—Trophonios, Amphiarios, and Orpheus—require *katabasis* into caves.[47] The Sibyls, prophetesses of Apollon not associated with one of His oracles, tended to live in caves. Asklepios, the son of Apollon who became the preeminent healing god, included caves in some of His most important sanctuaries.[48]

Nymphs frequently live in caves and bring wisdom to those who seek Them there. Heroes were often taught in caves by nymphs or other divinities.[49] Achilles lived and studied with Chiron, the wise centaur, in His cave on Mount Pelion. Philip of Macedonia gave a cave, sacred to the nymphs, to Aristotle to serve as the school where he taught Alexander the Great. Philip intentionally raised his heir to be a hero. Early philosophers, including Pythagoras and the Eleatic School in Sicily, were mystical ecstatics, usually dedicated to Apollon, and practiced initiatory *katabasis* in holy caves.[50]

Some caves, like the Ploutonion at Eleusis, are entrances to the Underworld. These caves may be places for asking the dead to share their wisdom or, as in the case of Eleusis, were places to learn the secrets leading to an auspicious afterlife.[51] From an ancient Greek perspective, the process of descending into sacred caves is a path to divine wisdom beyond what humans can achieve by their own effort.

Some ideas to connect with sacred caves:

- Go on a pilgrimage to a cave with the intention of seeking wisdom.
- Mimic the experience of going into a cave by ritually spending silent time in a space with blackout curtains.
- Visit a sacred cave on the astral.

---

47.   Ustinova, *Caves and the Ancient Greek Mind.*
48.   Håland, "Water Sources and the Sacred in Modern and Ancient Greece and Beyond," 83–108.
49.   Ustinova, *Caves and the Ancient Greek Mind.*
50.   Ustinova, *Caves and the Ancient Greek Mind.*
51.   Mylonas, *Eleusis and the Eleusinian Mysteries.*

Holy Springs

Every spring is enlivened by a naiad, which is a type of nymph. Every spring is sacred and must be approached as holy. Some springs are particularly powerful. The one I know best is Kastalia at Delphi, the most sacred spring in Greece. Before seeking an audience with Apollon, the petitioners purified themselves by bathing with water from the Kastalian spring. She can inspire poetry and drinking Her water is a blessing.[52] Wherever we are, there are enlivening spirits of our water source, and it is important to build healthy and appropriate relationships with Them. Many old prohibitions supporting the health of the springs come from understanding they are the home and part of the body of sacred beings.

Reverentially drinking local water—where safe—is an effective and meaningful way to attune to the spirits of a landscape. Areas that have poisoned their waters are, by definition, spiritually sick. I encourage you to learn about the source of your water, to reach out and give thanks to the naiads when you drink, and to defend the health of your waters and support others in defending theirs. May all water protectors be blessed and successful in their efforts. Their cause is holy.

Some ideas to connect with holy springs:

- Learn about your water source and go on a pilgrimage to meet the nymph/naiad.
- Create a prayer of gratitude to use when drinking water.
- Choose an action to defend the health of your water source and do it as an act of reverence.

Mountains

Greece is a mountainous country, and particularly high mountains were deemed divine. Olympus is the tallest and is located in northern Greece, with the great sanctuary of Dion, dedicated to Zeus and the Twelve Olympians, at its foot. Mount Parnassus, sacred to Apollon and Dionysus and the Muses' home, is the second highest. Mount Ida in Crete is sacred to Rhea and is where She gave birth to Zeus and hid Him from Kronos. A different Mount Ida in Asia

---

52.   Andronicos, *Delphi*.

Minor is sacred to the goddess Kybele. Mount Pelion includes the cave where Chiron lived. Many other holy mountains are places of pilgrimage. The process of *anabasis*, going up them, leads to spiritual elevation.

Some ideas to connect with mountains:

- Go on a pilgrimage to a mountain and approach it with the intention of spiritual elevation.
- Visit a sacred mountain in vision.
- Investigate pictures of mountains and choose one that calls to you. Learn about the mountain.

Trees and Groves

Like springs, trees are enlivened by nymphs. A sacred grove dedicated to a particular deity was a common feature in many sanctuaries. It is probable they were planted in honor of a deity rather than occurring naturally. Sometimes individual trees were deemed holy. A number of tree species in Greece grow slowly and live for hundreds, sometimes thousands, of years. Pausanias, the ancient travel writer, references trees considered ancient by the ancients that were often associated with legendary history. The first olive tree given by Athena stood on the Acropolis. Four giant plane trees, sacred to Artemis and the nymphs and putatively planted by Menelaus, still live in Karyes.[53] At Dodona in archaic times there were oaks, sacred to Zeus, who spoke His words through the wind in their leaves.[54]

Some ideas to connect with trees and groves:

- Find an old tree on your land or in a park that calls to you. Spend time sitting on the ground with your back against the tree's bole. Talk to the tree's spirit and introduce yourself.
- If you have land, plant some trees with sacred purpose.
- Remember an old tree you know or knew in the past. In vision, go to the tree and ask if you may enter it to get to know its spirit.

---

53. Pausanius, *Guide to Greece*.
54. Burkert, *Greek Religion*.

Pathworking to the Sacred Cave of Zeus

With your eyes closed, see the room in which you are sitting begin to fill with mists that get thicker and thicker until you can no longer see your hand in front of you. As the mists fade, find yourself on a mountain path walking up a hill.

There is a strong breeze blowing from your left. You feel the sun on your neck. The path is steep and winding, cutting through ground covered in loose stones and small shrubs whose small leaves emit a slightly acidic but pleasant scent. As you walk, you have to keep your eyes mostly focused on the ground so you don't fall, but in your heart, you feel yourself approaching the Lord of Olympus Himself. You feel His closeness and know He is waiting for you. The way is not easy. A goat crosses the path right in front of you and climbs to a shrub with such ease you envy its nimbleness. It is harder on human feet to walk with so many loose stones underfoot.

As you climb, snaking up the mountain, you see a spring ahead. You are grateful because it is hot and you are thirsty. When you reach it, you notice there is an ever-flowing fountain and a bench. Stop and thank the spring's nymph with a prayer. [Pause.] You drink, filled with gratitude for its cool refreshment. Recognizing this spring is close to the holy cave, you pray you may be purified and washed clean of anything not appropriate to take with you into the Cave of Zeus. You ask the spring if it is willing to purify you. Receiving its assent, you step back to the fountain and pass some water over your head and sprinkle water over the rest of your body, feeling all impurities being washed away. Thank the nymph for its generosity and walk on.

Beginning your ascent again, you see an eagle soaring overhead and feel your heart swell at this omen. Now the trail is steeper and almost straight. Before long, you come to a wall and open gate, indicating the entrance to the sacred precinct.

Entering the *temenos,* the trail veers to the left. You see the huge opening of a vast cave in front of you, like a wide yawning mouth. Stop for a moment, feeling the cave's power pulsing out from within. Finish climbing to its entrance. When you first step into the cave's mouth, you cannot see until your eyes adjust, then you realize the cave's floor slopes downward, into the dark.

You are here to meet Zeus, king of the Gods, father of gods and men, deep in the recesses of the cave of His birth. You feel a pulsing leading you toward the cave's center. You go down, down into the darkness. You can barely see anything, but you feel the power and are drawn to it like a magnet. Approach slowly, letting the dark seep into every bit of your being, filling the space between your cells. You become more aware of your senses of smell and hearing. The scent of dampness and the sound of fluttering that might be wings or could be a breeze in the distance feel like they are touching you. You register the sound of dripping water. You are drawn on, descending deeper into the cave.

Finally, you know you have arrived at the place you have been striving to reach—it feels almost like a room, an inner sanctum, made of stalagmites and stalactites. There is a flat area that feels like a table emerging from the floor of the cave itself. You sense you are not alone here in the dark. You notice in your hand you hold an offering for the Great Father. Give thanks to Zeus for His presence and lay your offering on the natural table and wait. Be open to whatever you now experience. [Long pause.]

Once you finish communing, give thanks for the grace you have experienced. Turn and begin to ascend out of the cave. Now you can see the light shining through the cave's mouth, and it is far easier and faster to climb back out than it was to descend into the darkness. At the mouth of the cave, stop again and give thanks, acknowledging you will take the wisdom and blessings you have received back with you into the mortal world. With confidence and joy, you walk to the opening in the wall and leave the sacred precinct.

Having climbed to the height of the mountain and then descended to meet mighty Zeus, you feel more sure-footed as you stride down the mountain, greeting the sacred spring as you pass it. Go down the path until you reach the place where it joins the main road, telling yourself you will remember and will fully integrate all you experienced here.

Mists begin rising from the ground, growing thicker and thicker until the fog is so dense you cannot see your hand before you. The mists dissipate. Find yourself back in your room.

SANCTUARIES

A sanctuary is a holy precinct. It can include multiple temples, shrines, and altars to various Theoi, a theater, a gymnasium, and other buildings or structures necessary for the cults. Often a sanctuary will have a main deity to whom it is dedicated, like the Sanctuary of Zeus at Olympia, but will also have temples and shrines to other deities as well. Sometimes the presence of a powerful natural feature—like a cave, spring, sacred tree, or mountain—gives rise to a human-built sanctuary and is incorporated within. However, the only essential aspects of a sanctuary are a *temenos*, an area set apart that has different rules than normal life, and a place where sacrifices and offerings are made within the *temenos*.[55] A temple, although common, is not a necessary part of a sanctuary.

While it is unlikely we will soon be creating elaborate sanctuaries, it is useful to understand their structure. First, we can set up resonances on a smaller scale in our physical sacred spaces. Second, many ancient sanctuaries continue to exist on the inner planes and we can go to them in vision. Third, we can construct sanctuaries in vision.

Altars

In ancient Greece the main area of religious activity was not the temple, but the altar outside. Altars were typically in open air. Most altars were rectangular and, if there was a temple, stood to the east. A sanctuary usually had a main altar and there might have been smaller altars for other deities. As sanctuaries evolved, simple altars were often replaced with more elaborate ones. Prayers were made, sacrifices and offerings given, and libations poured at the altar, not within the temples.[56]

Temples and Cult Statues

A temple (*naos*) is considered the God's house. If there is a cult statue or representation, this is where it is housed and seen. Holy statues are consecrated vehicles available to the Gods to give Them a place of physical presence, should They desire it. Cult statues are not the deity, but they could be embodied by the deity.[57] We do not worship the statues. We worship the Theoi who use the

---

55. Sourvinou-Inwood, "Early Sanctuaries, the Eighth Century and Ritual Space."
56. Kearns, *Ancient Greek Religion*.
57. Kearns, *Ancient Greek Religion*.

statues as a physical vehicles in order to be present in the material world with us. Some statues, like the unspeakably archaic olive wood statue of Athena Polias at Athens, were considered a gift directly from the Divine. Other cult statues were made and dedicated by human hands, like the Athena Parthenos, made by Phidias, that stood in the Parthenon. Temples may have evolved from palaces. Most places having a citadel, like Athens, eventually gave their *acropolis* to the Gods.

Once there is a sacred image hallowed as a vehicle for a deity to facilitate communication and worship, that image must have an appropriate home. It would be unthinkable to consecrate holy images and not take care of them. There are records of cities ritually decommissioning consecrated statues, sometimes because they were damaged. Usually, they were buried in blessed and dedicated pits.

Early temples consisted of a single room, sometimes with a porch. Eventually the elaborated form included a porch area (*pronaos*), the main room where the statue was located (*cella*), and sometimes a back room (*opisthodomos*). In some temples, there was a restricted room (*adyton*) that was the inner sanctum. Shrines (*naiskos*) were small and had a single room. Temples were oriented so the open door revealed the cult statue facing east with the altar in front of the porch.[58] Some temples vary from this pattern, like the Erechtheion on the Athenian Acropolis that incorporates numerous cult places, including the first olive tree, the salt lake given by Poseidon, and the grave of the divine heroes who were the first kings of Athens. As a result, the temple has an unusual shape.[59] There are rare instances where the landscape made an eastern-facing orientation unsuitable.

Propylaea

More elaborate sanctuaries might include a *propylaea*—a monumental gateway. Gates could be adorned with sculpture and often had templelike shapes.[60] The *propylaea* on the Athenian Acropolis incorporated an art gallery. Such monumental gateways included broad, shallow steps or a ramp as part of a processional Sacred Way. The scale of the broad steps and entrances gives permanent expression to the vast crowds in ritual processions, even when the sanctuary is empty.

---

58.   Pedley, *Sanctuaries and the Sacred in the Ancient Greek World.*
59.   Pedley, *Sanctuaries and the Sacred in the Ancient Greek World.*
60.   Pedley, *Sanctuaries and the Sacred in the Ancient Greek World.*

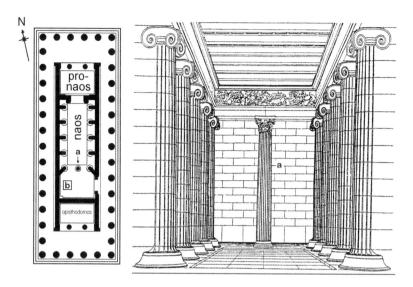

STRUCTURE OF A TEMPLE

Special Buildings and Places

Sometimes a sanctuary included specialized places designed for the particular cult's needs. For example, Delphi had structures called threshing floors that had to do with rites in which the spirit of Python was ritually re-killed every eight years by a boy embodying Apollon.[61]

In healing sanctuaries, such as those of Asklepios, healing baths and sleeping quarters for patients were included. In Epidauros, one of His main sanctuaries, a special building held His sacred serpents.[62]

Many sanctuaries had a *hestiatorion*—a dining hall where the deities were invited to join worshippers at a communal meal. These rites celebrated *theoxenia* (hospitality given to the Gods). Worshippers commonly shared the temple meat left from animal sacrifice. For many people, most meat they consumed was as part of rites of *theoxenia*.[63]

---

61.   Petsas, *Delphi*.

62.   Tomilson, *Epidauros*.

63.   Kearns, *Ancient Greek Religion*.

Votives and Buildings Supporting Activities in Honor of the Theoi

Votive offerings, including statues, works of art, and spoils of war, were on display all over the sanctuaries. These offerings were pleasing gifts meant to honor the Theoi while simultaneously increasing the giver's prestige.[64] While boasting (taking credit for what does not rightfully belong to you) was anathema, humility was not considered a virtue by the ancient Greeks. For example, Alexander the Great sent captured shields from the Battle of Granicus, his first victory in Persia, to Athens to be mounted on the Parthenon as an offering to Athena. Known throughout his life as being pious, this act thanked the Goddess for Her assistance—but it was also a statement to Athens (who initially opposed his rule) that he was the leader capable of uniting Greece and avenging the Persian destruction of Athena's temple on the Acropolis. Scholars who cynically view this as mere propaganda misunderstand the ancient Hellenic psyche. There is no tension between the two purposes. In large sanctuaries, small, richly decorated temple-shaped treasuries were constructed to house votive offerings. In Athens, the Parthenon was the votive treasury while the Erechtheion was the cult temple.

Pursuit of excellence in honor of the Theoi is a way to honor the Gods. The exquisite artistic votives, including architecture, honored the Theoi through excellence—as did excellence in theater, music, dance, and athletics. Many sanctuaries included a theater and a stadium to support these activities. Theaters were open air and included a circular orchestra, which is where the acting took place. Some sanctuaries had an enclosed auditorium for musical performances called an *odeon*.

Visitors

Sometimes there were other types of buildings outside the sacred precinct (*hieron*). Sanctuaries likely to draw numerous visitors might have *stoas* (long covered porticos providing shade) and guest quarters. Sanctuaries like Olympia, Delphi, Nemea, or Isthmia that hosted Panhellenic Games required athletic training facilities outside the *hieron*.

---

64. Pedley, *Sanctuaries and the Sacred in the Ancient Greek World*.

Pilgrimages to visit sanctuaries were common ways of expressing piety and travelers went to greet the Gods and appreciate the art and architecture. There were two sanctuaries, in particular, that were Panhellenic: Delphi and Olympia. These two were not under the control of any major *polis* and were largely responsible for the development of a "Greek" identity uniting individual city-states. In Delphi and Olympia, citizens from all over the Greek-speaking world would meet, get to know each other, compete, and forge a shared sense of identity.[65]

Exercise
CREATING AN ASTRAL SANCTUARY

You will create an inner plane sanctuary to interact with the Theoi and learn.

What You'll Need

A quiet place where you can work uninterrupted, a comfortable chair, a journal, and a pen. Optional: Art supplies.

Directions

The astral is the "dreaming" aspect of reality, where what begins as imagination is gradually given sufficient form to become independent. You will "dream" a sanctuary into being in co-creation with at least one of the Theoi. Building a sanctuary on the inner planes takes time. It requires you to go in vision regularly. At the end of each session, write down what you experienced.

Step 1: Choose which of the Theoi with whom you will work. Pray to the Great One, sharing your intention, and ask for partnership. Throughout this process, pay attention to your dreams and watch for omens and record what you receive in your journal.

Step 2: Choose your sanctuary's name.

Step 3: Cultivate a combination of daydream mentality with artistic creativity. In this state of sacred imagining, begin dreaming the landscape for your sanctuary. Is it in the mountains? By the ocean? In the woods? On a plain? By a river? What does the air feel like? What does the wind smell like?

---

65.   Scott, *Delphi and Olympia*.

Daydream yourself walking around and exploring the landscape. Write it down as creative writing. If you are artistic, draw or paint.

Step 4: As you explore your landscape, ask where the boundary of your sanctuary should be and how it will be marked. It could be a wall, a path, or boundary stones. Find them or build them. This demarcates your *temenos*.

Step 5: Create a protocol to get to the landscape like the entry we use to get in and out of pathworkings. For example, maybe find yourself walking on a path through the woods until you come to a low wall with a gate. Choose a consistent pathway and then use it every time to reach your astral sanctuary. If it helps you, write it down and record it, like the pathworkings. Be sure to always exit the way you came in, retracing your process.

Step 6: After you dreamt the *temenos*, explore the area, asking the Great One with whom you are working to help you find the correct spot for Their altar and temple. Let yourself be drawn to a location. Pay attention to what the area looks like. Dream a shrine or a temple. It can look like a particular historical temple or a basic one. In front of the temple, dream an altar. Imagine yourself making offerings there.

Step 7: Go inside the temple and note as many details as you can. Is there a cult statue? What does it look like? What are the decorations? Take notes on every session, either during or immediately afterward.

Step 8: Stabilize your astral sanctuary. Two things give an astral construct real power. First, you must use it regularly. It becomes more solidly real in the astral with repetition and continued energy. Creating manifest representations—like pieces of art, written descriptions, or stories—increases its power. Second, it becomes more real if it is being co-created with other beings on the inner planes. Check with the God and ask Them to come visit you there. Interact there, but also do things on the physical plane in Their honor to bridge the world of dreams and the physical. You can incorporate your astral temple into your daily practices of prayers and contemplation. Imagine yourself going to the inner plane sanctuary, and then do your prayers and meditations from there.

Step 9: Once your astral sanctuary feels stable after repeated visits, you can begin exploring and adding additional temples, shrines, or functions—like places for healing, study, or training. The more you use and explore your inner sanctuary, the stronger and more stable it will become.

PUBLIC SACRED SPACE IN DAILY LIFE

In every major *polis* there were sanctuaries in the city's center and sanctuaries in the rural areas. There were numerous shrines and altars throughout the city, and districts were typically named after the shrines and sanctuaries in their territory. For example, the Lyceum of Aristotle in Athens was in the district of the sanctuary of Apollon Lykeios—Wolf Apollon. Plato's Academy was in the district of the *alsos*, the grove, of Akademos, an important Athenian hero. Throughout the city and at crossroads and boundaries there were Herms—pillars with the head of Hermes and an erect phallus that warded liminal areas. Altars and shrines of heroes were scattered throughout the city. Little sanctified areas were embedded throughout the human-occupied space of ancient Greece. In addition to festivals that took members of the community to different temples and shrines on regularly recurring cycles, ancient Hellenes interacted with public sacred spaces on a daily basis. Greeting the deity of the *temenos*—be it of a temple, shrine, cave, altar, or grove—whenever passing by was common. The world was full of gods and spirits.

PATHWORKING THROUGH THE PANATHENAIA

The Great Panathenaia was an Athenian festival honoring Athena every four years. The power from the inner planes of the sacred geography of Athens is just under the surface. This pathworking takes you through the Panathenaic procession, giving you an entry into the astral form of Ancient Athens. Once you know it well, you can begin to explore on your own. It includes meeting places for the following:

- Hades, Persephone, and the ancestors
- Hermes
- All twelve Olympians
- Hephaistos, Athena, and Theseus
- Apollon
- Zeus
- Nymphs
- Hekate
- Demeter and Persephone

- Zeus, Apollon, and Pan
- Ares and the Erinyes/Eumenides
- Athena
- Artemis
- Kekrops
- Poseidon

With your eyes closed, see the room in which you are sitting begin to fill with mists that get thicker and thicker until you can no longer see your hand in front of you. As the mists fade, find yourself in the middle of a celebratory crowd. You are outside the city walls, the twin towers of the Dipylon Gates looming ahead. In front there is a small ship being pulled on wheels. The exquisite sail made of finely woven cloth shows the *Gigantomachy*—the war when the Theoi fought the Giants for the sake of the planet. The people will give this to Athena to be a garment for Her cult statue. Looking behind, you see the grave statues in the Kermamikos and realize you are standing close to the Temple of the Triptopatrion, the ancestors of Athens. This is where Athenians come to pray to the ancestors and where each newborn is introduced to them. The procession begins to move, and soon you are walking between the twin walls of the Dipylon Gates until you pass the threshold and enter the city.

Passing stoas and herms, you come to a break in the inner wall marking the beginning of the Agora; the great processional way cuts diagonally across. On the left, the Altar of the Twelve Olympians is decorated with painted reliefs that look alive. A little farther on the right, you see the Hephaisteion, temple of Hephaistos and Athena Ergane, patrons of the marketplace, standing on a hill. Their statues look down approvingly while the Athenian hero Theseus fights His mythic battles on the temple frieze. Below the hill is the little temple of Apollon Patroos—divine ancestor of Athens. Walking on, you see statues of the ten tribal ancestors, and in the distance on the right are the civic buildings and courts of the world's first democracy, a large altar of Zeus before them.

In the far corner of the Agora, diagonally across from where you entered, you come to the spring and fountain house. Greet the nymphs as you pass, hearing the merry water splash and inhaling the perfume of flowers. The climb is steeper now. On the left is a small shrine of Hekate at the place where the Agora meets the base of the Acropolis. Climbing past Hekate's shrine, you pass the Eleusinion, the temple of Demeter and Persephone from which the procession to Eleusis begins every fall for the Great Mysteries.

Your legs feel the strain of your slow ascent, but everyone begins singing songs of praise to Athena. Looking up, you see the caves—sacred to Apollon, Zeus, and Pan—on the northern slope of the Acropolis. Winding to the right, you circle the high city's base until you come to a large, barren hill, made of nothing but orange-red rock. This is the Areopagus, the Hill of Ares, with a temple for the Erinyes at the base.

The procession turns slightly, and you are before the entrance to the main sanctuary. There are broad shallow steps leading up the sacred hill. Climbing, you head toward the propylaea, the gatehouse that looks like a gleaming temple. On the right, jutting out on a wall, is the small and elegant temple of Athena Nike.

The hymns grow louder as you cross through the gateway and emerge on top of the Acropolis. To the right you see the temple of Artemis Brauronia, Artemis as the bear goddess who protects girls and women. In front, you see the giant bronze statue of Athena Promachos, the city's protector. The tip of Her upraised spear can be seen far at sea. There are smaller votive statues everywhere. In front of you there are two major temples.

The temple on the right is the Parthenon—the greatest offering to Athena, built by Phidias and containing the huge ivory and golden statue of Athena Parethenos. The western pediment shows the contest between Athena and Poseidon for the city of Athens's patronage in which Athena gave an olive tree and Poseidon struck his trident into the rock, bringing forth water. The Parthenon embodies mathematical perfection and artistic genius, but for this rite, you are heading to the most sacred site in Athens—the Erechtheion.

On the left, you see stones from the old temple of Athena Polias destroyed by the Persians—the Athenians left parts in ruin as a reminder of what had been done. Pass by the temple porch with its caryatid columns. Under this porch is the grave of Kekrops, the half-serpent half-man first king of Athens whom Athena pulled directly from the Earth of the Acropolis. The sacred serpent is kept in this part of the temple and honey cakes are offered to it on the porch above the grave. At the end of the building, you turn left and come to the altar of Athena Polias in front of Her temple.

The woven peplos is taken into the temple and given to the Goddess as She enlivens the ancient olive wood statue, a gift that fell from the Heavens—ancient in the time of the ancients. You gaze inside at the timeless statue pulsing with Her power and seeming to move and help as the women wrap Her in the new peplos. Put energy into this gift and ask if She will speak with you. Spend some time in communion with Athena. [Long pause.]

Thank Athena and go to the right. There are stairs going down, and you see an entire additional temple face on the building's right side. While walking down the stairs, you notice something strange. There is a hole in the porch's roof. You look down and realize there is a corresponding hole in the floor. Reaching out with your mind into the hole in the floor, you realize you are touching a saltwater pool. This is the Thalassa, the place Poseidon struck his trident into the Acropolis. Standing in front of this part of the temple, look down into your hand and discover an offering you give to Poseidon. Spend some time with Him. [Pause.]

Walking around the building, you see a small walled courtyard. Inside is an ancient olive tree—the first olive, given by Athena to the people of Athens. From inside the courtyard, you look back and see the Thalassa through an opening. On the other side, there is a door leading under the caryatid porch to the tomb of the Athenian kings. If you wish, go and meet the ancient king of Athens who came from the Acropolis itself. [Pause.]

Walk back toward the propylea, back through the gates and down the Acropolis, past the Eleusinion and the shrine of Hekate to the fountain of the nymphs. Mists begin rising from the ground, growing thicker and thicker until the fog is so dense you cannot see your hand before you. The mists dissipate. Find yourself back in your room.

CHAPTER SIX
SPEAKING TO THE GODS

Religion is about relationships and communication is the medium through which everything happens. Communication includes both speaking and listening. This chapter focuses on ways we communicate to the Theoi while the next discusses how we receive communication from Them. In Hellenic traditions, there are many ways of "speaking" to the Theoi. The most important is prayer, but the most famous and distinctive is the ritual complex of sacrifice, which combines numerous modes of communicating with the Theoi into a coherent pattern. The word *sacrifice* means "to sanctify" and is the most common translation for the Greek *hiera rezein*, "to do sacred things." It does not imply abnegation.[66] Anything done with the intention of communicating with or honoring the Theoi can be understood as "sacrifice," or "speaking" to the Theoi. Offerings, including votives, art, and performing arts created in honor of the Theoi, are "speaking." The pursuit of excellence as an act of dedication can be a way of speaking to the Theoi. Contests demonstrating this excellence are conducted as offerings. Individuals can undertake specific acts in honor of a god.

---

66. "Sacrifice," in *Merriam-Webster.Com Dictionary*.

Reciprocal Relationships

We are in reciprocal relationships with the Theoi. Making offerings is one method of establishing, maintaining, and deepening mutual relationships. Early Christian propaganda portrayed relationships between the Greeks and the Theoi as merely transactional. They pictured the Gods as susceptible to bribes. That was not how these relationships worked and is part of a smear campaign.[67] Unfortunately, many modern people read the ancient evidence through a lens distorted by this view. Any anthropologist studying gift economies can tell you they are not based in a market mentality but are rooted in a relationship mentality.[68]

Offerings are gifts, and gift-giving binds individuals together and knits communities to each other. In Bronze Age Greece, kings would make gifts to each other, the most precious and symbolic being large bronze tripods, which are three-legged cauldrons. These cauldrons are big enough to cook the meat from a large sacrificial animal, like an ox. Sharing a communal meal with the Theoi is a pious act. This gift from the head of one *polis* to another served the whole community, strengthening the entire society's divine relationships. The gift's quality and richness simultaneously honored the giver, the receiver, and both their communities. This is why the tripod is an important symbol in ancient Hellenic religion. It symbolizes sacred reciprocity.

In a reciprocal relationship, there is no requirement of a gift for a gift. There is an understanding that both parties are vested in the relationship, but the definition of a gift precludes a requirement to receive in return. The evaluation of a gift in a relationship based on mutuality is according to the means of the one who gives, not the value of the gift itself. What is most important is the care used in selecting or creating the gift, demonstrating the importance of the relationship. By contrast, in a market situation, the singular emphasis is on the monetary worth of the goods exchanged.

The Hellenic way of "speaking" to the Theoi is by doing things They will find pleasing. This can be giving Them gifts or by understanding Their agendas and doing things in honor of Them that are in alignment with Their larger goals. For example, the institution of "hospitality" is important to Zeus. Giving money to refugee services in honor of Him is pleasing and a fine act of

---

67.   Naiden, *Smoke Signals for the Gods.*
68.   Petrovic, "Deification—Gods or Men?" 429–43.

piety, as well as being a good thing to do. If one violates the laws of hospitality and earns His displeasure, repairing that relationship requires both feeling contrition and making appropriate reparations beyond what it would have initially "cost" to have been hospitable in the first place. It often requires publicly accepting responsibility for one's failings, which requires courage. This is not a bribe. It is a form of restorative justice focusing on repairing relationships, both human and divine.

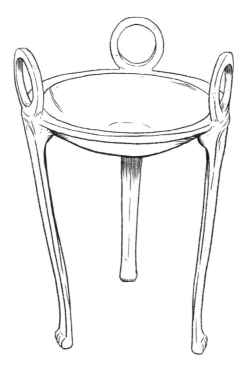

SACRIFICIAL TRIPOD

THE THREE QUALIFICATIONS

The Greek word *kalos* means "good" but also "beautiful." It has an aesthetic and a moral connotation. When "speaking" to the Gods, when "doing the holy things," everything should be as beautiful and good as it can be. There are three ways in which whatever is done should be *kalos*.[69]

---

69.   Naiden, "Sacrifice," 463–75.

Whatever is given to the Theoi, be it the performance of a hymn or the choice of an offering, should be as aesthetically pleasing and perfect as we can make it. If you are giving food, give the most perfect piece. Invest the time and effort to learn the song and sing it the best you can in the moment. Pay attention to the aesthetics of your ritual creation, practice, and prepare. Take seriously that They will be in your ritual as the most highly honored guests you could possibly have. Do your best.

Second, the worshippers must be *kalos*. This has to do with morality. It will not matter how beautiful everything is if the people speaking to the Gods are not moral. We should be *hagnos* (pure) and *agathos* (morally good and kind). The Gods care about the character of the worshippers.[70] As Aristotle taught, character is created by habit and habit is created by repeated action—so it is possible to purify and improve character.[71] People who are immoral should not come before the Gods.

Finally, the act of worship, whatever it is, should be appropriate to the divinity approached. In my experience, the Theoi are forgiving about technicalities we might get wrong in ritual, especially since we are learning and rebirthing anew. However, we should try to get to know the deity enough before the ritual to understand why we are asking Them to join the specific ritual. It should make sense.

Paying attention to our relationships with the Theoi and prioritizing doing things in Their honor and doing them in the right way is piety in the Greek tradition. Piety has a strong moral element since nothing one does will be pleasing to the Gods if one does not behave ethically and approach the Gods with the correct internal orientation.[72]

Prayer

Prayer is the single necessary part of all acts of worship. It is incorporated into every other form of "speaking." Prayer can stand alone, be anywhere, and is the true core of Hellenic religious practice.

Assuming an existing relationship, a prayer can be spontaneous and as simple as "Apollon, I love you!" or "Apollon, protect me!" Prayers should always be

---

70. Naiden, *Smoke Signals for the Gods*.
71. Aristotle, *Nicomachaean Ethics*.
72. Naiden, *Smoke Signals for the Gods*.

addressed to someone. Otherwise, there are no hard-and-fast rules, although there is a typical form.

Typically, the deity is called by name, including appropriate epithets as discussed in chapter 2. Naming the specific epithets alerts the Great One about which aspect is being called. The next part of a prayer makes the case for why the God should show up and care. This usually includes an appeal to the existing relationship the Great One has with the individual or collective. Sometimes a case is made, especially if there will be a substantive request, about how what is happening relates to the God's agenda. Finally, a request is made. The request may just be for *charis*—for the God to accept a gift and look upon it and the giver with kindness. If other requests are made, they should be reasonable and in alignment with the Great One's agenda, so far as the worshipper can understand it.

Prayers should be spoken aloud. Prayers done in silence were considered suspicious because they were assumed to be shameful.[73] I sometimes pray silently because in this culture it is not always appropriate to pray aloud, but I find when I am doing invocations (prayers asking a god to be present), speaking with volume and energy is more effective.

When praying, your stance should be physically open. It is a vulnerable stance but devoid of abasement and conveys we are not hiding on any level of being. The traditional stance is to stand up tall and straight with arms extended so the chest is wide open and unprotected. The stance radiates confidence and is unguarded. When praying to the Olympians, raise your arms and look toward the sky. When praying to the chthonic Gods of the Underworld, stretch your arms down toward the Earth and look toward the ground. If there is an enlivened statue or image, you may let your arms and gaze stretch toward the statue.[74]

HYMNS

Hymns are part of other rituals, but creating or singing a hymn is, in itself, an act of worship. Hymns obviously are sung. They often have instrumental accompaniment, but not always. Any instrument in the lyre family, especially the kithara, is sacred to Apollon. Flutes and reed instruments, like the *aulos*

---

73.   Versnel, "Prayers and Curses."

74.   Burkert, *Greek Religion.*

(a precursor to the oboe), are associated with Dionysus. Dancers frequently have percussive instruments, like frame drums, cymbals, and an instrument like castanets. Ritual processions often include hymns accompanied by dance. In ancient festivals, the nights were often spent singing hymns and dancing in honor of the Theoi.[75]

Hymns usually include praise of the God and tell the Great One's stories. Some hymns, like the *Homeric Hymn to Demeter* that gives the Eleusinian myth, provide information for specific cults.[76] Hymns tie the deity to the locale where the hymn is sung. Sometimes there are specific cultic hymn-forms. A *paian* is a kind of hymn sacred to Apollon, and the cultic cry of a *paian* is *"Io Paian! Io Paian! Io Paian!"*[77] Later, some of His family members, especially His son, Asklepios, also receive *paians*—but that is because of Their relationship with Apollon. A dithyramb is a hymn-form used for Dionysus and is believed to be the root of the tragic chorus and, therefore, the ancestor of theater.

OFFERINGS

Many types of offerings can be made to the Theoi as an expression of friendship, attention, and gratitude. Offerings are always about expressing and maintaining relationships.

Animal Sacrifice

Animal sacrifice was a significant part of ancient Greek religion, although less common than other kinds of offerings. Almost all red meat consumed by ancient Greeks was from sacrifices. Sacrificed animals were almost exclusively domesticated, the most common being sheep and goats. Oxen were the most prestigious sacrifices. Pigs were common, especially to Demeter, but less commonly given to heavenly Theoi. Domesticated deer were occasionally sacrificed. Poultry, especially geese, partridge, and chicken (once it joined the Greek farmyard at a comparatively late date) were sacrificed.[78]

The Pythagoreans were strongly critical of animal sacrifice. The Pythagorean school and those influenced by them were devotees of Apollon Hyper-

---

75.   Larson, *Understanding Greek Religion*.

76.   Athanassakis, trans., *Homeric Hymns*.

77.   Tomilson, *Epidauros*.

78.   Hitch and Rutherford, eds., *Animal Sacrifice in the Ancient Greek World*.

borios. Hyperborea was believed to be beyond the North Wind, past the land of the gryphons, where the sun shone twenty-four hours a day. It is home to a magical people who are wise and beautiful and bear a strong resemblance to Tolkien's high elves. Their god is Apollon and their goddess is Artemis. The Hyperboreans are vegetarian and Apollon Hyperborios receives only plant offerings.[79] Pythagoreans opposed eating meat on ethical grounds, similar to many spiritual arguments from other traditions that oppose eating meat. As such, they especially opposed animal sacrifice because they believed doing something spiritually degrading to one's soul in the name of a god was especially problematic.

Putting aside ethical arguments for vegetarianism, animal sacrifice is inappropriate for Modern Pagans, even those who do eat meat. In ancient Greece, people raised and cared for animals, most only ate meat as part of sacrifices, and had priests who were trained to slaughter in the most humane way possible. Most Modern Pagans live in urban areas, and the meat we consume comes from groceries and restaurants. For nonvegetarians in this culture, eating meat is not a rare and special occurrence. Our context is too different for animal sacrifice to be appropriate.

Animal sacrifice is unnecessary from the perspective of the Theoi. We know most sacrifices did not include slaughtering animals. If the purpose of sacrifice is to "speak" to the Gods in ways They will find pleasing, there are countless alternatives.

Nonanimal Sacrifices

Generally, offerings to heavenly Gods and Olympians are burned, those to chthonic Gods of the Underworld are buried or thrown in pits. Demeter crosses both realms. Libations were the most common form of offering. They are performed as a stand-alone ritual throughout daily life, as well as being part of a full sacrifice ritual.[80] Formal libations use a ceremonial cup, usually a *phiale,* which is a shallow bowl with a raised *omphalos* (navel) in the center, or a *rhyton* in the shape of a horn. Pray to the Theoi you mean to honor and then pour the drink on the fire or on the ground.

Informally, it is a pious act to share a sip of our drink with the Gods by spilling a bit on the fire or ground. In theory, most libations to the Olympians

79. Cole, *Landscapes, Gender, and Ritual Space.*

80. Naiden, "Sacrifice."

should go on the fire, but the ground is fine. In an indoor ritual, pour your libation into a cup or bowl and then take it out at the end. Historically, most libations were wine, but milk mixed with honey was frequently given to chthonic, especially agricultural, deities. Water on a hot day is appropriate. I sometimes give coffee or other things. If you are visiting an archaeological site, *only* use a bit of water surreptitiously spilled on the ground and leave no other substances. Be respectful of Their sites.

Any food can be given to the Theoi if it tastes and looks good and is desirable. Historically, cakes and cookies were almost always included in sacrifices. Incense could be offered alone as a sacrifice.[81] When burning incense, include prayers so it is clear for whom you are burning it. Things you make yourself are better received because your effort and time make the gift more powerful.

OFFERINGS OF THANKS

When you ask for help and your prayer is granted, follow up by making offerings of gratitude. Similarly, when you receive abundance or blessing from some aspect of reality under the purview of one of the Great Ones, you should express your gratitude. Here are some traditional ideas.

First Fruits

The first fruits from the harvest were sacrificed in thanksgiving for the Earth's bounty and the blessing of the crops.[82] For grains, it is best to spend the human effort to turn them into cakes. First fruit sacrifices are not just about food; they include crafts and trade. A weaver might give her first acceptable piece of weaving to Athena. A blacksmith might give his first acceptable sword or cauldron to Hephaistos.

Life Transitions

In gratitude for Her protection during childhood, young women sacrificed their toys to Artemis in their coming of age ritual. A way to rebirth this would be having children who have outgrown certain toys ritually dedicate them to Artemis—the protector of children—and then giving them to a charity or shel-

---

81.   Naiden, *Smoke Signals for the Gods*.
82.   Kearns, *Ancient Greek Religion*.

ter. When women survived a dangerous birth, they gave Artemis their favorite possession or spent time weaving a garment to sacrifice.[83]

On the opposite end of life, craftsmen going into retirement sacrificed their tools to Hephaistos. Retiring soldiers sacrificed their weapons to Ares. Similarly, someone retiring could give their "tools" to a young person just starting out in the profession.

Dekate: The Tithe

The tenth part of a successful venture was usually offered to one or more of the Theoi who supported the success. Sometimes the tithe was for a risky trade venture, but most often it was the tenth part of battle spoils. Gifting battle spoils to a god meant they would be displayed and bring honor to the giver.[84] Humility is not a virtue in this worldview. We should never claim credit for deeds we didn't do or excellence we don't have, but we should be proud of our accomplishments and not hide them. Ideally, they will inspire others.

For example, at the Battle of Marathon's end when the Athenians won against overwhelming odds, Miltiades, the Athenian general most responsible for the victory, sacrificed his helmet from that battle to Zeus at Olympia. We know this because it is in the museum—complete with dedicatory inscription. This gift gives thanks to Zeus for His help, and honors Miltiades by memorializing his victory.

Art and Architecture

Art and sacred architecture were common offerings of thanks. Statuary was rarely created for purely mundane purposes. Most statues were offerings to the Gods, sometimes in thanks for victory. This includes statues of the Gods, some of which were cult statues or shrine statues receiving worship, but many of which were votive offerings. Cult statues tend to face straight forward and, although they have identifying elements, they are not usually engaged in activity.[85] Statues of people could be given in thanks—for example, the many *kouros* statues of youths dedicated to Apollon.

---

83. Burkert, *Greek Religion*.

84. Kearns, *Ancient Greek Religion*.

85. Larson, *Understanding Greek Religion*.

Votive relief carvings were common. These are scenes carved and mounted in walls, niches, and in rocks and caves. Sometimes they were substitutions for animal sacrifice. In healing cults, votive reliefs often testify to the healing the patient received.

The temples, shrines, and sanctuary buildings, like treasuries, were also offerings. They were typically richly decorated and made to look as elegant and beautiful as possible. Sometimes they were paid for by individuals and sometimes by an entire *polis*.

The emphasis for all these artistic creations is on making them *kalos*. They must be as beautiful and perfect as possible, and all the people involved must be pure, good, and kind. For your practice, creations of any form of art, including the performing arts, are worthy offerings. You have to dedicate them to whichever god you are honoring, naming the God whom you are honoring aloud in prayer.

THE "SACRIFICE" RITUAL COMPLEX

The Hellenic ritual of sacrifice is a complex of ritual actions linked into a coherent pattern. *Hiera rezein*, "to do sacred things," is the most common Greek phrase describing this ritual complex.[86] The ritual of sacrifice has various levels of elaboration, from the largest Panhellenic festivals held every four years over the course of many days to a personal sacrifice ritual at a household altar. Most sacrifices that were part of major festivals were offered at the sanctuaries on behalf of the entire *polis* and most of the population participated.

As a modern person, I do not endorse animal sacrifice and do not recommend re-creating the ancient sacrifice ritual in its old form. However, because it is the most common template for ancient Greek ritual, there is value in knowing sacrifice so we can take appropriate pieces and connect with lines of power when creating new rituals.

Reasons to Sacrifice

Each *polis* had its own calendar replete with festivals. A festival is a recurring date on which sacrifice was offered to one or more of the Theoi. The festival

---

86.   Naiden, "Sacrifice."

may have additional activities, but they all included sacrifice. Not every festival required multiple hours, but some went on for days.[87]

Sacrifice could be offered at need. Most often this was for an individual. If someone was sick, if they were about to go on a business venture or travel, if they were getting married, if a child was born—truthfully, for almost any major life event, it was appropriate to sacrifice and pray. A *polis* or organization, like an army or a trade expedition, might sacrifice at need. There were always preliminary sacrifices before any meeting of a governing council. When there was plague or the possibility of war (as either the defender or aggressor), the community would make sacrifices. A sacrifice might be used to ask the Theoi to witness something, like an oath.[88]

Finally, it was appropriate to sacrifice in thanksgiving. In fact, if we make a prayer and it is answered, it is bad manners not to give thanks. Thanksgiving sacrifices were incorporated into the calendar as festivals, including those tied to the agricultural year and on anniversaries of important historical events where the Theoi had intervened to bless the life of the *polis*.[89]

Description of the Traditional Sacrifice Ritual

While this description includes animal sacrifice, I recommend adopting the form for other offerings, including fruits, vegetables, and baked goods. Although elaborations are possible, the essential components of sacrifice are the preparation, procession, purification, prayers, giving the offerings, watching for signs the sacrifice is accepted, and communal feasting. Sometimes these were simple and sometimes complex.

Preparation

Preparation is the sacrifice ritual's beginning. Everything had to be aesthetically pleasing. Inspecting and selecting the offerings was part of the ritual. In animal sacrifice, the inspection and selection were especially formalized. The animal had to be beautiful and healthy and have lots of vitality. Other offerings were the best available.[90]

---

87.   Gawlinski, "Athenian Calendar of Sacrifices," 37–55.
88.   Rice and Stambaugh, "Sacrifices and Festivals."
89.   Naiden, *Smoke Signals for the Gods*.
90.   Naiden, "Fallacy of the Willing Victim," 61–73.

Additionally, the participants were clean, in their best clothes, traditionally wearing wreaths on their heads. They had previously purified themselves from any *miasma*. The preliminary preparations gave them a chance to move into the mental and emotional space closest to the Theoi. The offerings were arranged beautifully. In a large sacrifice, the horns of sacrificial oxen were sometimes gilded. Garlands of flowers were placed around the necks of sacrificial animals and adorned trays of offerings.[91] All this took place outside the *temenos*, but the activity of conscious and careful preparation helped shift focus away from everyday ways of being.

Procession

The procession (*pompe*) itself was an offering of performance art. Functionally, the worshippers carried the offerings into the *temenos* to the altar. It was a ritual boundary-crossing, involving purification at the edge of the *temenos,* then stepping out of the mundane and into sacred space. Through the procession, the worshippers moved closer and closer to the Gods by singing hymns, dancing, and physically crossing the threshold. In large festivals, the entire community processed a specially laid out Sacred Way, trod over and over by generations. The great processions in some Catholic countries have their roots in this ritual form predating Christianity. In a household, the procession may begin in a hallway, then lead to the altar in the courtyard or in another room—but the movement and transition is important.

Purification

Once the altar was reached, all participants ritually washed their hands.[92]

Invocation

The priest or priestess prayed to the Great One and asked the God to be present. This invocation was absolutely necessary. In polytheism, it is essential to specify which Great Ones are being worshipped and invite Them to be present.

---

91. Burkert, *Greek Religion.*
92. Burkert, *Greek Religion.*

The Sacrifice

In an animal sacrifice, after invoking the Great One for whom the sacrifice is meant, the animal was tested to see if the God would send an omen of acceptance before it was slaughtered. The signs usually involved specific behaviors, like shivering in particular patterns when sprinkled with liquid, or particular types of movements in relation to food being put before them.[93]

Placing incense on the fire was a preliminary offering. In animal sacrifices, once the omen from the God demonstrated the animal was acceptable, grains of barley were sprinkled on it, on the altar, and on the participants. The priest or priestess cut a few hairs from the animal's head and placed them in the fire. This consecrated the animal to the Great One.[94]

In animal sacrifice, the knife hidden in a basket carried by a priestess was used to swiftly kill the animal. The animal should not see it coming and ideally should not be distressed. At the moment of the killing the women gave the ritual *ologymos*, which in Latin is "ululation." It is a high-pitched trilling cry of emotional intensity. If the animal was small, it was held over the fire so blood dripped directly onto the fire and the altar; if it was larger, the blood was caught in a bowl and poured on the fire.[95]

Watching for Signs

The animal was then taken away and butchered. The priest and leading participants observed the fire and examined the liver and entrails for signs the deity accepted the sacrifice. The Greek practice of *hepatoscopy* (liver examination) was not as detailed as what the Romans developed. It mainly determined if the God was pleased.[96]

After butchering the animal, the "God's portion" was burned. This was usually the tail and the bones of the hip girdle and thighs wrapped in fat. Often some organs were put on the fire. The smoke pleased the Theoi. In fact, the Greek word *thuein*, which refers to killing an animal for a God, literally means "to make smoke."[97]

---

93.   Naiden, "Fallacy of the Willing Victim."
94.   Burkert, *Greek Religion.*
95.   Burkert, *Greek Religion.*
96.   Naiden, *Smoke Signals for the Gods.*
97.   Naiden, *Smoke Signals for the Gods.*

Sometimes the entire animal was burned and given to the God, called *holo-kauston* (the whole burned). This is not normal but might be done for several reasons. The first is the person or people who are sacrificing are in dire straits and are desperately calling for help. In this instance, the communication is the loudest broadcast signal possible to get the attention of the Theoi. Sometimes the entire animal is burned because it is to a chthonic spirit of the underworld and, since mortals are susceptible to dying, eating food dedicated to the dead or Theoi of death is considered dangerous. Finally, when a sacrifice is made to seal an oath—which is really a suspended curse one places upon oneself to be enacted if one breaks the oath—it is considered dangerous to eat the animal.[98]

Libations, usually wine, were poured on the fire. There were usually other types of food offerings as well as more incense put on the fire for the Gods. In a nonanimal sacrifice, the various cakes, fruits, libations, nuts, and other food made up the main sacrifice.[99]

Throughout the offerings, the lead participants watch the flames, observing how they burn in order to determine whether or not the God is pleased. Although the emphasis on this chapter is on "speaking" to the Theoi, in practice we always need to be listening, especially when speaking. Omens occurring during sacrifice have special gravity.[100]

Feasting

Finally, the participants come together, with the God present, to share a communal feast. Sometimes it would include full *theoxenia*, a rite in which a banqueting couch and table were laid out for the God among the participants. The Great One, enjoying the smoke, was believed to participate in the feast.[101] In many festivals, feasting was followed by music and dancing well into the night.

REGULAR PRACTICES FOR HONORING THE THEOI

Incorporating regular practices into your life will help you build strong relationships with the Theoi and keep the lines of communication open and

98. Graf, *Magic in the Ancient World*.
99. Burkert, *Greek Religion*.
100. Kearns, *Ancient Greek Religion*.
101. Kearns, *Ancient Greek Religion*.

strong. You can do this by developing excellence in honor of the Theoi, by cele-brating festivals, and by developing a daily practice.

Pursuit of Areté

The Greek word *areté* is often translated as "virtue," but it also means "excel-lence." If we think about the way "virtue" is used in herbalism, it leads us toward a better understanding of what *areté* truly is. The virtue of a plant is the rarefied essence of that living being. *Areté* is the rarefied human essence. To pursue *areté* is to strive for your own perfection as a human. Aristotle lays out the moral vir-tues in *The Nicomachaean Ethics*, but the pursuit of *areté* should be present in all arenas of human potential.[102] We should always strive for excellence.

If there is one common agenda in relation to humans among the Theoi, it is that They want us to be good, fully developed humans. Striving to be as excellent and godlike as we can be is a way to honor Them. Strive for excellence in your activities as an act of piety and seek the support of the Great Ones in doing so. Identify areas in which you have special abilities and focus attention on perfecting them—both for your own intrinsic satisfaction and as devotion. The ability to self-consciously develop our talents makes us human.

While excellence in any area is valuable, excellence in the moral domain is essential. Part of the role of philosophy—literally the "love of wisdom"—is to pursue *areté* of character. Philosophy is the training of the mind, the character, and is the pursuit of spiritual excellence. I discuss the process of developing *areté* more thoroughly in chapter 14 but note that one can pursue the develop-ment of excellence as an offering.

Agon: The Contest

Celebrating pursuit of *areté* in honor of the Theoi was regularly incorporated into religious festivals in the form of sacred competitions. The word *agon* (from which we get "agony") means "struggle," but it also means "contest" or "com-petition."[103] Placing contestants who have achieved excellence together in com-petition facilitates the development of greater excellence in the competitors than they could achieve alone. Although each competitor wants to do their best and win, they want their opponents to do their best. There is no honor in

---

102.   Aristotle, *Nicomachaean Ethics*.
103.   Nagy, *Ancient Greek Hero in 24 Hours*.

winning against a weak competitor. The ultimate goal is the advancement of the whole frame of what excellence looks like.

While we know the most about the great athletic competitions, like the Olympics, if any area of excellence could be turned into a contest, it was. There were competitions for baking, beauty, weaving, blacksmithing, and everything you would see at a state fair. From a religious perspective, these competitions, as activities to honor and please the Theoi, have a communal and an individualistic element. The individual, by pursuing *areté* and then sharing their excellence in a sacred context, honors the Gods. The community as a whole has to make choices to give individuals enough *schole* ("leisure" time freed from the work of production) so that they can be free to pursue excellence. Therefore, when a community makes a choice to invest its collective resources in freeing up an athlete to train, a musician to practice, a weaver to perfect skills that are more labor-intensive than are necessary for producing work clothes—the whole community is sacrificing and is rightly proud of their fellows' achievements.

The most well-known competitions are the Games. The ritual cycle of the Games is derived from Bronze Age funeral games, like those represented in Homer.[104] The four great Panhellenic festivals, held every four years, were the Olympic Games at the Sanctuary of Zeus at Olympia, the Pythian Games at the Sanctuary of Apollon at Delphi, the Nemean Games at the Sanctuary of Zeus at Nemea, and the Isthmian Games at the Sanctuary of Poseidon outside Corinth. The Panathenaic Games dedicated to Athena in Athens never quite became fully Panhellenic but were close to that stature. The stadium in Athens where the modern Olympics were reborn is, actually, the restored Panathenaic stadium.

The athletic contests included footraces, chariot races, the discus throw, the long jump, and various forms of combat sports like wrestling, boxing, and the *pankration* (mixed martial arts). The Games usually included other contests as well. The Pythian Games of Apollon included highly prestigious musical contests, and most Games had some musical and dance competitions.[105] Rhapsodes—poets who performed epic poetry—competed.[106]

104.   Burkert, *Greek Religion*.
105.   Burkert, *Greek Religion*.
106.   Nagy, *Ancient Greek Hero in 24 Hours*.

Outside the Games and in a different set of festivals dedicated to Dionysus, the great theatrical performances were turned into a contest. The creation and performance of tragedies, comedies, satyr plays, and dithyrambs were all ways to honor the Gods, especially Dionysus, through performing art. All performances are an offering, and the contest is part of the ritual context.

For Modern Pagans, encouraging excellence and creating ritualized opportunities for community members to present their excellence to the Theoi in ways that inspire others is in keeping with Hellenic tradition. It would not be effective to have competitions, even if they mimicked the ancient events, unless the competitors train and dedicate themselves to excellence. It is the development of human excellence that honors the Gods. The Games were just a method for achieving excellence.

Festivals

A festival is an offering and collective communion between the Theoi and the community. Sacrifice was part of every festival and may have been the entire content of a festival. The major festivals, however, contain other ritual activities and specific purposes.

Each *polis* had its own festival calendar using lunar months, but the agricultural festivals were tied to the fixed stars to keep them aligned with agricultural cycles. The calendar used in Athens is what we know best, although the calendar from Delphi is also well preserved. As Modern Pagans, I suggest constructing our own calendars that are meaningful to our particular communities rather than choosing one from an ancient city.

Each calendar includes monthly sacrifices that are regular touch-points with various Theoi in order to maintain our relationships, and these vary from *polis* to *polis*. The first day of the new moon, Noumenia, is propitious and a day of rest. There would be small state sacrifices and sacrifices in the home.[107] The night before, the dark of the moon, was Hekate's feast of Deipnon. The house was swept clean and a meal left for the restless dead outside the household's door or at the crossroads. The proper form is to put the meal down and walk away without looking back. The poor sometimes ate the meal, although that is not the original purpose. Some current practitioners make donations to food

---

107.   Panopoulos, Panagiotopoulous, and Armyras, *Hellenic Polytheism*.

banks for the poor on Deipnon in Her honor, whereas others believe this practice strays from the emphasis on purification and honoring or appeasing the restless dead. Regardless, Deipnon, the night before the beginning of the new month, is a time to do what is needed to start afresh, and then on Noumenia, begin anew. Hekate stands in those transitional spaces.[108]

There are numerous festivals tied to the seasons that have specific purposes. Dedicated to Demeter and Persephone, Thesmophoria was a three-day fertility festival attended only by women that linked human fertility to the Earth's fertility. The rite was secret. Thesmophoria was tied to the agricultural year but in some places was tied to the sowing and in others to the reaping. Piglets were sacrificed, thrown into a pit, and left to rot for a year. The next year they were retrieved and used to fertilize the soil.[109]

While it is unlikely we would re-create ancient Hellenic agricultural methods, there is value in ritually rebirthing a sacred understanding of food and the Earth's holiness and linking it to human fertility. This is especially important given our often disrespectful and destructive methods of modern food production and our spiritual distance from it. In more than one oracular session, Apollon has said Triptolemos (the demigod tasked by Demeter and Persephone to spread the knowledge of agriculture) must ride again. His comment was directly linked to combatting environmental degradation. Rebirthing a festival for Demeter and Persephone meeting these requirements would be a worthy endeavor.

Exercise
CREATE YOUR OWN FESTIVAL CALENDAR
Create your own festival calendar that makes sense in your community. It is not a bad thing if there is variety among communities—it did not harm the ancient Greeks.

What You'll Need
A calendar that includes solar and lunar information and possibly astrological information, a journal, and a pen. A quiet place, preferably at your altar. An offering (incense, candle, or a libation).

---

108.   Johnston, *Hekate Soteira*.

109.   Evans, "Sanctuaries, Sacrifices, and the Eleusinian Mysteries," 227–54.

Directions

Create an annual calendar based on particular functions rather than re-creating specific ancient festivals. Make an offering of incense, a candle, or a libation and pray and listen to what the Theoi want. Generate a list of functional festivals that you want to incorporate into your calendar. Functionally, consider developing rituals for the following:

- A spring festival celebrating the Earth coming back to life. For example: Anthesteria (Dionysus) or Theophania (Apollon).
- A festival of thanksgiving for bounty. It can be first fruits or it can be toward the harvest's end.
- A festival linking the Earth's fecundity with humans. In ancient times, fertility rites were solemn because if food didn't grow, people died. The precariousness feels different than how most Modern Pagans envision "fertility festivals." For example: Thesmophoria (Demeter).
- A festival dedicated to the Theoi of the *polis* focusing on building and strengthening relationships between the whole community and the Gods of the *polis*.
- A festival for the ancestors and heroes.
- A festival celebrating excellence. For example: the Games, sacred contests, sacred performance festival
- If you or your community has a particular patron, a festival honoring that deity.

There is a lot of room for creative inspiration in this type of approach. Based on what makes sense for you and your community, tie your festivals to the seasons and/or the lunar cycles and link them to a date. It is best if it is a cycle in natural time (tied to solar, lunar, or astrological cycles). Document your new calendar.

Once you have established your overall calendar, at least a month ahead of time, with each one, work with the Theoi and begin by creating simple rituals or traditions fulfilling the purpose. You can take inspiration from ancient sources and lore or you can build your own working with the Theoi.

Start simple and allow the traditions to evolve over the years. The first cycle, you may just perform prayers of gratitude for all but one, which you focus on developing into something more complex.

DAILY PRACTICE

This whole chapter has covered ways in which we communicate with the Theoi, but it is the daily practice that keeps the relationship open, developing, and real. The most important thing is to actually talk to Them, especially to those Great Ones with whom you have special bonds. This can be by going to your altar, making an offering of a candle or incense or a libation, saying a prayer to connect you, and then listening. It can be taking some time to travel to a place on the inner planes and spend time in communion with Them. As with any relationship, if you want it to be living and deep, you have to actually talk regularly.

In addition to your specific formal practices, as you move through your day, be aware of what is important to the Theoi with whom you are in relationship and look for opportunities to do things They will appreciate. When you see and take an opportunity, make a quick prayer, even if it is just "Hera, I honor you" to call Her attention and turn that moment into an offering. Similarly, as you are going through your day, pay attention to the domains in which you are working and don't be shy about asking for assistance. For example, when you are traveling, ask Hermes to bless your way. Not only may you receive assistance, you are strengthening Hermes's human-user interface and your connection to Him, so it is beneficial to Hermes. Remember, we have to ask the Theoi for help. They respect our autonomy and won't interfere unless we give Them permission.

As an example, my formal daily practice includes consciously going into my *temenos* and lighting candles on my altars in front of my consecrated images of the Theoi. The candles are an offering. I say prayers and usually offer incense. My prayers align with the standard form. I call the Gods by name with epithets. I usually just ask for Their presence and blessing and give thanks for our relationship. I typically include prayers for my *polis*. Because I am specifically devoted to Apollon and Athena, I ask for Their help in ensuring I am able to serve Them well. Sometimes I may have a more specific request on behalf of myself or others. Sometimes I ask for assistance in seeking clarity when I don't know what to do about a certain situation. I may ask for support, but I never ask Them to do my work for me. I never try to pawn my responsibility off on Them. I listen and pay attention to omens. Then I go about my day following the advice I received.

Exercise
DESIGN YOUR DAILY PRACTICE

Design two versions of your daily practice. The biggest obstacle to a successful daily practice is a lack of time and exhaustion. Having elaborate expectations for yourself will make it more likely you will avoid your practice. Design two versions of a daily practice for yourself. One is very simple and should take you less than five minutes and maybe less than two, if needed. The second is a more elaborate version for when you have the time and energy.

What You'll Need

A journal and a pen.

Directions

Go to a quiet place where you can be uninterrupted, preferably at your altar.

Step 1: Create a fast version of a daily practice that can be done in less than five minutes and functionally

- gets the attention of the Great One(s) with whom you are closest.
- tells Them you value your relationship.
- makes a request (it can just be to accept your gratitude or to bless you in your day).
- includes listening to anything They say.

Take notes and make your instructions for what you will minimally do each day.

Step 2: For the more elaborate version, think about what would please Them and engage you. You can determine if you want to make regular offerings and, if so, what types. You can write more elaborate prayers. You can include time working in vision. You may want to include Great Ones other than just those with whom you are closest. Use your imagination and don't be afraid to change the form of your practice if it gets stale. Take notes and make your instructions for what you will do if you have time and energy for your more expansive practice.

CHAPTER SEVEN
LISTENING TO THE GODS—OMENS, ORACLES, AND VISIONS

Listening is the most essential relationship skill. In our relationships with the Theoi and other spirits, listening is complicated because They are not normally operating through physical bodies. However, They communicate with us regularly. Sometimes we initiate contact through acts of "speaking" as described in the last chapter. Paying close attention and "listening" while speaking is the crucial difference between talking "at" the Gods and real communication. Communication initiated by Them is easily overlooked.

Pitfalls

Barriers to effectively listening to the Gods come from our socialization. Our culture associates hearing or seeing things others don't as a sign of mental instability. Clearly there are people who suffer from hallucinations, but all unusual experiences get painted with a broad brush. I suggest the determining factor should be whether you are able to function well in the world, not what inner experiences you have. Any of us socialized in modern "Western" cultures have been trained from a young age to ignore perceptual input that doesn't fit with consensus reality. It takes effort to break through that socialization. It helps to be in a community where you can reinforce each other while also having more objective eyes who will tell you if you are beginning to live in dysfunction. Having honest, courageous peers who will tell you what you need to hear, not what you want to hear, is the basis of true friendship.

Another piece of socialization we have to break through is to undo the legacy of strains of monotheism emphasizing the unworthiness of humans in their relationship with God. Christianity teaches that God loves humanity so much He sent His only son, who is an aspect of Himself, to suffer and die for humanity's redemption. This necessitates a vision of humanity as fatally flawed because otherwise one doesn't need a redeemer. Feelings of unworthiness are not a good basis for healthy relationship for anyone, including between humans and the Theoi. They get in the way of perceiving when one of Them is reaching out to make contact and can make us fear being arrogant just for receiving communication.

Finally, many of us carry around the idea that God is so vast that our personal concerns are too trivial to be worthy of divine attention. This is a variation of the worthiness problem and also comes from projecting our human limitations onto the Gods. Apollon once directly addressed this with me when I was apologizing about bothering Him with something. He stopped me and said, "I'm not that small." I was taken aback and said, "I know you're not small, that's why I feel ridiculous bothering you with…" to which He broke back in and said, "No. I mean, I'm not that small. It's not as though I cannot attend to you and be with you, individually, and many others, and still attend to the cosmic scale. I'm not that small. I don't have that limitation." The image that arose in my mind was a painting of Krishna and the Gopi maidens where Krishna is individually with all the Gopi maidens at once.

Make a direct effort to counter these forms of socialization. If possible, being in community with like-minded others, even if they are not directly on the same path, is helpful. It helps you avoid two dangers. Once you realize you are in a mutual relationship with one of the Great Ones, you may have inappropriate ego inflation. If you begin feeling more worthy than other people, check yourself. It is natural for humans to be in relationship with the Great Ones. The fact many are not is an unnatural aberration due to wounds from our culture, not due to inherent lack of worthiness. The other danger is becoming superstitious. Superstition is when you begin seeing signs or communication everywhere. It is an overcorrection. Again, being in like-minded community can help with this. The danger of superstition is the temptation to cede your responsibility as a human to exercise your critical judgment. We are supposed to be fully responsible spiritual adults. There is nothing wrong with seeking counsel to help us make better decisions, but there is something badly wrong with asking others—humans or the Gods—to take on our responsibilities for us.

Once you begin listening, watch your state of mind—if it is regularly anxious or afraid, then back off the psychic development and deal with your anxiety first. While you can receive warnings from the Theoi and spirits, They are not constantly communicating doom—regular portents of doom are probably manifestations of anxiety more than communication.

TYPES OF LISTENING

The ancient sources distinguish between technical and natural divination.[110] Natural divination is communication that is a gift and does not require training. One form available to everyone is communication coming through dreams. Possessory oracles, like the Delphic Oracle, are natural because being possessed by a god is not learned—it is a direct gift from the God. An epiphany (*epiphaneia*) or theophany (*theophaneia*) when one of the Theoi show up and make themselves known, often speaking directly without a medium, is a natural form of communication. The technical forms of communication can be learned by anyone, although there are some who have especially high levels of mastery. These are interpretive arts like the ability to read omens and portents or using formal divinatory systems, like astrology, dice, or, in our times, tarot.

In reality, the natural and technical are often mixed. Dreams and oracles often require interpretation, and skillful interpretation can be learned. People who sit as *mantis* (those who are possessed by the God and allow the God to speak and act through their body) are often not as good at interpreting what is said as someone else is. Speaking from experience, if they were thinking about what something being said through them means, it would get their personality in the way and taint the oracular process. The job of *mantis* is to step back and try to stay out of it.

I think of the types of listening as being a spectrum ranging from those that are most common, take the least energy, but are also most likely to be misunderstood up to the forms that are least common, take the most energy, but

---

110.   Johnston, *Ancient Greek Divination*.

are least likely to be misunderstood. Omens and portents are the most common. They take the least energy to create but are the most likely to be misinterpreted (or just plain missed). From there, dreams and visions achieved in trance states take a bit more energy, are still fairly common, but usually require interpretation and can be mixed with weird dream imagery. Possessory oracles are a chance to directly ask one of the Great Ones specific questions and receive answers in language rather than imagery. They take a fair amount of energy and a committed working partnership between one of the Theoi and a *mantis* that involves, among other things, modification of the subtle physiology of the *mantis*. Finally, an epiphany or theophany where one of the Great Ones physically shows up in our world is very rare, takes a lot of energy, but also tends to be unambiguous.

RELIGIOUS SPECIALISTS

In ancient Greece, almost everyone had some technical knowledge about reading omens and portents and dream interpretation. There were ways of "provoking" an omen, like most of our modern forms of divination. You could provoke a dream through dream incubation. While technical methods included a learnable skill set, there were some people with high levels of spiritual intuition who were masters.

For example, Aristander of Telmessos was Alexander the Great's main seer. He was gifted at interpreting omens.[111] While officially a form of technical divination that can be learned, Aristander regularly departed from all the other seers and from known "rules" about omens to give original interpretations that were reliably accurate. His form of interpretation was a high mystic art rather than a rational science, and he had high integrity, sometimes telling Alexander things he didn't want to hear but needed to hear. Aristander was always listening on behalf of Alexander, and the excellence of his service significantly contributed to Alexander's astonishing successes.

Each possessory oracle, most of whom were for Apollon, had at least one *mantis*. The specialists at the oracular temples were chosen by the specific God, vetted, and typically lived the rest of their lives in the sanctuary.

---

111. Flower, *Seer in Ancient Greece*.

There were itinerant freelance specialists who offered possessory oracles.[112] Because they lacked official vetting and weren't associated with a particular cult, they had an ambivalent status. When you were in Delphi, you could have confidence you were talking to Apollon because He would not accept the insult of an imposter in His temple. The same could not be said about a random *mantis* in the streets; however, consulting a God through one of them did not require a pilgrimage. Some of these itinerate specialists had a good reputation for being helpful and honest. Interestingly, there were some—the "belly-talkers"—who claimed to have beings who were highly evolved but not necessarily gods with whom they symbiotically shared their bodies permanently.[113] For those who are interested, the description is similar to what later occultists call "in-dwellers."

Chresmologues were specialists who recorded and compiled oracles.[114] They acted as scribes so those who received an oracle would get the accurate text of what was said. They also compiled oracular utterances and used them as a form of bibliomancy, giving people a "fortune." While it was valuable to have good recordings of what was said in an oracular session, when they strayed into distributing oracles for others, they were often considered shady.

The most highly regarded seers and mediums/*mantis* often came from families that had a reputation for related gifts.[115] The relationship between these gifts and particular bloodlines is a common thread in many cultures.

Natural Omens

Natural omens are any of the signs in the world through which one of the Theoi is trying to communicate. The most powerful omens are those where one of the Theoi is initiating contact, but they are often the easiest to overlook because we are going about our day and not watching for them. Make a conscious effort to pay attention and be open. Keep a journal and ask yourself what you noticed each day. As you begin to recognize communication, pay close attention to how it feels when you are receiving a message—especially how it feels in your body. Spend time encoding those feelings into your

---

112.   Vlassopoulos, "Religion in Communities," 257–71.
113.   Johnston, "Oracles and Divination," 477–89.
114.   Stoneman, *Ancient Oracles.*
115.   Larson, *Understanding Greek Religion.*

memory. Our somatic/body intelligence can help us activate conscious awareness if we learn what certain things feel like.

For example, while driving on a freeway, a crow, sacred to Apollon, flew from
the side, dipped, and turned right in front of me, and I felt, almost in language,
"Be careful!" My attention snapped into focus, and seconds later, the tire of the
car in front of me blew out. If I had not been as intensely attentive as I was, I
might not have swerved into the other lane in time to avoid an accident. That
feeling of communication was so clear and visceral, the memory of it helps me
recognize the sensation now. Look for anchor points in your experiences.

While the Theoi can use almost anything to communicate, there are several common forms that are easy to start with.

Birds

Interpreting bird behavior as a mode of communication from high spiritual
beings is common in many cultures, including ancient Greece.[116] While there
were some ancient rules (e.g., bird of prey on the right is auspicious, on the left
is inauspicious), I find getting rid of rules and just seeing what they say to you is
better. It helps if you know which birds are sacred to whom. Eagles are sacred
to Zeus, but an eagle can be used by any Great One for communication. When
I notice an eagle, the highest-flying bird, it is a reliable sign someone is trying
to communicate with me and often comes as confirmation of "big" messages.

While I believe a bird can be used by any of the Theoi, especially birds of
prey, here are some traditional associations.

- Eagles: Zeus
- Falcons: Hera
- Crows and swans: Apollon
- Owls: Athena
- Doves: Aphrodite

---

116. Burkert, *Greek Religion*.

Kledon

Another form of omen that is easy to begin with is *kledon*. *Kledon* is bits of speech you overhear that have meaning.[117] If you are aware of it, it is a common form of omens. Your attention is being manipulated to create communication. When your attention is drawn and you overhear something, notice what you heard and the sensation. I'm sure many of you have experienced this with music where suddenly songs on the radio make sense in relation to what you have been thinking about. Pay attention to misspeaking, especially when it is in a ritual context. When you get communication involving the names or images, including company logos, of one of the Theoi, pay attention.

Omens in Ritual

Traditionally, anytime you are making offerings or praying, you should be watching for signs from the Theoi, because you know They are already present in the ritual. If you are burning anything as offerings, paying attention to the flames and how things burn can reveal messages. Any *kledon*, especially misspoken words, can be signs. Note anything unusual happening during the ritual.

PROVOKED OMENS

Provoked omens are systems where you can ask questions and get answers by allowing one of the Theoi to intervene in a controlled but meaningful way. In order for it to be one of the Theoi and not just your own spirit, you do have to ask one of Them to use the system and then verify They are by seeking confirmation.

Provoking Kledon

In ancient Greece, a worshipper would go to a shrine or temple, pray to a god, and ask for guidance on a particular issue. Then the petitioner closed up their ears and went out of the sanctuary. Once outside the temple gate, whatever was first heard was the counsel.[118] This is easily adapted to modern practice. When you have a question for one of the Theoi, pray and ask for guidance. Relax and, over the course of your day, let your attention be drawn to a sign in your environment. It may be verbal, it may be your mind drawn toward something in

---

117.   Larson, *Understanding Greek Religion.*
118.   Larson, *Understanding Greek Religion.*

writing, or it may be your mind being drawn to an image. The *kledon* practice is the same as natural *kledon*, except you are asking a specific Great One to send you a message in that format.

Kleromancy

Kleromancy is divination by dice or drawing lots.[119] In Delphi, the Pythia was only possessed one day a month for nine months of the year. The rest of the time, she let her hand be guided by Apollon in a state of being overlit and drew lots to answer questions.[120] A bag of light or dark stones of roughly equivalent size and texture or black and white beans were used.[121] The idea is to create something truly random, invite the God to guide the outcome, and then it is no longer random.

Most of our current forms of divination, like tarot, rune readings, ogham, and I-Ching can be used this way so long as you first ask one of the Great Ones to guide it. Many of these systems have more context than the yes-no questioning from lot sorting (or using a pendulum). You can get more depth in the answers, but simple clarity is often sacrificed in the process.

Regularly using divination to communicate with the Theoi gives Them a channel to communicate and the more symbolically complex methods, like tarot, can be a good way to let Them start a conversation. The ancient Greeks learned and adopted from others all the time. Even though the tarot comes from outside the ancient Greek tradition, I have no hesitation in using it and a pendulum in conjunction with more traditional methods to increase the efficacy of communication and deepen sacred relationships.

Exercise
OMEN TRAINING

This practice will help you learn how to recognize omens and build a relationship with one of the Theoi.

---

119.   Stoneman, *Ancient Oracles*.
120.   Andronicos, *Delphi*.
121.   Parke, *Greek Oracles*.

What You'll Need

A pendulum, a small notebook or app you can have with you during the day, your altar, a candle, and an image of the deity with whom you are striving to build a relationship.

Directions

Do this exercise daily for at least a month.

Step 1: Train your pendulum to answer yes and no. Take your pendulum in your dominant hand and say, "Show me yes," and observe. Then say, "Show me no," and observe. This is a form of provoked omen. What is manipulated is the movement in your body operating below the threshold of conscious awareness. I use pendulums to double-check myself a lot. If I'm worried I might bias things, I close my eyes while I ask the question and only open them to observe the answer that is already in motion. It does not always move the way I think it will move.

Step 2: Go to your altar each morning. Light the candle in front of the Great One you are trying to build a relationship with and say,

Great One, I am seeking to develop a relationship with you. I am striving to be open and recognize whenever you are communicating with me. I am focusing on learning how to recognize your signs. I ask you to send me a sign today. Help draw my attention toward your sign. Help me recognize it for what it is. Help me remember, understand, and learn how it feels. Thank you for your support and for the gift of your friendship.

Step 3: Go through your day and pay attention. Immediately record anything that seems to be an omen in your notebook or app.

Step 4: At the day's end, go back to your altar and light your candle again. Pray to whomever you called on that morning.

Great One, thank you for working with me today. Please help me understand and recognize your communication. Guide my hand with this pendulum so I may receive correct information. Thank you.

Using a pendulum, ask yes-no questions. Go through your list of omens you think you received. For each, first verify it was indeed an omen. Talk about how it felt in your body and try to get specific. Ask for feedback about whether you are perceiving correctly. Verify or discover the omen's source. Test any interpretations you are making. Record all of it in your journal.

Step 5: At the end of a month, review your progress. You should have a much better sense of omens, know how it feels in your body when you are receiving one, have built or deepened a relationship with one of the Theoi, and have more open awareness. If you feel it has been insufficient, ask the pendulum if you need to continue for longer or if you should try to work with another deity.

DREAMS AND VISIONS

The ancient Greeks saw dreams as a way through which the Theoi would communicate—the Greek word is *oneiromancy*.[122] They paid close attention to their dreams, took them seriously, and studied them. Many early philosophers, including Aristotle, theorized about dreams.[123] All the theorists were aware most dreams seemed to be random mental processes that lacked divine meaning. They knew that all sorts of physical conditions, like what one ate before sleep, could shape dreams, but also realized sometimes truth comes in dreams. Dreams were divided between dreams in which things are happening and those in which the dreamer receives teachings. Teaching dreams are considered to be of divine origin. They sometimes include a Great One directly, and the meaning is often pretty clear.

By contrast, enigmatic dreams can be important but difficult to decipher. Some are true and some are not. Some are communications and some are perceptions of something beyond our waking consciousness. In Homer's *Odyssey*, the imagery of the twin gates of horn and ivory is used. The dreams coming through the gates of horn bring truth and those coming through the gates of ivory bring falsehood—but it can be difficult to know the difference. Porphyry explained you can cut a horn into a very thin slice and see through it, whereas no matter how thinly you slice ivory, it is always opaque. Therefore, the ivory

---

122.   Stoneman, *Ancient Oracles*.

123.   Aristotle, "On Dreams," 729–35; Aristotle, "On Divination in Sleep," 736–39.

gates do not show us truth, whereas the horn can, but the dream symbolism still colors how truth is seen.[124] Similarly, dreams can sometimes reveal truth beyond what we can know by ourselves, but they are colored by the individual dreamer's psyche.

Dreams having divine origin tend to be vivid. Pay attention to your dreams, and if you have a "big dream," note how it feels. When I am "dreaming true," when I am seeing something real, when I am being taught by some being that is not a human, or when I am clearly in direct communication and interaction with a Great One in the part of my being that is temporarily free from my body, there is a specific tactile sensation that is different than my regular dreams. Recognizing that sensation means I can call on my ability to remember more strongly.

To do this work, we have to take care of our bodies and figure out our personal best sleeping conditions. When I am exhausted, I neither remember my dreams nor have big dreams. When I am too hot, I am more likely to have nightmares. I have more big dreams when I am alone, in real darkness, not using many electric lights a couple of hours before, and away from city noises. When you have a big dream, take note of the physical conditions that enabled it to come through to understand how you are wired.

Dream Incubation

In numerous cults, especially the healing cults of Asklepios we will discuss in chapter 11, the ancient Greeks created practices for incubating or provoking "big dreams." Even if we cannot manage to have regular good sleep hygiene, it behooves us to periodically practice dream incubation.

The ancient model is to go someplace set aside for this purpose away from where you live. Historically, it would be a sanctuary of a dream oracle. These included the sanctuaries of Asklepios and the initiatory caves dedicated to Apollon. The dream oracle of Amphiaraios of Oropos was another sanctuary that practiced dream incubation. Petitioners went on a pilgrimage, searching for guidance or seeking healing from one of the Great Ones in their dreams.[125]

In our contemporary rebirthing, we do not currently have dream incubation sanctuaries, but we can still practice dream incubation. The place you go

---

124.   Anghelina, "Homeric Gates of Horn and Ivory," 65–72.

125.   Ustinova, *Caves and the Ancient Greek Mind*.

should be peaceful, in a tranquil setting. There should be quiet, and at night it should be dark and away from the sounds of technology.

Exercise
SILENT RETREAT DREAM INCUBATION
This is a quest for spiritual guidance.

What You'll Need
Find a place where you can go on retreat for a few days away from noise—someplace dark and where you can be left alone. Bring a journal and a pen.

Directions
Make a commitment to yourself that you will not speak aloud, you will not engage with others, and you will not take in language. Other than emergencies, do not use technology. You may journal. Before you leave, say a prayer in which you set your intention to focus on listening to the Theoi. When you arrive, take a purifying bath or shower then pray and make offerings. Conclude your prayer, saying these will be the last words you will speak until you leave the retreat, except in a true emergency. From this point, pray silently and move your communication inward.

When the time is right, with full intention, go into a special place and sleep, expecting to receive a dream. Pray as you fall asleep. Immediately upon waking, write down your dreams in as much detail as you can. During your retreat, allow yourself to be led and your nervous system to detox. Don't be surprised if the first couple of days of being in silence are actively painful—I usually end up crying uncontrollably without content in the first couple of days as my body releases the stress it is carrying. This is usually preliminary to my body relaxing enough that I can have a big dream. We are so used to overstimulating our nervous systems that the unwinding is uncomfortable. If there is running water nearby where you can be without engaging with other noise or people, allow its sound to help repattern your etheric body. Let yourself sleep whenever your guidance and your body tell you to sleep.

When you are ready to leave, you may speak your prayers of thanks aloud to the Theoi, to any spirits who assisted you, and to the land that nurtured you during your stay. This ends your rite.

Scrying/Katoptromancy

You can induce a type of waking dream through scrying. Intentionally allow your physical gaze to relax and shift until you see waking dreams begin to emerge. To scry, you need to gaze at something providing a backdrop for images to appear. An ancient method involved pouring the blood of a sacrificial animal into a shield and scrying into the blood. This was used prior to battle. Similarly, you could pour oil into a shield and scry.[126] In current practice, I tend to use milk or water with a bit of squid ink. I prefer food-based substances that can be safely libated.

In addition to interpreting flames of a sacrificial fire as an omen, you can scry into the fire and allow visions to emerge. *Katoptromancy* is scrying into mirrors. Pausanias reports that at the temple of Demeter at Patras, petitioners gazed into a mirror against the water of a fountain.[127] Scrying is similar to dream incubation in that you are striving to create an opportunity for contact by intentionally shifting your mental state away from normal waking consciousness with an invitation.

Theophany and Epiphany

The word *theophany* means "to see one of the Theoi." The definition of epiphany is a bit broader, meaning "when a deity reveals Themselves."[128] In both, the God is present and makes that presence visible (e.g., Athena doesn't send the owl as an omen, She is present in the owl). These forms of communication are the rarest, although not unheard of. They are the purest because we see the God face-to-face.

Historically, there were two circumstances in which the Theoi tend to reveal themselves this way. One is within the context of a cult, often at the founding of a cult.[129] Demeter appeared in Eleusis in disguise. When She revealed Herself,

---

126. Stoneman, *Ancient Oracles.*

127. Pausanias, *Pausanias Descriptions of Greece.*

128. Platt, "Epiphany," 492–504.

129. Platt, "Epiphany," 492–504.

She gave instructions for founding the Eleusinian Mysteries. Athena appeared in Athens and vied with Poseidon to be the city's patron. Apollon appeared at Delphi. These were accepted as literal truths.

Once a cult has been established, there are opportunities to ritually invoke a deity through rites celebrating *theoxenia*—giving hospitality to the Gods. This provides a circumstance in which multiple people may perceive Them.[130] The climactic moments of some Mystery initiations are likely to have involved situations in which a deity makes Him or Herself visible.[131]

The second set of historical circumstances in which theophanies tended to occur is during crisis when one of the Theoi intervenes because there is an emergency.[132] Many recorded tales of theophanies are related to battle and war, like the story of Pheidippides and Pan discussed earlier.

ORACLES

Hellenic oracles, like the oracle of Delphi, were a crucial part of ancient Greek religion and an example of tremendous compassion on the part of the Great Ones. This section is about the possessory oracles in which one of the Gods, usually Apollon, temporarily possesses a *mantis* and speaks directly through the medium.

Oracles derive authority from the being possessing the *mantis* and speaking.[133] As discussed earlier, the advantage of specific oracular cult centers is that when a worshipper would go to Delphi or Didyma, they knew they were talking with Apollon. When they went to Dodona, they knew they were talking to Zeus. There are some oracles associated with particular heroes or the dead, but the vast majority of oracular cults are Apollon's.

Apollon is the Lord of Light, and Light is synonymous with transcendent Truth. He is the prophetic god. In the *Homeric Hymn to Apollo*, He claims the right to prophesy to mortals the "unerring will of Zeus."[134] He is also a healer and the god of music, philosophy, and all the human arts and areas of higher

---

130.   Platt, "Epiphany," 492–504.

131.   Ensdiø, "To Lock Up Eleusis."

132.   Platt, "Epiphany," 492–504.

133.   Johnston, *Ancient Greek Divination*.

134.   Athanassakis, trans., "Homeric Hymn to Apollon," 15–47.

knowledge.[135] One of His most important titles is *Iatromantis*, which means "physician-prophet."[136]

A profound realization I had since serving as Apollon's *mantis* is the way in which His oracular work is another manifestation of His healing work—it is deep soul-healing work. He is helping us deal with and heal from the limitations accompanying human *moira* and the suffering arising from our limitations.

Oracles are not about telling the future. They provide counsel for decisions. An oracular utterance implies action and the possibility for change. One seeks an oracular consultation so their actions can be informed by things humans cannot know through reason alone. Apollon and Zeus are the two Great Ones who have the title *Moiragetes*, the leader of the Fates.[137] They see *themistes* more clearly than any others—both "what is" and "what is right"—and see how to close the gap. The "unerring will of Zeus" is "what is right"—Divine Cosmic Order.

We do not have that clear vision. As discussed in chapter 1, it is human *moira*, our essential nature, that we are not omniscient, but we are held accountable by the law of causation for the outcomes of our actions. This makes us vulnerable to *hamartia*, the tragic mistake, where despite our best intentions and efforts, we can accidently destroy everything we hold dear. Through His unfathomable compassion, Apollon (and Zeus at Dodona) have chosen to speak directly to mortals to give us information we need to avoid *hamartia*—the tragic mistake—and to cleanse and heal *miasma*. Through oracles, these Theoi give us guidance beyond what can be known by human reason.

In Plato's philosophy as enunciated in the *Laws*, all matters of Divine Law and morality are under the guidance of Apollon.[138] In providing guidance to humans about how to avoid *hamartia*, achieve success, and cleanse *miasma*, He regularly gives humans advice about what they need to do to maintain and deepen good relationships with the Theoi or heal wounded relationships between mortals and the Gods or other classes of beings.

---

135.   Athanassakis, trans., "Homeric Hymn to Apollon," 15–47.

136.   Graf, *Apollo*.

137.   Petsas, *Delphi*.

138.   Plato, "Laws," 400–482.

When to Consult an Oracle

Both states and individuals consulted oracles. When Apollon asked me to serve as *mantis* in the capital of the United States, part of the agreement was that every session included some questions for the greater good of our society as well as the questions for and by the individual seekers.

The purpose of oracular consultations is that there are decisions to be made but reason is insufficient to make an informed choice. It is not a test nor is it just for forecasting. Historically, ancient Greek states consulted oracles whenever they were considering major changes in policy. Individuals did the same whenever they were either facing or considering changes in life circumstances.[139] For a state, this included new policies, war, peace, truces, treaties, colony formation, and all major matters of state.[140] Delphi is rightly the most famous because of its critical role in so many seminal moments in Greek history—including the creation of democracy, which was largely guided by Apollon through his oracle at Delphi. Individuals historically consulted an oracle over questions of career, health, marriage, and relationships or when someone or something was lost.[141]

Consulting an oracle is advised if there are concerns about relationships with any of the Gods. It is appropriate to consult an oracle when there is any indication of *miasma*, either as an individual or a group. The intention of such a consultation is twofold: to get an appropriate diagnosis, and then to learn what needs to be done to rectify the situation, which is a form of healing.

Oracular Answers

In an oracular session, specific questions are asked, and usually those are the questions then answered, but we have historical records in which Apollon has not answered the question but basically said, "This is what you need to know." I have encountered that in my work as well.

We have quite a few oracular responses in the written record, although more given to states than to individuals. The recordings taken by *chresmologues* given to the states ended up in state archives, increasing their likelihood of

---

139.   Stoneman, *Ancient Oracles.*

140.   Fontenrose, *Delphic Oracle.*

141.   Fontenrose, *Delphic Oracle.*

being preserved. We have more from Delphi than from anywhere else, but Delphi was the Panhellenic oracle used by everyone, so it deserves its reputation.[142]

The answers are direct counsel on matters of state and individual concerns. Many answers provide ways of purifying *miasma*. Opinions were rendered on religious matters and advice was given on the relationships between humans and the Gods. Some oracular answers provided knowledge a human could not know or discourse about some aspect of reality. The record preserved examples of all these topics.[143]

Originally, answers were given in dactylic hexameter, which is the meter of Homeric epic. By the time of Plutarch, the Delphic oracle spoke in plain prose speech. Plutarch wrote an essay speculating as to why this might be. His conclusion was that by his day— during the Roman Empire—formal speech would be viewed as affected and would create barriers to belief.[144] In my experience as *mantis*, Apollon adopts a conversational and deeply personal tone. Based on Plutarch's reflections and my own, it seems the form varies depending on what is needed to meet Apollon's main intention, which is to effectively communicate and build relationships.

One of Apollon's epithets is Loxias, which might be related to a word for "ambiguous" but may be related to the verb "to speak." There is no doubt that unclear prophecies make for good theater. However, the historical oracles we have are quite unambiguous. Even the dramatic ones that required some interpretation were not ambiguous.[145] The counsels given by Apollon during the second Persian War as reported by Herodotus are interesting examples because they directly influenced decisions that fundamentally shaped our history.

Delphic Oracle and the Persian Invasion
In 480 BCE, the Greeks knew they were facing an imminent invasion from the world superpower, Persia. The Greek city-states were vastly outnumbered. Persia had a professional army; Greece had the equivalent of a militia with few seasoned soldiers. The Spartans sent a delegation to Delphi to ask Apollon for counsel.

---

142. Fontenrose, *Delphic Oracle.*
143. Fontenrose, *Delphic Oracle.*
144. Plutarch, "Oracles at Delphi No Longer Given in Verse," 255–345.
145. Fontenrose, *Delphic Oracle.*

Either your famed, great town must be sacked by Perseus' sons,

Or, if that be not, the whole land of Lacedaemon

Shall mourn the death of a king of the house of Heracles.[146]

This prophecy was alarming but not ambiguous and would have been understood by any Spartan hearing it. Apollon made clear Sparta's choice—to lose its freedom or its great king. A suicide stand would save Sparta. Anyone knowing the geography would recognize the pass of Thermopylae as the place to make that stand. The Spartans held the Persians for seven days, and when they were finally overwhelmed, the Spartan king, Leonidas, told most of the troops to retreat and stood with his three hundred Spartans, seven hundred Thespians, and four hundred Thebans, covering the retreat. Every one of the rearguard, including Leonidas himself, chose death in battle while slowing down the advancing army. Sparta did not fall.

The Athenians also sent a delegation to Delphi and received a terrifying and specific oracle.

Fools, why sit you here? Fly to the ends of the earth,

Leave your homes and the lofty heights girded by your city…

Nothing endures; all is doomed. Fire will bring it down,

Fire and bitter War, hastening in a Syrian chariot.

Many are the strongholds he will destroy, not yours alone;

Many the temples of the gods he will gift with raging fire,

Temples which even now stand steaming with sweat

And quivering with fear, and down from the roof-tops

Dark blood pours, foreseeing the straits of woe.[147]

There is nothing remotely vague about this oracle. Apollon is saying the Persians are going to utterly destroy all of Athens. They will burn the Acropolis and the temples. What the Athenians need to do is run is because anyone who remains will die.

---

146.   Herodotus and Sélincourt, trans., *Herodotus*.

147.   Herodotus and Waterfield, trans., *Histories*.

The delegation from Athens went back again to Apollon as suppliants, begging for more information. They received a second prophecy.

Pallas Athena cannot propitiate Olympian Zeus,
No matter how lengthy her prayers, or how cunning her entreaties.
So I tell you again, in words that will bear no distortion—
While everything else will fall that the borders of Cecrops' land
Contain, yes, and the ravines of most holy Cithaeron as well,
Yet to Tritogenia far-seeing Zeus grants a wooden wall.
Only this will stand defiant, a succor to you and your children.
Do not, then, abide the coming of the cavalry, nor the foot,
Still in the face of the vast landside host. You must retreat instead,
And turn your backs. And yet, for all that, you shall meet them face to face.
Divine Salamis, the sons of women will be destroyed by you
When the grain is scattered—or else, when the harvest is gathered in.[148]

This response does not contradict the first but gives new information. Importantly, the activity was not limited to the mortal sphere alone. Athena was actively working hard to protect Her people. She won a wall of wood to protect the Athenians. The delegation returned from Athens. During a meeting on the Pnyx, the meaning of the wooden wall was debated. Some thought they should go to the Acropolis and build a wooden fence. However, Apollon clearly reinforced His first counsel—that the Athenians needed to run. Themistokles convinced the Athenians that the wooden wall must mean their ships and they should take the sacred statue of Athena Polias, the people, and evacuate. He argued that the Athenians should make a naval stand in the straits at Salamis because it would not have been called "Divine" if it did not favor an Athenian victory.[149] The Athenians evacuated; the Persians killed those few remaining and burned the whole city, including the Acropolis and all the temples. When the Athenians made a naval stand in the straits of Salamis, their smaller more maneuverable triremes gave them a significant advantage and they triumphed over a vastly larger navy. The oracle did not tell the future, it helped create the future.

---

148.   Herodotus and Holland, trans., *Histories*.
149.   Stoneman, *Ancient Oracles*.

Delphic Oracle

Delphi was the most important oracular cult and, thanks to the writings of Plutarch, we have more documentation about how it worked than other oracles. Delphi was Panhellenic and governed by an amphictyony, in which a league of states shared responsibility for the sanctuary.[150]

A high priest and another priest who often had philosophical inclinations were responsible for the sanctuary. Apollon is also a god of philosophy.[151] A woman over the age of fifty (past menopause) but dressed like a young woman served as Pythia, the *mantis* for Apollon at Delphi.[152] The Pythias were not specially educated but were recognized as being especially pious and virtuous women. They were chosen by Him and likely had something in their composition making them appropriate as mediums.

On the day of possessory rites, one day a month for nine months of the year, the Pythia got up early and bathed in the sacred spring, Kastalia. She then went to the temple and waited. The questioners went to the Kastalia and washed their hair and did initial purification work. Each bought a *pelanos*, which is a special barley cake and was the "admittance" fee. The cost of the *pelanos* was sliding scale, ensuring everyone, no matter how poor, could consult Apollon. In a procession, they climbed The Sacred Way, singing *paians*—the sacred hymns to Apollon.[153]

Once they reached the altar in front of the temple, there was a special sacrifice that was also an omen. The attendants dripped water on the head of a goat. If it shivered in a particular pattern, this indicated Apollon could possess the Pythia that day.[154] They sacrificed the goat and the Pythia went into the temple. Under the temple's main floor was a vault-like artificial grotto. There was a small pool of water and a crack over which sat a tripod seat, which is a cauldron but with the bowl being made into a seat. The *omphalos* was in the chamber, as were two golden statues of Zeus's eagles and the grave of Dionysus before He was resurrected as a god. Just outside the chamber was another small room where the priest, questioners, and *chresmologues* sat.[155]

150.　Scott, *Delphi and Olympia*.

151.　Fontenrose, *Delphic Oracle*.

152.　Parke, *Greek Oracles*.

153.　Stoneman, *Ancient Oracles*.

154.　Parke and Wormell, *Delphic Oracle*.

155.　Andronicos, *Delphi*.

The Pythia climbed up and took her seat on the tripod, her feet above the ground. She held a bowl of water from the spring and a twig of Daphne (bay laurel) while wearing a crown of laurel leaves.[156] Sometimes a noticeable sweet scent rose from the Earth. The priest watched for the signs the Pythia had stepped back and Apollon was present, which seems to have been a slight trembling of the laurel branch. He welcomed the God and then asked questions on behalf of the petitioners. At no point was the Pythia raving, going crazy in ecstasy, or any other weird fantasies Victorian writers seemed to have about her. The voice coming from her spoke clearly and, by Plutarch's time, plainly.[157]

There is evidence marshaled by archaeologist John Hale and his geologist colleague Jelle Zeilinga de Boer that the fumes Plutarch discussed coming from the crack were ethylene.[158] [159] Ethylene was used as an anesthesia and creates a mildly euphoric state. As someone who is doing this kind of work, ethylene alone does not make an oracle. The ethylene would help the *mantis* get into a dissociative state so she wasn't in the way of the possession. That is essentially what I am doing without the drugs, which have their own health risks. The evidence suggests the goat omen was important because Apollon was communicating whether it was safe for the Pythia to be in the vault with the gas flow, which, as Plutarch reports, varied in intensity. As mentioned earlier, Plutarch tells of one incident before his time in which the omen said it was not okay for Apollon to possess His *mantis*, but a high-ranking dignitary sought the consultation. The priests kept dumping water on the goat until it eventually shivered the right way, but the omen had been forced. The Pythia went into the chamber and everything went wrong.[160] At higher doses, ethylene causes frenzy and death—which is what happened in that instance. Plutarch recounted this as a warning so his successors would remember.

156.   Connely, *Portrait of a Priestess*.

157.   Plutarch, "Oracles at Delphi No Longer Given in Verse."

158.   Boer and Hale, "Geological Origins of the Oracle at Delphi, Greece," 399–412.

159.   Boer, Hale, and Chanton, "New Evidence for the Geological Origins of the Ancient Delphic Oracle," 707–10.

160.   Plutarch and Babbitt, "Obsolescence of Oracles," 348–501.

Other Oracles

In Ionia, the western part of modern-day Turkey, there were two important oracles of Apollon. Didyma was outside of Miletos and Klaros was in Colophon. Klaros was older and had a male *mantis*.[161] The oracle was probably similar to Delphi. There was a lower-level constructed grotto, a sacred well, and a tripod and *omphalos*, both of which are symbols of oracles of Apollon. The oracle was possessory. The founding myth of Klaros is that Apollon, through his oracle at Delphi, commanded the family of Teiresias, the famous blind seer, to sail from Thebes and found the oracle.[162]

The oracle of Didyma originally had a male *mantis*.[163] Next to Delphi, Didyma was the most important oracle. Originally, there was a small temple in a grove of laurel trees along with a small spring. In 493 BCE, when the Persians conquered Miletos, Darius burned the temple and took the cult statue. This effectively closed the oracle. In 334 BCE when Alexander the Great recaptured Miletos from the Persians, He re-consecrated the oracle at Didyma. Since all knowledge of the procedures had been disrupted, Alexander had experts from Delphi restart the oracle. From then on, the *mantis* was female as in Delphi.[164] During Hellenistic times, Miletos began building a new gigantic temple enclosing the old temple, the laurel grove, and the spring in the new temple's courtyard.

There were many smaller oracles of Apollon, but these three are notable for their influence. The other oracles of Apollon likely operated on a similar model.

Possibly the oldest oracle in Greece is Dodona in Epiros, which is in north-central Greece. Dodona is the oracle of Zeus. The oldest descriptions of the oracle at Dodona are from Homer. There was an ancient oak of Zeus. The *Selloi*—priests who don't wash their feet and sleep on the ground—cared for it. It seems likely the priests heard Zeus's voice in the wind blowing through the oak leaves, but it isn't certain.[165] At some point, the original oak died, and

---

161. Stoneman, *Ancient Oracles*.
162. Johnston, *Ancient Greek Divination*.
163. Stoneman, *Ancient Oracles*.
164. Stoneman, *Ancient Oracles*.
165. Johnston, *Ancient Greek Divination*.

then we have an oracle talking about the oak grove and the "doves" of Zeus. It seems as though the cult shifted to having a female *mantis* of Zeus.[166]

When visiting Dodona, I had the strong impression of Zeus but in a serpent form, like Zeus Meilichios. I do not have any good historical evidence for that impression, but it was strong. If someone with the correct subtle physiology and character went there, He wants a *mantis* again.

Serving as a Mantis

In the Hellenic sense, you cannot choose to be a *mantis*, you have to be chosen. It is a long-term partnership with one of the Theoi, typically Apollon. This is different than some other traditions in which one may serve as a general medium. That does not involve the same level of entanglement as a long-term relationship as *mantis*. To be clear, if you feel called, you can say no, and I advise you to seriously consider the consequences of accepting. This type of relationship requires changes to your nervous system, changes to your behavior, and, in opening this type of door, others close.

If you feel led to offer yourself for this kind of work, then make a deeper study of oracles than you can get from just this book. Read everything you can and intensify your devotional work with Apollon or the being you want to serve. However, even if you are in a deeply personal and loving relationship, there is an additional piece that can only be seen from Their side that has something to do with being able to "wire in" safely.

After the Call

If you feel you have received the call for this kind of work, verify it through omens. Begin working diligently and daily in vision with the Great One who has called you. In all likelihood, you will begin to have your subtle physiology altered, and there will be quite a bit of preliminary work. Apollon spent two years modifying my subtle physiology before I could begin sitting as *mantis*. Be sure to ask, during this time, about what you need to be doing, and understand new restrictions.

---

166.   Stoneman, *Ancient Oracles*.

Challenges in Service

Part of the challenge of serving as *mantis* is it requires you to open yourself up in a way that can make it challenging to move through the world. Traditionally, if you were a cult *mantis*, you would move into a sanctuary and spend the rest of your days in a rarified and spiritually protected environment. You would not be out in the world in a state of greater openness dealing with all the stress and strain of mundane existence. You certainly would not be in leadership positions in the work world. As contemporary people, we don't have that luxury.

I got a tattoo covering the area where my cervical and thoracic vertebrae meet, because that is an entry point for spirits. Although I perceive Apollon as coming in through the top of my head, the tattoo is keyed specifically for Him so no other spirits can enter. I recommend doing something similar if you will be opened up this way.

As a *mantis*, the most important thing is to step back and be out of the way when serving. It is important to figure out any obstacles you might have for successfully stepping out of the way. For some, it may be a fear of losing control. For others, like myself, worrying about getting in the way ironically makes it harder to get out of the way. Learn your psychology enough to know your obstacles and develop a plan to address them.

Preparation

You will need to develop your ritual formula. I do a lot of purification, including the whole week beforehand. Bathing in Daphne tea every day for a week is good practice. Train yourself with various cues that will help you step back. I recommend having specific clothes you only wear when sitting as *mantis*. Special incense is a useful cue. I burn a lot of bay laurel and have an assistant who blows it in my face at various intervals to help me get back and stay back. You will need to figure out what works for you and develop a pattern.

Oracular Sessions

You need to develop a ritual structure that works for you. You will need at least one assistant to help you with your cues, manage the process of asking questions, and be the one to thank the deity when it is time for the rite to end. It is incredibly helpful if your assistant knows your energy well, recognizes when things have shifted, and greets the deity. The reassurance that someone who can see this will help you really let go. Prior instruction should be given to those in attendance to only speak to the Great One and not to use your name. This will help you stay out of the way.

Apollon prefers for me to be conscious, although not in control. There are some traditions in which the medium is completely gone during possession, but He seems to like me to observe. I directly perceive some of His emotions and sometimes I will see something He has difficulty putting into words that I can then try to explain in more detail later. He is frequently doing work on the questioners on an energetic level—often some form of healing. The words themselves are not always the significant part of what is happening. When you are sitting, if you are conscious, avoid trying to interpret the content—just observe. Getting your mind engaged will typically bring you forward and taint the process.

Aftercare

Have someone else take care of logistics and practical things for the next couple of hours. Don't drive or operate any heavy machinery for a couple of hours. Drink water and eat protein. If you are having trouble getting fully back, put some salt water on your head and the back of your neck.

CHAPTER EIGHT

HOUSEHOLD PRACTICE

The fundamental building block of ancient Greek society was the *oikos*—the household. All larger units of society—the *phratry* (fraternity), the tribe, the *polis*—are composed of households.[167] The organization of the *oikos* goes back into prehistory and was more resistant to change than other social forms. It is the social unit that most easily translates into other cultures around the world. In most modern Western cultures, we have experienced tremendous change in our household and family structure, for good and for ill. This chapter explores household religious practices and considers adaptations for our current context.

What Is the Oikos?

The Greek word for family combines the words for "house" and "lineage" into a single concept. An *oikos* includes the physical house (or estate if the lineage owns more than one), the property (perishable and imperishable), and the household's members, which includes the ancestors.[168] In a fundamental way, the *oikos* owns the members, not the other way around. The household's members are the temporary caretakers of the *oikos* and are responsible for both building and maintaining the household. There is honor if you die leaving your household stronger

---

167.   Sofroniew, *Household Gods*.
168.   Cox, *Household Interests*.

than when it came into your care and shame if it is weaker. This is not just about physical property but, more importantly, the character and moral reputation of the household's members.

For our purposes, it is unnecessary to get into the historical specificities since I would actively oppose re-creating an ancient patrilineal and patriarchal structure. However, it is important to note the historical *oikos* is an extended family structure that included ways to bring people into the *oikos* beyond blood and marriage. These included fostering, where a child might live with the family of a parent's dear friend for a period of time for any number of reasons. Bonds of hospitality could develop into membership in an *oikos*. Friendships, both between families and individuals in different regions, were strengthened through long visits as houseguests. During these visits, the guest may be treated as a member of the *oikos* and be received as such in return on a future visit. Sometimes these relationships were formalized and these friends served as ambassadors if from different states.[169]

Finally, there is the bosom friend. Friendship was considered one of the highest virtues in ancient Greece. Not everyone had this type of intimate friendship—but among those who did, the friends often had roles in each other's *oikos*.[170]

OUR CURRENT SITUATION

Changes in the family and household structure are behind many of our major social shifts over the last couple of centuries. At this point, people rarely live with three generations under a single roof, and many of us do not even live in "nuclear" families. This is both good and bad. A strong predictor of female empowerment in a society is a high divorce rate. It reflects that women have financial and other means to get out of bad relationships, which is important given the high levels of violence against women around the planet. I am grateful women have more options. I am grateful my many LGBTQIA+ friends can now create an open family life more or less free from scrutiny. All of this is only possible because the prevalent systems and ways of defining families have collapsed.

---

169. Cox, *Household Interests.*
170. Cox, *Household Interests.*

As an unmarried, childless, postmenopausal woman, I am grateful for my freedom and am suspicious of any uncritical look backward into "the good old days." However, as I age, I am simultaneously aware that there is no clear pattern of what support in old age looks like for people like me—and we are legion.

We are collectively immersed in an epidemic of lonely alienation. Many people work all day, go home alone, passively consume media, and go to sleep—just to wake up the next day and start over. People who can't work are denied even those social interactions. It is easy to invest in relationships mediated by the internet and neglect face-to-face relationship building, but a long-distance friend cannot help you after surgery. One reason many nuclear families fail is because partners find themselves increasingly isolated with only each other to rely on—and one person is not a support network. Our elderly are often left behind and alone as they age. This kind of alienation would not have happened in family systems that included more people living together, but we are unlikely to ever go back to the old *oikos* system.

The way forward is for us to create new forms of the *oikos*. Human beings are social by nature. We cannot thrive in isolation and we require more forms of intimacy than just a romantic partner. A powerful thing we can do is dedicate ourselves to developing deep in-person friendships and then consider how we might want to arrange our lives in order to spend our time and energy deepening those relationships. There are many ways we could arrange our lives that would give us better support than what we have right now, and I think figuring this out should be a priority, individually and collectively.

On a ritual level, there are many aspects of household practice you can integrate, even if you do live alone. However, I encourage everyone to consider who the other members of their household would be, including bosom friends, and to create opportunities to be together regularly. Some quick ideas:

- Create a rite of formal introduction for each of your bosom friends in which you introduce them to your hearth-flame and explain what doing this means to you in terms of how you understand your relationship.
- Rotate hosting meals for each other at a regular interval and make it easy to do; you can order in or do a potluck.

- Choose a day a month in which you have a standing "date" with your bosom friend group to participate in a cultural activity, like attending a movie, a play, a musical event, a festival, or a symposium. Rotate responsibility for choosing the event.
- Select one event or holiday a year where you will host a party.

THE GODS AND SPIRITS OF THE HOUSEHOLD

There are a number of Great Ones and other spirits who are important in household practice. The most important of all is Hestia.

Hestia and the Hearth

You met Hestia in chapter 3. Hestia is both the eldest of Chronos and Rhea's children and Zeus's youngest sister because she was vomited up last.[171]

Unlike Vesta—the Roman version—Hestia is occasionally given iconographic form in Greek art, but most often she is worshipped as the hearth-fire itself. The hearth-fire is the spiritual heart of the home. It provided warmth. It was where ingredients were turned into food. The household's spirits were present at the hearth. Except in certain ritual circumstances, the hearth-fire was not permitted to go out. In ancient Greek households, the hearth was often not in a stable location. In hot weather, the hearth-fire was in the courtyard. In cold weather, it was kept in braziers that were moved around the house as needed. Hestia was wherever the hearth-fire was, and that was the center and heart of the *oikos*. Hestia protects and blesses the *oikos* in which She is honored.[172]

New members were brought into the *oikos* by ritually introducing them to Hestia at the hearth.[173] This process included introducing new babies, new spouses, new foster children, and new hearth friends. No one could participate in the rites of the *oikos* without first having been introduced at the hearth.

Hestia is gentle, pure, and kind. There are rules of courtesy and respect that should be obeyed around Her.[174] The rule of thumb is, if you wouldn't do it in front of your grandmother because it would be rude or upsetting, don't do it in front of Hestia.

---

171. Sofroniew, *Household Gods*.
172. Sofroniew, *Household Gods*.
173. Dillon, "Households, Families, and Women," 241–55.
174. Instone, *Greek Personal Religion*.

A *prytaneion* is a building in the *polis,* which is the seat of government. There is a central hearth-fire in the *prytaneion,* which is the hearth-fire of the *polis* and a manifestation of Hestia.[175] The famous temple of the Vestal Virgins played that role in Rome. Some temples of other deities, like Apollon's temple at Delphi and the Temple of Athena Polias in the Erechtheion on the Acropolis of Athens, kept undying flames that were sacred to Hestia. Hestia's fire was the source for sacrificial fires. Most often, in a household, sacrifices were held in the courtyard. Hestia's fire in the *prytaneion* was the source for sacrificial fires for the *polis.*

Zeus Ktesios

Next to Hestia, the most important household deities are a couple of forms of Zeus. Zeus Ktesios protects the prosperity of the *oikos* and the household property and appears in the form of a snake.[176] The object that forms the connection between Zeus Ktesios and the *oikos* is a *kadiskos*. A *kadiskos* is a small lidded jar with a handle on each side that look kind of like ears. This jar should never have been used for any other purpose. The *kadiskos* becomes an aniconic cult statue that is regularly refreshed. It is used as the interface point between the *oikos* and this aspect of Zeus that protects the household.

Traditionally, each Noumenia, you feed the *kadiskos* by putting in olive oil, fruits, and other foods, pouring spring water over it, and sealing it. You then clean it each Deipnon (the dark of the moon, the night before Noumenia). A modern adaptation, since our household wealth is usually in the form of money, is to keep some cash in the *kadiskos*. When you need cash, talk to Zeus and borrow money from the *kadiskos*, but then replace it with extra as soon as possible. This way, your household wealth increases, even while being used. Keep your *kadiskos* on a household altar, at the hearth, or in a pantry.

Exercise
Make a Kadiskos

A spell to make a tool for Zeus Ktesios to bless the prosperity of the *oikos*.

---

175. Sofroniew, *Household Gods.*

176. Deacy, "Gods—Olympian or Chthonian?" 356–67.

What You'll Need

A small piece of pottery with a lid. If it has "ears" or a face and it feels like Zeus would like it, that is best. If it has handles, traditionally it is adorned with white and yellow thread. Incense. Cash.

Directions

Light the incense. Hold the pottery and say,

> *Zeus Ktseios, Protector of the Household Stores, Guarantor of our Wealth, I ask you to bless this oikos! I offer you this vessel as a way to commune with you.*

Pass the vessel through the smoke. Place the cash inside the jar and say,

> *Zeus Ktesios, I ask you to protect the wealth of this household and help it grow. Thank you, Mighty Zeus, father of gods and men.*

Put the *kadiskos* on your household altar, at the hearth, or in the pantry.

Zeus Herkeios

Zeus Herkeios guards and blesses the boundary and courtyard/yard of the *oikos*. Most household rituals were conducted in the courtyard, and, in good weather, it was the main place where the members of the household did their work. Zeus Herkeios guards your home's boundaries.[177]

Exercise
CONSECRATE BOUNDARY STONES FOR ZEUS HERKEIOS

This is a protection spell for your property.

What You'll Need

A trash bag, incense, and four stones you will ritually collect.

Directions

While traditionally, the stones would be collected from the sacred waterways, this can harm fragile ecosystems. Therefore gathering stones from the area you live and then bringing them to the nymph will link the powers.

---

177.   Larson, *Understanding Greek Religion*.

Step 1: In the area where you live, find four stones. If you live in a house, they can be larger stones. If you live in an apartment, they should be smaller. Let yourself be led to the correct stones.

Step 2: Take the stones to a creek or waterway, preferably where you have built a relationship with the nymph. Pick up trash as an offering to the nymph. When you have gathered as much as you can, ask the nymph if you may wash the stones in Her water. Thank the nymph and be sure to dispose of the trash properly.

Step 3: Consecrate the stones to Zeus Herkeios by passing the ritually cleared stones through incense while saying,

> *Zeus Herkeios, guardian of the fence and courtyard, I call to you and ask you to bless this oikos. Accept these stones as your vessel and protect this house and household from all danger on all levels of being.*

Step 4: Place the stones. If you live in a house, place them at the four corners of your property. If you live in an apartment building, you can put small stones in the four corners of the building lot or, if you cannot do so discreetly, in the four corners of your apartment. See Zeus standing in the corners. Thank Him for His blessing and protection.

Step 5: Feed the links by creating a habit in which whenever you pass in or out of your home, you greet and thank Zeus Herkeios for keeping the household safe.

Apollon Agyieus

Apollon Agyieus is Apollon "of the streets." He protected the boundaries between the *oikos* and the world outside and kept the *oikos* safe and pure. Apollon Agyieus protects the streets and public places. The fronts of ancient Greek houses were directly on the street with courtyards on the inside. Right at the boundary between the *oikos* and the public space was a white obelisk sacred to Apollon Agyieus often adorned with garlands.[178] If you have property where you can place such an obelisk, consecrate it along the pattern given for the boundary stones for Zeus Herkeios.

---

178.   Graf, *Apollo*.

Household Guardians

Agathos Daimon, or "good spirit," and Tyche Agathe were spirits who blessed the fortune or "luck" of the *oikos*, including blessing the sources of the family fortune—especially fields and orchards. Agathos Daimon often takes the form of a snake. In general, snakes and beings who take the form of snakes are guardians. They had an important place in many temples as well as in the home. You can use a snake-shaped object on your household altar or near your hearth to honor Agathos Daimon and pray for the luck of your household.

Ancestors

Many extended families held common burial grounds. *Kohes* are libations poured to the ancestors as well as to the Theoi of the Underworld. During the transition from when a member of the *oikos* died to when that member became an ancestor, specific rites were undertaken. At Anthesteria (in February), the dead were believed to temporarily return, and sacrifices were made to honor the ancestors.

Most lineages had at least one hero(ine) who was regularly honored. A hero is one of the dead who could be called upon for intercession. The hero(ine) was often venerated by the whole community. The rites of the *oikos* maintained strong and healthy relationships with these beings.

BASICS OF HOUSEHOLD PRACTICE

There are many ways we can adapt household practices and make them appropriate for our current context, like creating a household altar and daily prayers or offerings.

Altars

You need something that functions as the hearth of your *oikos*. If you have a fireplace, then making the mantle into an altar and consecrating the actual hearth is ideal. If you do not, then creating a small household altar, including a flame, will work. While it is traditional in Greece even today to keep an oil lamp going at all times, I think this is unnecessary and creates a fire risk when unattended. I use tealights within a special votive holder. The altar can be on a shelf, on a small table, in a specially made altar cabinet, or in a little nook. This altar is for the well-being of your *oikos* and is different than a personal devotional altar, unless the main deity you work with is Hestia.

For your household altar, I recommend the following:

- A flame for the hearth (essential)
- A statue of Hestia
- A *kadiskos*
- A snake object for Agathos Daimon
- A place for incense
- Pictures of family members, ancestors, and members of the *oikos*

Praying and Making Offerings

In your daily practice, light your hearth candle (or go to your hearth if you are using something you feel comfortable leaving lit) and make prayers and offerings to the different beings who are concerned for the well-being of your household. Thank the spirits of your *oikos* and ask for Their protection. Pray for the well-being of the members of your *oikos,* even if they don't live with you. This includes blood relations, bosom friends, ancestors, and other spirits who are part of your *oikos*. During my prayers, I thank the spirits of the house and household and ask for Their protection. Listen for any feedback you receive.

When entering or leaving your home, say hello and goodbye to the spirits of the *oikos*, acknowledging Zeus Herkeios when you pass the boundary. When traveling, take a link to your household altar with you and check in on the well-being of your household and all the spirits. The link can be a small consecrated figure in the shape of a snake or whatever your household spirits lead you to consecrate. When traveling, hold the link and, in vision, enter your house and walk all around it, spreading light throughout.

Cleaning and Purification

Cleaning and doing repair work with the spiritual intention of serving the *oikos* is spiritually powerful. Try keeping an inventory of belongings and strive to take seriously the idea that you are a steward of the household's resources. I seek to repair things, keep them in working order, and not to accumulate wastefully. These are old ways of thinking about belongings, but I think they are healthy and I feel good responses from the spirits. In addition to physically cleaning the household, energetically and spiritually clean it. Sea water is always purifying. Using bay water is purifying. Burning frankincense and bay laurel for purification rarify the atmosphere to the point where nothing that does not match its spiritual vibration can remain.

Exercise
CREATE THE HEARTH OF YOUR OIKOS
This is a spell to create the ritual center of your household.

What You'll Need
A location for your hearth (either a fireplace with a mantle or one of the other options for an altar). A candle and candleholder (I recommend a votive holder with tealights), either bay leaves or frankincense, and a firesafe vessel. If using frankincense, you must have charcoal. Optional: A *kadiskos*, a statue of Hestia, a permanent incense vessel, a representation of a snake for Agathos Daimon, and pictures of ancestors and members of the *oikos*.

Directions
Thoroughly clean the location and cense it with frankincense or bay leaves. If you are using a candle for your hearth-fire, pass the holder through the incense. Say the following prayer aloud:

> *Divine Hestia, great goddess of the hearth, bless and inhabit this hearth of my oikos. Claim this as Your own and bring peace, tranquility, prosperity, luck, and peace to my/our household. I light the holy fire of the hearth of my/our oikos, divine Hestia. Be present, be present, be present! This is my/our hearth. This is the heart of my/our oikos. It is so.*

Add any other parts to your household altar, passing them through the incense smoke and repeating what they are and how they are present in your *oikos*. Place everything where it is beautiful and not overcrowded. When you are done, thank Hestia and all the other spirits of the *oikos*.

CHAPTER NINE
RITES OF PASSAGE

Many traditional rites of passage are about admitting new members to the *oikos* or transitioning them out. While the traditional three forms are births, weddings, and death, if there are beings you want the household's guardians to welcome even in your absence, formally introduce them to the household altar, which is your hearth. Depending on your practice, this may include various spirits who work with you and who may need access to your household uninvited.

Birth

Historically, several days after birth, the family of a newborn celebrated the rite of Amphidromia. During this ritual, the child (who is now deemed likely to live) became part of the *oikos*. The participants either ran around the fire with the baby or put the baby down by the hearth and then ran around it.[179] The point is for household members to introduce the baby to the spiritual heart of the *oikos*. The child was also given a name. There was typically a feast and relatives gave presents to the family.

---

179.   Sofroniew, *Household Gods*.

Ritual
WELCOMING A BABY INTO THE OIKOS
A ritual making a baby a spiritual member of the *oikos*.

What You'll Need
A drink for libations, water with sea salt that is comfortably warm to the touch, the hearth of the *oikos*, and a feast.

Directions
Light the hearth of the *oikos* and gather all the members of the *oikos*, including extended family and bosom friends, with the parent(s) holding the baby. Together, say,

> We call to Hestia, great goddess of the hearth and household, to Agathos Daimon, to all the Household Guardians, and to the Ancestors; we ask you to be present! Be with us as we welcome a new member of our household. We bring this infant before you, pure and cleansed.

Rub a little salt water on the baby's crown.

> In the eyes of the Theoi, the Ancestors, and all members of the household and its Guardians, we name our beloved infant, [baby's name]. Hestia, Guardians, and Ancestors, recognize and accept [baby] and bless [baby] as a member of this oikos.

Either circle the hearth with the baby, hold the baby close to the hearth, or circle the hearth candle around the baby. Whatever is both logistically possible and safe.

> We call to Artemis, the guardian of children, to watch over [baby], protect [baby], and ensure [baby's] healthy growth.
>
> We, the members of this oikos, swear to help [baby] thrive. Here, before our sacred hearth and all those assembled, seen and unseen, we will speak our wishes for [baby] and ask for these blessings to become manifest.

Each member holds the baby (or the parent holds the baby down to younger household members) and speaks a wish as a prayer. Each prayer is ended with, "This blessing I wish for you." Everyone answers, "May it be so."

For example:

> [Baby], I wish for you that whenever you face life's struggles and disappointments, you fully learn and integrate all the right lessons that will help you be resilient and happy. This blessing I wish for you.

Answered by all, "May it be so."

Pour the libation or place any offerings in the hearth or on the altar.

> Hestia, great goddess of the hearth, Agathos Daimon, Artemis, Ancestors, and all those who have come in spirit to bless [baby], please accept our gratitude and our love. We offer this to you and invite you to stay with us as we celebrate the growth of our household.

Then have the feast.

WEDDINGS AND NEW HOUSEHOLDS

In ancient Greece, the main point of a marriage was bringing a woman into a lineage so the *oikos* could continue through children. The woman formally remained part of her father's *oikos* and brought with her a dowry that remained the property of her birth family. If the marriage fell apart, it went back with her. However, if she remained married and had children, it would eventually pass to them upon her death. Although the new bride went to live in her husband's household, she maintained close relationships with her birth family. Sisters were often especially close to their brothers.[180]

The wedding typically took several days. The bride and groom were ritually bathed and purified. The wedding feast included much merriment and a large public procession after sunset in which the bride was taken from her father's home to the home of her husband. The lead torchbearer was "best man" and primary witness of the marriage. Wedding processions were pieces of performing art, torchlit with songs and dancing and a festival atmosphere. At the groom's house, the groom's mother received the new wife. Ceremonially

---

180.   Cox, *Household Interests*.

gripping the bride by the wrist, her new husband led her to the hearth, where they knelt together, introducing her to the spiritual heart of the home. As the groom removed the veil from his bride, the new couple was showered with symbols of prosperity and fertility, like nuts, coins, and dried fruits.[181]

The old rituals focus on a woman joining her husband's *oikos*. Now most marriages are between people who are already living on their own and are blending households. In fact, quite commonly committed couples create a new, blended *oikos* without it necessarily involving marriage. There is value in ritualizing this process, either in conjunction with a wedding or on its own.

Ritual
CREATING A NEW, BLENDED OIKOS

This rite is for creating a blended household and has no necessary relationship to marriage. I expect there to be many more experimental forms of households, which may or may not involve erotic partnerships. The appropriate timing is whenever more than one adult decides to blend households with at least one other in a way meant to be truly committed and long term.

What You'll Need

A taper candle for each adult member of the new household and a candlestick for each taper where they can safely burn down, a new vessel for the hearth-fire (recommend a special votive holder with tealights), bay leaves or frankincense, and a safe vessel to burn the incense in. Each member contributes one item for the new household altar. Optional: *Kadiskos*, statue of Hestia, permanent incense vessel, vessel for libations, pictures.

Directions

Prior to the rite, all members of the new *oikos* create a name for the new household and select the location for the hearth altar. Each member creates a sentence of their vision of the new *oikos*, all of which will be blended together. For any members of the new *oikos* who have an old household hearth altar, light a taper candle from the old altar and burn it partway, then put it out while seeing the flame still burning in your mind's eye This will

---

181. Sofroniew, *Household Gods*.

be the hearth-fire from your previous household. Gather all members of the new household to create your new household altar.

As described in the ritual for setting up your household altar in chapter 8, find and cleanse the space and the items for your altar with the other members of your new *oikos*. Each member of the new *oikos* should have a taper, either carrying the old hearth-fire or a new taper. Say together,

> *Divine Hestia, great goddess of the hearth, bless and inhabit this hearth of our new oikos. Claim this as your own and bring peace, tranquility, prosperity, luck, and peace to our household. Together we take the light of our separated households and blend them into the one light that is the holy fire of the hearth of our new oikos, [name of household].*

From the candles of your old hearth, join in a single flame that is your new hearth. Set the old candles aside in a safe container and let them burn all the way out or as far as is safe.

> *Divine Hestia, be present, be present, be present! This is our hearth. This is the heart of our oikos. It is so.*

Add any other parts to your household altar. It is best if either you create them together or if each household member contributes something. In each case, smudge it and then say together, "This is the [x] of our *oikos*. Welcome!"

Once your household altar is set up, go back and forth and introduce the household members, including ancestors and spirits by saying, "Hestia and Guardians of the *Oikos*, I introduce [x] and say they are welcome."

After all members and spirits of the *oikos* have been introduced, each household member proclaims their vision of the *oikos* and asks for a blessing, ending with, "We are stronger together. It is so." The other members of the household echo, "We are stronger together. It is so."

Pour the libation or place any offerings in the hearth or on the altar.

> *Hestia, great goddess of the hearth, Agathos Daimon, Ancestors, Guardians, and all those who have come in spirit to bless the founding*

of our new oikos, [name of oikos], please accept our gratitude and our love. Thank you. This rite has ended.

If it is not safe to burn the tapers all the way down in the candlesticks you have, bury them. After the rite is over, you can create a material object that includes the name of your *oikos* and the various vision sentences the members created to further bless the *oikos*.

LEAVING THE NEST

In ancient times, adult children did not leave the nest in the same way, but now it is an important rite of passage. A ritual to bless this transition would be useful. It is a significant transition for both the newly adult child and the parents. In this ritual, the parents give the child a blessed vessel for Hestia (a nice votive holder with a candle or an oil lamp) to ritually carry some of the hearth-fire to the child's new home. A parent could give their child their own vessel to use as a *kadiskos*.

Ritual
LEAVING THE NEST

To ritually bless the transition as a young person leaves the household.

What You'll Need

On the altar, place a new *kadiskos* made by the young version, the vessel having been gifted by members who are staying and fed by them with seed money, including small bills. A favorite beverage for a libation offering and any other offerings desired. A consecrated new hearth-fire vessel to be given as a gift, a taper candle. A prepared feast. Invite all members of the *oikos*, the extended family, and bosom friends.

Directions

If you wish to have gifts, tell the guests to give something practical to help the young person set up their first household. Gather everyone in front of the household altar.

Parent/Elder: We call to Hestia, great goddess of the hearth and household, to Agathos Daimon, to the Household Guardians, and to the Ancestors; we ask you to be present! Come be present as our beloved [x] leaves us today to begin their own *oikos*. We invite the beloved who are present to come forward before the members and spirits of this household and share with [x] today something they see in them that makes them proud and to make a wish for their future.

Each person says something affirming and voices a wish. Each prayer is ended with, "This blessing I wish for you." Everyone answers, "May it be so."

Parent/Elder: [X], while you will always be part of the hearts and lives of the members of this household, you are ready to begin your own household. It is right and proper you should lead the prayers and the offerings to the Theoi of this household before you leave.

[X] speaks the prayers of their heart and makes offerings.

Parent/Elder: [X], you will carry the sacred flame of this household into your own with all the blessings of everyone here and the Gods of this household. We give you this vessel for your hearth-fire. May it be blessed. Come and light your hearth-fire from our sacred flame.

Have the young person light the candle from the sacred flame on the taper candle. Have them gaze into the flame for a minute or so.

Parent/Elder: See the fire burning bright and spend some time gazing into the heart of this household, you will carry its power in your heart. [Pause.] Now, seeing the flame burning strongly, extinguish the flame while still seeing the light trapped inside the candle. You will carry this with you to your new home, and when you use it to light your own hearth-fire, you will know it is the fire and love from this hearth you carry. We, the members of this household, invite all of you and all the spirits of the *oikos* to join us in a feast in honor of this sacred and blessed transition.

Proceed to the feast.

DEATH AND DYING

The dying process is when a member of the *oikos* transitions to becoming an ancestor. There are two considerations: dying and death.

Dying

In cases of sudden death, the beginning of the process is clear. Often, then as now, it is murkier and characterized by a growing realization that someone will not get better.

PRAYER FOR THE DYING OR RECENTLY DEAD

If someone is sick, it is usually best to pray to Asklepios and Apollon. However, there are times in which it is not clear if it is more compassionate to pray for healing or for a swift and merciful death. In such instances, light a candle and pray:

> *Gentle Asklepios and merciful Hermes Kthonios, guide of souls, [X],*
> *who is loved by me, is suffering. Please bring to [X] whatever is best for*
> *their highest good, be it healing or a swift and painless death. Hermes*
> *Psychopompos, whenever the time of death arrives, soon or in the dis-*
> *tant future, I ask you to guide their soul to its blessing.*

Death and Funeral Rites

When someone you know dies, light a candle and pray to Hermes Psychopompos, always naming the individual about whom you are praying. Traditionally, once the person was believed to be dead, the body was cleaned, dressed with oil, and covered with a shroud and the face with a cowl. The head was wreathed and a coin placed in the mouth. The body was typically laid out in the house for three days so family and friends could say goodbye.[182] The delay of three days ensured the person was not merely deeply unconscious.

Before sunrise after three days, the family and friends processed with the body to the pyre or the cemetery. If the body was burned, the bones were gathered and inhumed. The laws of Solon forbidding a bunch of ostentatious

---

182. Humphreys, *Family, Women and Death.*

practices give us a good sense of what Athenian funerals looked like before he intervened.[183]

In Solon's vision, the closely related bereaved would tastefully and modestly take the body to the grave where they would bury their beloved with solemn dignity—perhaps including a few tasteful grave goods. Libations would be poured and a reasonable animal sacrifice might be made. It would be a modest and dignified affair.[184]

Based on what he specifically forbade, we can extrapolate that a wealthy funeral included a large procession with a lot of women loudly lamenting, tearing at their hair, wailing, and lacerating themselves. These women were not only close relatives, but many others—probably including professional mourners. They would heap grave goods in with the corpse and sacrifice an ox at the graveside. After burying the dead, the mourners would make a day of it: wandering through the cemetery, wailing loudly, and telling stories of the other dead and generally ensuring a major spectacle. After the funeral, a marker commemorated the person and became a focal point for ancestor reverence. Many of these tombstones survived and are extraordinary works of art. They bring honor to the *oikos* who commissioned them but could also become extravagant.

In Homeric times and in Macedonian culture, which was more Homeric than Athens, the dead were cremated and might have been honored with funeral games.[185] The Myceneans and Macedonians buried the cremated remains in tumulus structures, often with extensive grave goods.

After the funeral, the hearth-fire was extinguished and the whole household, including the members, was ritually cleansed. New fire was brought from the city's hearth. This all honors the fact that something fundamental has ended for the whole household and a new pattern must be established.[186]

It is healthy that the ancients did not try to hide from the fact of death or from dealing with the body. At least in the United States, our culture obscures the facts of death instead of facing them, even though death is the inevitable outcome of life.

---

183.   Plutarch, "Solon," 109–110.

184.   Humphreys, *Family, Women and Death*.

185.   Burkert, *Greek Religion*.

186.   Panopoulos, Panagiotopoulous, and Armyras, *Hellenic Polytheism*.

There are stages of mourning that take time. During the laying out process, the friends and families are with the bereaved. There are a lot of things needing to be done rapidly after death—right when those who are closest to the deceased are in the least capable frame of mind. The presence of community in those moments by people who are empowered to step in is important. Later, there is a more public remembrance during the funeral. The ritual transition of taking the body out of the household and either cremating or burying it marks a transition in a visceral way. Crucially, it includes the first ritual acts to honor the deceased as an ancestor, to honor the Gods of the Underworld, and to ask Them to receive the beloved dead.

Finally, grieving does not end immediately after a funeral. Additional rites were conducted during the first year at increasing intervals. These rites included communal meals and sacrifices to and on behalf of the dead. For example, there was a wake for the first three days, the funeral was on the third day after death, and there might be another ritual on the ninth day and then at the end of a month. After that, there was another at three months, six months, and then a year. Once a year is reached, an annual offering, maybe on the deceased's birthday or on the anniversary of death, would be appropriate, as well as acknowledging the new ancestor at the overall ancestral sacrifices.[187] This structure gave a frame for continuing the grieving process while ensuring the most intimately bereaved were regularly in contact with and supported by community. We can create similar rituals that honor the grieving process.

Ritual
NINTH-DAY MEMORIAL
To grieve the loss of a beloved one and support the bereaved.

What You'll Need
A libation of something the beloved dead enjoyed.

Directions
Nine days after death, gather at the hearth of the beloved dead's *oikos*, at your hearth, or at the gravesite. If possible, this is best done with those who are experiencing the most grief and who can support each other.

---

187. Humphreys, *Family, Women and Death.*

Hades, Persephone, Hermes, Hecate, we pray to you for the well-being of our beloved [X]. We have gathered to honor [X], beloved in life, beloved in death, and now an ancestor. Please accept our offering.

Pour the libation.

We ask for the strength, courage, and grace to feel our grief with hearts that are soft and strong, accepting that this is part of the mystery of human moira. May we find comfort in the love of our community and our Gods.

Open the space for anyone to say what they need to say—to the beloved dead, to the Gods, to each other; whatever serves the process of grieving. At the end,

Loving Theoi, thank you for being with us in our grief. Beloved [X], we miss you. To this precious community, thank you for gathering and supporting each other. Our love makes us strong. Thank you to all the beloved spirits both in bodies and not. We give thanks.

Something similar can be done at thirty days, three months, six months, and a year.

CHAPTER TEN
THE *POLIS* AND CIVIC DUTY

The Greek word *polis* formally refers to an ancient city-state, like Athens or Sparta, but it can mean the forms of community beyond our families to which we have duty. We are all members of groups. Those groups are made up of their individual members, but they have a type of coherence that maintain identity even when individual members leave.

For us, that typically includes our local communities as well as our nations. For those who, like me, work in a large organization, the perspective of the *polis* can be a useful lens for determining your duty. We essentially live in villages. If you consider the people with whom you interact across your normal year and add them together, I propose those people are your village. This includes your duty to other members of your religious communities (kindreds, covens, groves, etc.) of which you are a part and duty to other members of organizations of which you are a part, like your colleagues.

The ideal of the *cosmopolis* asks us to understand ourselves as citizens of the whole cosmos in addition to belonging to a specific *polis*. This ideal drove Alexander the Great, and he was striving to manifest it. The same ideal drives me.

CITIZENSHIP AND DUTY

What does it mean to be a citizen? In the ancient world, the eligibility of citizenship was far too restrictive, often only available to sons of prior citizens. In this historical moment in the United States, there are people who have lived here for many years, paid taxes, and contributed to society, but who are denied citizenship, like the so-called Dreamers. At the same time, an appalling number of American citizens don't perform even the most basic duty of voting or they try to get out of jury duty. Problematically, our current understanding of citizenship focuses almost exclusively on rights rather than responsibilities.

In a broader sense, being citizens means being true members of the groups to which we belong. To the ancient Greeks, duty to the various collectives of which you were a member was central to an individual's self-concept and reputation. The ideal of citizenship is that the citizen is responsible for the collective. The citizen shows up and takes responsibility for the health and well-being of the community. The citizen stands up and holds the community to high ethical ideals—opposing and, if necessary, attempting to remediate that which degrades it. When making decisions, the citizen considers the long-term impacts on the community. The citizen does not pursue self-interested aims at the collective's expense and recognizes they are perceived by the Theoi and the rest of the world as a representative of the collective and acts honorably. From the ancient Greek perspective, if you are not a good, responsible citizen of your collectives, you are not a good person.

Citizen Oaths

In Athens, one powerful expression of the citizen's duty is conveyed by the oath taken by the *epheboi*, the young men who were entering their period of mandatory military service. This oath, taken in the cave of Aglauros on the eastern slope of the Acropolis, was sworn to numerous Theoi.[188] In direct experiences with Aglauros, She expressed interest in working with us to reinvigorate the ideals of civic responsibility and engagement in modern democracies.

The oath sworn is as follows:

> *I will not shame my holy weapons, nor will I abandon my comrade wherever I take my stand. I will defend things both sacred and proper, and I will not leave my country lesser, but greater and better, both as far as I myself can, and in company with all. I will obey those who at any time exercise power reason-*

---

188. Kearns, "Nature of Heroines," 96–110.

ably, the laws which have been laid down, and those which shall in the future
be reasonably laid down. If someone tries to abolish them, I will not permit it,
either myself or in the company with all, and I will honour the ancestral holy
things.[189]

I want to call attention to a couple of important aspects of this oath. First, there is a requirement that the citizen exercise judgment and not be blindly obedient, either to those in power or to laws. The laws and the rulers must be reasonable and just. If not, the citizen should, by implication, oppose them. Two great heroes of Athens were Harmodios and Aristogeiton, two lovers who stood against tyranny at the cost of their lives.[190] Second, the oath talks about both individual and collective effort and responsibility.

The oaths sworn by jurors demanded that individual citizens exercise judgment to defend the Rule of Law and democracy. Jurors were enjoined to oppose tyranny and oligarchy, even if it would make the individual juror unpopular.[191]

Gods of the Polis

There are a few of the Theoi who are especially concerned with the *polis.* The three most important are Zeus, Athena, and Apollon. The call to service I answered from Athena and Apollon to found and hold a center for them in Washington, DC, is specifically related to Their desire to help us create a healthier and more appropriate civic life. These Great Ones want us to reclaim and prioritize our duty as citizens and our general sense of responsibility for our collectives.

Zeus and Athena

Zeus Boulaios and Athena Boulaia oversaw the government's integrity.[192] Athena is typically the guardian of the *polis,* and democracy was born under Her aegis. Athena, as the patron of the *polis,* often has a specific name or iconography tied to the particular community. In the United States, Her form is Columbia, and I call Her Athena Columbia when I invoke Her as the goddess of the

---

189.   Kearns, *Ancient Greek Religion.*

190.   Larson, *Understanding Greek Religion.*

191.   Larson, *Understanding Greek Religion.*

192.   Pedley, *Sanctuaries and the Sacred in the Ancient Greek World.*

United States. Zeus, as the god of kings, is concerned with the Rule of Law—human and divine—and ensuring rulers are held to the laws of immortal justice.

Apollon

Apollon is deeply interested in political life. Apollon Nomimos is the great law-giver. Apollon bore responsibility for preparing young men for citizenship and training them in their duty. In His form as Apollon Alexikaikos, the averter of all evil, He guarded the places of assembly where decisions were made. Apollon is also the great diplomat, diplomacy being a form of healing between collectives.[193] Finally, Apollon, through His oracles, counseled representatives from communities that ran afoul of the Theoi. He told them what they needed to do to heal those relationships. A significant portion of surviving records of the utterances by Apollon through His oracles gives instructions to communities about how to purify and heal *miasma* and restore right relations with the Gods and spirits.[194]

Ares and Athena

The military is primarily under the guardianship and leadership of Ares and Athena Areia. Every able-bodied citizen was expected to willingly sacrifice himself in defense of the *polis* if needed. Although I have concerns about our modern military, I note that the ethics of honor, sacrifice, and self-discipline generally seem more evident among military personnel than among the general populace.

Judicial Theoi

Themis, Dike, the Erinyes/Eumenides, Athena, and Apollon are particularly concerned with the judicial system. The iconography of Themis—blind, holding scales and a downward-pointing sword—is present in many courthouses, and She remains easily invoked in such circumstances. Dike is the daughter of Zeus and Themis and has the same iconography as Themis. The Erinyes/Eumenides uphold the Rule of Law and pursue the guilty, including oath-breakers.

---

193.   Graf, *Apollo*.

194.   Fontenrose, *Delphic Oracle*.

THEMIS

Heroes and Heroines of the Polis

Heroes and heroines are divine ancestors for entire groups, not just for those who are descended from Them by blood—many of Them don't have physical descendants.[195] They are often guardians of certain territories or a particular society that can branch out to other groups later. So, for example, Theseus was a hero of all of Attika. Alexander the Great is a hero who is working from the other side pressing for the realization of the ideal of the cosmopolis and has been revered by many cultures as a holy man or hero, including being mentioned as such in the Koran (Duh-al-Qarnayn). Aglauros, mentioned earlier, is a heroine of Athens but has offered to expand Her mission to promoting the ideals of civic duty in other democracies. In the United States, George Washington and Martin Luther King Jr. function as heroes. They both have protective roles and call us to higher ideals.

THE POLIS AND RELIGION

Most great rituals we know about were undertaken by the community to ensure good relationships between the community as a whole and the Theoi. Rituals accompanied virtually every aspect of public life, and each was under the protection of certain Theoi. In a secular, multicultural society, it is not appropriate—and in the United States, unconstitutional—for religious rituals to be conducted by the equivalent of "the state." However, individual religious communities can conduct rituals for the purposes of nurturing right relationships between their broader communities and the Theoi. There are ancient precedents.

While we are most familiar with large-scale rituals, there are others performed by only a few people on the entire community's behalf. Many had to do with nurturing deep relationships between a particular god and the community or undertaking purification/healing rites. Leaders, acting as the entire community's representatives, performed some of these rituals, while religious specialists conducted others. The more potentially dangerous rituals were conducted in secret by only a few people acting on behalf of the whole community. One example is the Arrhephoria in Athens in which two young girls carried out a secret ritual on the entire city's behalf.[196] Another is the Plynteria, during which

---

195.   Nagy, *Ancient Greek Hero in 24 Hours*.
196.   Vlassopoulos, "Religion in Communities."

the most sacred cult statue of Athena Polias was taken to the sea and bathed.[197] During this ritual, everyone else in the city stayed indoors.

As I will discuss in chapter 15, magical practitioners can perform private rites that spiritually serve the *polis*. I consider this to be my duty as a magical citizen. I have listed the Theoi associated with each area of community life for your use in supporting your village. Make offerings and prayers as needed at your altar.

Oaths

An oath is a suspended curse you lay upon yourself in the event you break your word.[198] Oath-taking is an important aspect of public life and should never be taken lightly. Traditionally, oaths were sworn upon becoming citizens. This was a rite of passage for natural-born citizens. Upon taking a public office, the incoming official swore an oath to ethically perform the duty of office. In courts, juries and witnesses swore oaths. Members of the military took oaths. We still take oaths for most of these purposes, the exception being for natural-born citizens.

You should never take an oath that requires you to suspend your judgment—especially your moral judgment. You should never take an oath you cannot realistically fulfill.

The general form of an oath is this:

- Invoke the appropriate gods to witness and uphold the oath.
- Swear your oath—which is a promise. Be specific. Be careful in your wording.
- Specify what you are calling on yourself, should you break your oath.
- Make your offering and don't consume any of it yourself or allow anyone else to do so. The whole offering goes to the Gods because an oath is a suspended curse.

In the old days, those swearing oaths would swear that if they broke their word, havoc would be visited upon their families and descendants too. I implore you not to do that, even if it is traditional. It creates problems for

---

197.   Kearns, *Ancient Greek Religion*.
198.   Kearns, *Ancient Greek Religion*.

people who are not you and can go on for generations. Don't be a future fool-ish ancestor.

Even though oaths should never be sworn in a cavalier fashion, they have an important function, and that is to give us more strength in fulfilling our duty. It is not a bad thing to swear oaths of duty to your communities. Just be careful and reasonable in what you promise. Additionally, be careful and aware of the oaths you swear in other aspects of your life.

Deities of Oath-Keeping: Erinyes/Eumenides, Dike, Themis, Zeus

Voting

In ancient Athens, the Pnyx, where the citizens of Athens met in Assembly and made decisions, was directly in the sightlines of the Acropolis. They knew they were making decisions as citizens under the eyes of Athena. All meetings of the council or the generals were also in these sightlines. Additionally, each meeting began with sacrifices to Athena and Zeus and prayers to the ancestors.[199]

While I absolutely oppose having state-sponsored prayers or activities, I think it is completely appropriate for me, personally, to pray and make offerings for our citizens to embrace their duty, show up, vote, and use their power wisely.

I believe it is my duty to stay informed and engaged beyond voting. In particular, I keep an active altar for the *polis* and work to shine Light. If I perceive that any elected officials are undermining the integrity of our democracy, I report them to the Gods of the *polis* and do what work I can for healing—both magical and through mundane activities. You can do the same.

Deities of Voting: Athena, Zeus, Helios, Apollon

The Courts

Every lawsuit included sacrifices to the Gods and oaths in the trial's beginning. When it comes to upholding Rule of Law and seeking justice, work with Themis, Dike, Athena, and Apollon. The ancient Athenian law courts were open air because it was believed no untrue thing can withstand the Light of the sun. Working with Apollon and Helios to "bring the Truth to Light" is advisable, including if you are on a jury.

---

199. Vlassopoulos, "Religion in Communities."

Deities of the Court: Themis, Dike, Helios, Athena, and Apollon

The Military and Protection

Athena Promachos is Athena the protector. You can pray to Her for the protection of the *polis* and to defend the integrity of your various governments. In the United States, there are federal, state, and local governments, and often the most impactful government is the one closest to your immediate community. If you or someone you love is in harm's way because they are acting as a guardian of the *polis*, working with Athena Promachos and Athena in Her aspect as the nation's guardian (Athena Columbia, Athena Britannia, Athena Marianne, etc.) is advisable. In ancient Greece, any campaign was accompanied by formal sacrifices made by military leaders and the omens were taken seriously.[200] This is obviously not the case now. Prayers and offerings for the protection of soldiers to help them uphold their honor and exercise ethical restraint in stressful circumstances are appropriate. Many of our veterans need support with healing.

Deities for Protection and Veteran Support: Athena Promachos, National
form of Athena, Apollon, Asklepios

OATH-KEEPING

While much of the ancient *polis* religion is impossible or inappropriate to replicate, the lines of power can be tapped and forms adapted to meet the needs of the *polis* now. Following is a ritual I created that serves as a case study of this type of modification. As an American, I am concerned about how many elected officials are either directly working to undermine the integrity of our democracy or are complicit by allowing it to happen. Combining techniques from magic (which in ancient Greece is usually by and for individuals) for the purposes of serving the *polis*, this ritual uses methods similar to ancient magical judicial workings.

This is an example of adapting methods from magic that can serve the *polis* while not embracing state religion and can function as a combination ritual/ protest. Substitute the appropriate documents.

---

200.   Larson, *Understanding Greek Religion.*

Ritual
Oath-Keeping

A ritual to call on appropriate Theoi to hold public servants to their sworn oaths.

What You'll Need

Salt water and copies of the oaths or governing documents the officials have sworn to uphold.

Directions

Go to the location of your civic building or call forth the appropriate location in vision. Purify yourselves with salt water.

Invoke Athena:

Bright-eyed Pallas Athena, great maid of wisdom. I call to you by your names of old. Hear me, know me, answer my call. Athena Polias, Athena Boulaia, Athena Promachos, Athena Themis, Athena Nike, come, great goddess of the polis, divine guide of human civilization, wise counselor, You who bless the ekklesia, the gathering of the demos. Great protector, shield of the people, upholder and bringer of justice. Come be with us during this rite of oath-keeping. Bring us your wisdom. Bless us with discernment and clarity of purpose. We ask that you aid us in seeing, claiming, and using our power as citizens and residents of this nation, so we may best be of benefit to all beings with whom we share this Greater Earth. Athena Nike, may we rise up and meet this great challenge in full confidence knowing that through You, victory is inevitable. We call to you today, great goddess of wisdom, to help us stand by our principles and defend the integrity of our democratic norms and processes. Athena, help us dare to stand as a people in the best parts of our national character and be the courageous, hopeful, daring, open and generous people this world needs us to be. Athena Themis, hold up to us your vision of both what is and what is right, and fortify our strength so we never stop working until those images match.

Invoke Apollon:

Phoibos Apollon, Moiragetes, Lord of Light, of enlightenment, hear me and answer my call. Apollon Nomimos, great lawgiver, through your counsel and your oracles you directly shaped the foundations of the polis. Shining One, You directed humanity to found courts, construct constitutions, articulate rights, abandon the cycles of vengeance for Rule of Law, and embrace isonomy, equality before the law. Through your oracle at Delphi, you approved and provided guidance for the reforms of Cleisthenes and the construction of the Athenian constitution, giving birth to Democracy, the rule of the demos, the people, for the first time in human history. We call to you, Apollon Nomimos, be present and guide us during this rite of oath-keeping. Apollon Alexikakos, averter of all evil, you are hagnos, absolutely pure, and no unwholesome thing can withstand your holy presence. Be present with us during this rite and be present in our nation. Avert all evil from without and within. Thank you, blessed and loving Apollon.

Call to the Upholders:

Here before the People's House we stand, citizens united in our devotion to the Rule of Law and the Constitution. All our leaders and civil servants swore oaths to defend the Constitution. We are here to call on the Gods to insist on their observance.

Themis, hold your scales up and measure their oath. Dike, great goddess of the vows sworn by men, Pallas Athena, Apollon, and all Bright Gods, witness their troth. To the Underworld Court of Judges, we call. Hades, Persephone and Erinyes, dark Furies, we give you the oath-breakers. Remove them; make them fall.

Hold up copies of oaths or governing documents.

To the Empyrean Spirits, to the Gods Below, witness and know that willful ignorance does not lessen the bonds of a sacred oath. To those who have sworn: This is your oath; bear witness, bear witness. [Repeat thrice.]

Read a section from the official documents together and then repeat, "This is your oath; bear witness, bear witness." Repeat thrice.

At the end of the final three chants about the oath, switch to "Hold them accountable" and raise energy.

Closing prayer:

> *To all the Great Ones who are present, who have witnessed this rite, who have witnessed the oaths sworn by our leaders in all branches of government. We ask for your protection. We ask you to uphold the oaths and defend the integrity of our democracy. We register with you all our leaders who are oath-breakers, who violate or undermine the [governing document] and ask for your justice. We pray to you to keep an ever-watchful eye on those who have sworn. Hold them to their duty. Thank you, Great Ones. We give thanks.*

CHAPTER ELEVEN
HEALING

Mortals will, by definition, experience illness and death. Health is one of the highest goods but is ultimately temporary. Health is more than just a state of the physical body—it includes psychological and spiritual health. A society or an ecological system can be understood as being healthy or unhealthy. Healing gods are typically among the most compassionate and intimate with humanity. In the Hellenic context, this is Apollon, His son Asklepios, and Their family. Perspectives on health and healing from the ancient Greek world can enrich our current understanding, and some ancient Hellenic religious healing techniques, especially rites of incubation, could be complementary to modern medicine.

My experiences with both Apollon and Asklepios indicate They work with modern medicine and would not want people to abandon medical advances but use them wisely in an empowered way. A patient should be a partner in their own healing. Galen trained as a priest of Asklepios at His temple in Pergamon and is the founder of Western scientific medicine.[201] The intercession of Apollon and Asklepios, especially in visions, often drove the advance of medicine through disclosing new techniques, medicines, and methods of diagnosis.[202] It is completely counter to that spirit to abandon such advances in favor of

---

201. Ustura, *Pergamon Asklepion.*
202. Graf, "Healing," 505–18.

lesser technologies for treating disease. Ancient Hellenic methodologies have a profound emphasis on what we now call "preventative medicine."

THE CONCEPTS OF HEALTH, DISEASE, AND HEALING

Health is a state of being in balance on all levels. Ancient physicians embraced the theory of the humors—the four liquids associated with the elements—and their need for balance within the body. While that theory, at least on the physical level of observing the bile and blood and so forth, has been discredited by science, the metaphor of balance as an approach to health is useful.[203]

Physically, it means observing the balance of diet and liquid, of activity and rest, of exertion and relaxation. For optimum health, there needs to be work-life balance with the realization that all necessary labor—like cooking, cleaning, errands, and child- and eldercare—all fall on the "work" part of that scale. We should strive for an appropriate balance of time in which our attention is externally focused and internally focused in activities like contemplation, daydreaming, meditation, and enriching our own internal landscape. We are not in a society that encourages balance, and its achievement may not be possible without significant societal changes.

Health, as appropriate balance on all levels of being, requires constant attention and is always temporary. We will all get out of balance and then have to work to restore it. What is required to maintain balance is always in flux. In ancient Hellenic medicine, doctors recognized that stage of life and seasonal environmental conditions were two major factors shifting what is necessary to maintain health.[204]

In our culture, disease is often portrayed as an external invader that must be "fought." Metaphors of conquering disease come from a radically different mindset than metaphors about restoring health. In focusing on disease as battle, we create an intolerable situation. At some point, we will all lose. It makes disease and death strangers instead of part of life and encourages us to focus on "beating" a particular ailment while paying inadequate attention to actual health. This is a recipe for situations where we overlook side effects and quality of life in the quest to "win" against an ailment. Furthermore, it shifts almost all

---

203. Edelstein, *Ancient Medicine.*
204. Edelstein, *Ancient Medicine.*

our attention to intervention when one is sick rather than focusing on empowering people to maintain health.

Dietetics, which included exercise and routines of rest as well as what we think of as "diet," was the mainstay of daily Hellenic health practices.[205] Ancient physicians believed most ailments could be addressed early by adjusting dietetics. For us, we need to prioritize enabling people to take care of themselves. This is more than an individual issue. It has to do with how we design our society. Our culture's propensity to treat fitness and health like an individual moral issue is part of our soul-sickness. We have undermined the integrity of our food, poisoned our environment, and created a culture of mandatory overwork. If we want to be healthy, we have to redesign our society.

Disease, or the physical effects of being out of balance, can come from *miasma*. *Miasma* can cause disease on an individual or a communal level, like a plague.[206] For many years, contemporary scholars have viewed the idea of plague being caused by *miasma* as superstition. I think it contains profound wisdom. We are just beginning to understand the effects of environmental degradation, which is a form of *miasma*, on health. I think the ancients were correct in understanding that the root of such degradation is a spiritual pollution arising from wounded relationships requiring purification and healing. It is not accidental that Apollon, the Lord of Light, the prophet who tells humanity how to purify and avoid *miasma*, is the great healer. The metaphor of "healing society's ills" is apt.

THEOI OF HEALING

Most of the Theoi involved in healing are in Apollon's lineage. The healing cults of Asklepios, the son of Apollon, always include at least an altar to Apollon. Over time, the cult of Asklepios took on more physical healing for individuals, while Apollon remained the primary god addressing healing on a societal level and individual healing at the soul level.

Apollon the Healer

Apollon has many aspects, including being the great healer. In Homer, He both brings and releases plagues. Paian (Paean or Paeon) is one of His epithets as

---

205.   Edelstein, *Ancient Medicine.*

206.   Graf, "Healing."

the god of healing and is the sacred hymn of Apollon. The *paian* is only sung to Apollon or in the cults of His son, Asklepios. The names of most Olympians are found in Linear B and are clearly already present in Mycenean culture. Apollon is not a name in the script; however, the healing god, Paiawon, is present. Scholars debate whether or not Paiawon, which clearly became Paian, was another name for Apollon or was a different being whose cult became assimilated to Apollon.[207] The Homeric epics are stories from the Mycenaean culture's latter days, and, by that time, Apollon is present and is a healer.

In addition to Paian, two other common epithets of Apollon referring to His role as a healer are Iatros (Doctor) and Oulios (provider of Health). Individuals prayed to Apollon for health or when they were ill. Infertility was a grave problem in Hellenic culture, and prayers and sacrifices were given to Apollon to ask for his intercession. A common name is Apollodorus, which means "the one whom Apollon has given."[208]

Many oracular utterances in which Apollon speaks directly through His *mantis* addressed questions about illness and *miasma*. They typically contained information about the *miasma's* causes and remedy. In His oracles He addresses *miasma* on a personal level, but also ways in which entire communities can heal. If the cause is spiritual pollution or is in any way cosmic, then it requires assistance from Apollon.[209] I call on Apollon Maleatas as the Healer of Souls and Societies. Apollon Maleatas is His cultic name from Epidauros, which became the most important healing sanctuary of Asklepios.

Asklepios

If the cause is a physical defect, then it became the purview of Asklepios. As previously discussed, Asklepios was born as a mortal from a mortal woman but was taken by His father, Apollon, and raised to be a healer. Apollon arranges for Asklepios to be trained by Chiron, the wise centaur and foster father of heroes. Asklepios, although mortal, receives His healing powers from His father.[210]

Asklepios was the greatest physician of all time. He could heal maladies beyond the skill of any other mortal and He is always portrayed as intensely

---

207.   Graf, *Apollo*.

208.   Graf, *Apollo*.

209.   Graf, *Apollo*.

210.   Pitruzzella, "Drama and Healing in Ancient Greece: Demeter and Askleios," 74–86.

compassionate. One day a king came to Asklepios about his recently deceased son and begged the great physician to heal his son from death for the sake of his whole kingdom. Asklepios went into the woods to think. While sitting in contemplation, He saw a serpent climb up his staff. He killed the serpent, but then watched as another serpent brought an herb to his fallen companion and revived it. Asklepios took the herb and made a drug to revive the dead.[211] The serpent-entwined staff became His symbol.

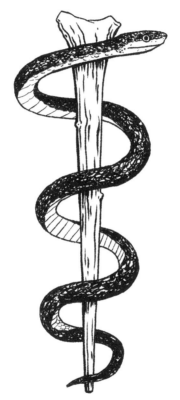

THE STAFF OF ASKLEPIOS

Zeus is protector of the Cosmic Order and, in raising a mortal from the dead, Asklepios violated a foundational part of the cosmic structure. It was not safe to have this ability in the hands of a mortal, so Zeus killed Asklepios with a thunderbolt. Zeus granted Asklepios *apotheosis*, making Him a god. He

---

211.   Graf, *Apollo*.

married Epione, the daughter of Herakles, and had a number of children who joined His healing cult. Asklepios is intimate with mortals, having begun His life as a mortal and having mortal sons and immortal daughters. He possesses tremendous empathy and understanding of humanity's plight.

Hygeia

The most important child of Asklepios is His daughter Hygeia, the goddess of health. At every temple of Asklepios, both Apollon and Hygeia are also worshipped. Hygeia is Her father's partner in healing and is associated with hygiene. Healing baths were a regular part of any treatment. She is depicted with a snake, and the symbol of pharmacists is the Bowl of Hygeia, a cup with a serpent wrapped around it, giving its venom to be used in manufacturing medicine. Snake venom is an ingredient in many potent curative drugs.[212]

Other Healing Theoi

Other daughters of Asklepios include Panakeia (Panacea), who is associated with a drug that can cure all things. Iaso is a goddess who assists in the processes of recuperation. Akeso is the goddess of the entire process of healing, and Aigle, which means "dazzing light," is the goddess of health restored. While these goddesses are all present in the cults of Asklepios, They do not have the same cultic importance as Hygeia.[213]

Another healing deity is Telesphoros, who is the god of recuperation. Whether He is part of the family of Asklepios is unclear, but He is worshipped in the sanctuaries of Asklepios and is responsible for the patient's safety during recuperation.[214]

Finally, Chiron the centaur was the foster son of Apollon. He learned healing, music, archery, gymnastics, prophecy, and philosophy from Apollon. Chiron is the revered teacher of heroes and was the foster father of Asklepios.[215] In some sanctuaries of Asklepios, sacrifice was offered to Chiron. Chiron is the ultimate pedagogue, so I recommend calling on Him if you are striving to learn—especially if you are learning medicine or any allied healing art.

---

212.   Ustura, *Pergamon Asklepion*.

213.   Ustura, *Pergamon Asklepion*.

214.   Ustura, *Pergamon Asklepion*.

215.   Pitruzzella, "Drama and Healing in Ancient Greece."

THE ROLE OF THE PHYSICIAN

From at least Homeric times, ancient Greece had doctors—specialists who served as healers. Itinerant healers, like other skilled craftsmen, wandered from place to place, temporarily staying in and serving communities. Larger cities and towns had physicians with stable practices. Armies employed physicians who accompanied them on campaigns. Finally, there were the priest-physicians of Asklepios who served at the healing sanctuaries. Typically, doctors went to the patients, except for the sanctuaries, where the patients undertook a pilgrimage to seek healing.[216]

Ancient Greek medicine had three major branches: dietetics, pharmacology, and surgery. Health can be maintained, strengthened, and often restored through dietetics, which includes diet, movement, and noninvasive bodywork practices like massage and hydrotherapy. Galen wrote extensively on food and diet and was especially known for inventions in surgery.[217] Dietetics had a particularly respected place—not only in what we recognize as preventative medicine, but also in curative medicine. Pharmacology is the use of drugs to treat medicine. Ancient Greece left us a great deal of pharmacological knowledge.[218] Because of the dangers of blood loss and infection, surgery was the treatment of last resort, but we have the essential tools of surgery present, especially at the major sanctuaries of Asklepios where the physician-priests were also surgeons.[219]

Amulets were sometimes included in medical care. While not part of Greek medicine, there was a strong appreciation for the psychological aspect of healing, so doctors typically would not discourage such things if they made the patient less afraid and more hopeful.[220] Indeed, while modern medicine dismisses things like amulets as just having a placebo effect, placebos have real physical impacts. In fact, asking why placebos work at all indicates a magnificent mystery about the nature of embodied consciousness. Set and setting is important. A significant aspect of ancient Greek medical training concerned

216.   Edelstein, *Ancient Medicine*.

217.   Galen, *Galen*.

218.   Scarborough, "Pharmacology of Sacred Plants, Herbs, and Roots," 138–74.

219.   Ustura, *Pergamon Asklepion*.

220.   Edelstein, *Ancient Medicine*.

how to interact with patients in ways that create the best psychological conditions for healing.

MEDICAL ETHICS

Most of us are familiar with the Hippocratic Oath, which dates back to ancient Greece and governs the ethical dimensions of medical practice. However, that oath does not represent the ethics of most ancient Greek physicians. It is based on Pythagorean ethics, which were not widely held. The Hippocratic Oath forbids three major categories of common work for doctors—assisted suicide for the terminally ill, abortion, and surgery. These restrictions are about specific tenets concerning spiritual pollution that were outside the ancient Greek cultural norm.[221] The Hippocratic Oath gained lasting importance because Pythagorean ethics aligned easily with the emerging Judeo-Christian ethics at the fall of the classical world.[222]

Abortion

There was no stigma surrounding abortion unless undertaken for reasons of vanity or to conceal adultery. Surviving sources make it clear women could procure an abortion of their own volition.[223] In fact, many great thinkers, including Plato and Aristotle, believed birth control, including abortion, was necessary for a well-functioning society. Keeping the human population in balance with the environment was a moral imperative. Parents who were past the ideal age for having children were counseled to abort. This was considered the responsible course of action.[224]

Physician-Assisted Suicide

Similarly, there was no stigma against suicide for those who were suffering with a terminal illness.[225] Two areas of ancient medical research were improving the efficacy of prognostication—the art of understanding and correctly predicting the course of a disease—and developing drugs that could give a painless death.

---

221. Edelstein, *Ancient Medicine*.
222. Haarman, *Roots of Ancient Greek Civilization*.
223. Edelstein, *Ancient Medicine*.
224. Aristotle, *Politics*.
225. Edelstein, *Ancient Medicine*.

Recognizing humans are mortal and death can never be defeated, doctors focused on treating what they could and then helping the patient understand the course of the disease beyond what they could treat. Doctors worked with dying patients to give them an accurate prognosis so the patients could get their worldly affairs in order. Based on their understanding of the course of the disease, a patient could plan their end-of-life care with confidence, potentially including requesting poison.[226]

Refusing Treatment

When human physicians determined the patient could not be helped by human medicine, they still gave prognostication but would refuse to treat the ailment that was beyond their capacity. This was the case for terminal illness, for certain chronic conditions normal human medicine could not treat, and sometimes for illnesses where normal treatments had failed. In these cases, the patient would be directed to seek divine help. If there were reasons to believe the illness had any kind of cosmic cause, including punishment from angry gods or spirits, or if there was a plague, Apollon would be consulted. If the causes were bodily, then the patient would go to a sanctuary of Asklepios.

THE RITE OF INCUBATION

Anyone needing healing was welcome in the sanctuaries of Asklepios. Men, women, children, slaves, foreigners, the wealthy, and the poor were all treated equally. The expectations of payment were dependent on means and healing was not denied to those in need. We are aware of almost three hundred sanctuaries of Asklepios, all of which had a common and deeply intimate mode of healing: incubation. The earliest temple to provide this particular form of healing is Epidauros.[227]

The Sanctuary

The sanctuary at Epidauros included several types of buildings in addition to the usual temples and altars. Sometimes patients remained for an extended period, requiring dormitories. There was a large banquet hall in which the patients, priests, and attendants joined in communal meals with the Theoi.

---

226.   Edelstein, *Ancient Medicine.*
227.   Tomilson, *Epidauros.*

There were quarters for particular types of healing activities, including baths and surgeries. There was a mysterious but obviously important *tholos* building that probably functioned to bridge the Underworld's power into this one and likely served as home to the sacred healing serpents. Next to the *tholos* was an *abaton*, a two-floor dormitory where the dream incubation rite took place.[228]

Preparation

Upon arriving at the sanctuary, the patient knew they were going to seek an encounter with Asklepios through a healing dream. The patient met with the physician-priests of Asklepios and underwent various preliminary preparations, including a healing and purifying bath. The patient sacrificed and prayed to Asklepios, asking Him to come in a healing dream, and petitioned Mnemosyne to help remember the dream and Themis to help the dream be correctly understood.

The Dream Incubation Rite

The incubation ritual's core is that the patient, properly prepared and with appropriate expectations, enters the *abaton* and goes to sleep. The priests instruct the patients not to move if they hear anything in the night. It is possible the sacred snakes were released into the *abaton*.

Sometime during the night, Asklepios visited the patients in their dreams. Usually it was Asklepios Himself, sometimes with an assistant.[229] Sometimes the patient was visited by one of His animals, like a temple snake. We have numerous descriptions of these dreams. Asklepios, the master physician, made His rounds. He came to each patient and examined them. Sometimes He gave them a treatment plan. Sometimes He healed them directly in the dream, often by giving the patient medicine or performing surgery in the dream. There were times in which a patient was given a new formulary for a drug that had not previously existed.[230]

The patients recounted their dreams to the priests upon awakening in the morning or after being awakened by the priests. In the *abaton* at Pergamon, each patient had a semiprivate cubicle and a priest-tender probably sat with

---

228.   Tomilson, *Epidauros*.
229.   Pitruzzella, "Drama and Healing in Ancient Greece."
230.   Graf, "Healing."

each patient, awakening them when their dream was over to help capture it before it could be forgotten.

Following the Dream

The physician-priests would follow up on whatever was revealed by Asklepios in the dream. If He told the patient to get a specific surgery, the priests operated. If Asklepios told the patient to follow a pharmacological regime, the drugs were produced. Any specific requirements for other therapies or changes to diet were recorded.[231] At the incubation's end, the patient shared a sacrificial meal with Asklepios. If there were additional parts of the treatment requiring the physicians at the sanctuary, the patient stayed until the convalescence was over.

Giving Thanks

After being healed, many patients gave thanks to Asklepios through votive dedications, often made in the shape of the body part that was healed and sometimes recording their story in detail. These testimonies were installed all around the healing sanctuaries, increasing the patients' confidence and their psychological preparedness for a healing dream.

COOPERATION BETWEEN "SHAMANIC" HEALING AND MEDICINE

From surviving inscriptions left by grateful patients, we see that many patients' experiences bore a strong resemblance to what those trained in "shamanic" healing see and do in their journeys. In the case of dream incubation, individuals who had not been trained and may never have had other shamanic experiences had an unmediated vision of their own healing. For example,

> *Gorgias of Herakleion and suppuration. He had received an arrow-wound in the lung during battle, and for a year and a half discharged so great a quantity of matter as to fill fifty-seven dishes. In sleep he saw a vision. He thought the god extracted the arrow-point from his lung. When day came he departed, holding the point of the arrow in his hand.*[232]

---

231.   Ustura, *Pergamon Asklepion.*

232.   Hamilton, *Incubation.*

What is historically remarkable about the healings at the sanctuaries of Asklepios is the cooperation between the spiritual healings of Asklepios and science. We know Asklepios does not only create miracle healings, but he also gives diagnoses and treatments to be followed in medical cases that were beyond the knowledge of human doctors without divine assistance. Divine instructions were given directly to patients who conveyed them to the doctors, who then followed those instructions. Many physicians used this revealed knowledge to advance the science of medicine.

LESSONS FOR REBIRTHING

There are aspects of ancient Hellenic healing worth rebirthing. I am greatly appreciative of modern medicine and, like the ancients, do not see science and religion as in opposition, but as complementary. I am grateful for the advancements in diagnostics and surgery. I am grateful for modern pharmacology, not only for advances in creating drugs, but also for the fact dosage is so much more easily controlled.

Societal Revisioning and Reorientation

Hellenic medicine's emphasis on balance and empowering people to maintain wellness—including recognizing the importance of adapting to changes in the environment—is something to take from ancient Hellenic medicine. We have created a society optimized for machines and treat humans as machines, expecting the same thing from them day after day, with no attention paid to the rhythm of our bodies or the seasons. We ask people to have good diets and exercise, but we don't investigate the systems that make it hard to incorporate good diet and exercise into our daily life. We do not match our diet to the state our individual body is in at any moment but believe what is "good" is good for everyone all the time. When we fail at being healthy, it is treated as an individualistic moral failing. If we deeply reconsidered what it means to be healthy and prioritized designing a society to maximize human health and happiness, we would see dramatic changes.

Rebirthing Healing Dream Incubation Cults

We could rebirth the healing cults in a way that is complementary to modern medicine. My experiences with Asklepios in numerous locations indicate He is eager to rebirth His cults of dream incubation. I suspect rebirthing these cults could help with diagnosis of ailments that are not straightforward by indicating paths to pursue and helping people learn how to manage chronic conditions.

Requirements

To be successful, rebirthing this type of cult has certain personal and spatial requirements.

1. People need to feel called to rebirth the incubation cult of Asklepios. It is specifically about creating a space and a protocol for Him to come to people seeking dreams. This requires a personal connection to Asklepios.

2. These cults require the correct space. Sacred bathing as purification is an essential preliminary rite. In some places, the baths use water from sacred springs; in others, ritual bathing is in the ocean. This consecrated water is from a divine being. It is likely the water source will dictate the sanctuary's location.

3. A simple altar and *temenos* is minimally required.

4. The patient needs someplace special and set apart for this form of healing to serve as the *abaton* where they can experience deep sleep. Ideally the *abaton* would be kept separate and only used for that purpose. The sleeping area should be comfortable, soothing, completely dark, possibly with running water, and somewhat cool.

Structuring a Dream Incubation Rite

The research on therapeutic uses of psychedelics clearly demonstrated "set and setting" is essential for visionary states to be meaningful and healing.[233] In the case of dream incubation, the patient must be prepared with the clear expectation of a healing dream. They have to feel safe and have a setting in which they will sleep well. The setting needs to be sacred and feel sacred.

1. The patient should treat the entire experience as a pilgrimage, including planning for it, going somewhere different with intention, and treating all activities as part of the holy rite.

---

233.   Pollan, *How to Change Your Mind*.

2. The patient should be given a series of preparatory activities.

- Basic body care, like ensuring adequate hydration and abstaining from practices that harm sleep, including blue light and caffeine.
- Preliminary ritual bathing.
- Perhaps preparatory bodywork to open to experience, like massage.
- A ritual to connect with Asklepios, including offerings, prayers, songs, and sacred stories of Him, His compassion, and His healings to help set the stage.

3. The priestly healer should strengthen the expectation the patient will have a healing dream, remember it, and reinforce that if anything in the experience is disturbing, it is part of the healing and they should not fight it.

4. Send the patient to sleep in the prepared space.

5. As soon as the person wakes from the dream, they should recount what they have experienced to the priest(ess), who should write it down and ask clarifying questions as necessary.

6. The next day, the patient should think of some personally meaningful way to give thanks to Asklepios. A communal meal should be shared, inviting Asklepios to partake.

7. The priest(ess) should remind the patient to consult a medical professional and do their research before ingesting anything or putting any unknown substance on their body. They should be encouraged to work with their medical healing team.

I hope someone who has access to the correct kind of land will feel this call and rebirth a sanctuary of dream incubation. Building a place of power will make this practice much more reliable and powerful.

Exercise
HEALING DREAM INCUBATION PILGRIMAGE

Here is a rite for incubating a healing dream that accommodates lack of access to a healing sanctuary.

What You'll Need

A place to go on retreat for a couple of days—someplace dark and away from noise where you can be left alone. You can do this at home, but then you will need to be more mindful of not slipping into your routines. Ideally, the place has a pure water source for bathing. An offering for Asklepios. Incense you find soothing. A journal and pen or recording device. A meal you can share with Asklepios. Optional: Massage or other bodywork.

Directions

Approach the experience as a pilgrimage. Before you leave, say a prayer in which you set your intention to seek a healing dream from Asklepios. Once you arrive, do not use technology other than for emergencies. When you arrive, take a purifying bath with the intention of being open and receptive for a healing dream. Go to a place that feels correct and pray to Asklepios for healing. Make an offering to Him. Spend time talking to Him. If you have access to massage or other bodywork, you may pursue it as preliminary work. Remain in a holy mindset.

Burn incense in the bedroom where you will be, get as comfortable as possible, and make it as dark and silent as possible. Be sure you have the ability to rapidly record your dream. When you are tired, say another prayer to Asklepios for a healing dream and tell yourself you will have one. When you awake the next morning, thank Asklepios. Spend time in meditation and share a meal with Him. This can be done by having a meal in which you lay some aside for Him while being in silent communion. At the meal's end, give thanks once more and end the rite.

CHAPTER TWELVE
THE MYSTERIES

The Mystery Religions are a Hellenic and, later, a Hellenistic religious form. The word *mystery* comes from the Greek *mysteria*, which is the term for this type of cult.[234] The Eleusinian Mysteries of Demeter and Her daughter, Kore, are the oldest.

The Mysteries have specific characteristics that set them apart from other forms of Hellenic religion. Unlike civic cult or household cult, the mysteries are personal and their effects are individual. The mysteries are initiatory and, therefore, they are optional. An individual must seek out the mysteries and undertake a path to initiation. The content of those initiations is kept secret. Most importantly, the fundamental claim of the mysteries is that something is altered during the process of initiation affecting the individual in the immortal part of their being in a way that offsets the burden of mortality. This change either results in or is caused by divine intimacy between the Theoi associated with the Mystery Cult and the initiates.[235]

There are two types of Mystery Religions. Some are site specific, including sacred geographies that are part of the initiatory process. The Eleusinian Mysteries are the most important of these, but this also describes the Mysteries of Samothrace and the Andanian Mysteries.

---

234. Burkert, *Ancient Mystery Cults*.
235. Burkert, *Ancient Mystery Cults*.

Other mysteries are not rooted in a specific sacred geography so could be celebrated anywhere—the most important being the mysteries of Dionysus and the Orphic mysteries, which are related to each other. There are some later mysteries related to non-Hellenic gods, but the "Mystery" form of their cult is newer than the worship of these Gods. For example, the goddess Isis is very ancient, as is Her worship, but the Mysteries of Isis are comparatively new, arising in Hellenism when Greek and Egyptian cultures were melded. Some other mysteries of this sort are the Mysteries of Cybele and the Mithraic Mysteries. [236]

Influence of the Mysteries on Wicca

I came out of the broom closet in the mid-1980s. One of the first descriptions I ever heard of Wicca is that it is "a Mystery Religion." Some distinctive features of Modern Paganism, especially initiatory Wicca, are directly inspired by the ancient Hellenic Mystery Religions, in particular the Eleusinian Mysteries.

Most importantly, the entire idea of initiations that are not life-stage rites of passage but rather are meant to cause spiritual change at the immortal level of self derives from the Mystery Religions. Mystery Religions include vows of secrecy in which initiates swear not to divulge the contents of initiatory traditions to those who are uninitiated. Some practices used in Wiccan initiations, like blindfolding and initiatory oath-taking, are part of ancient Hellenic Mystery Religions.

However, for all these similarities, modern Wicca is not functionally the same as the ancient Mystery Religions. It is inspired by them, but I argue Wiccan initiations are not causing the same kind of changes in the initiates. They do not inherently alter their experience after death. This does not detract from the importance of Wiccan initiations. I am a third-degree Wiccan priestess and have experienced initiations that have moved and changed me, including on the immortal levels of being—but differently, I think, from initiations in the ancient mysteries. I understand my Wiccan initiations as accelerating my personal spiritual evolution, but if I am correct about what the Hellenic Mysteries were doing, they have yet to be reborn.

---

236. Larson, *Understanding Greek Religion.*

THE CLAIMS OF THE MYSTERIES

In order to understand what the mysteries are claiming, I want to share some revealing statements from ancient authors about what initiation into the Eleusinian Mysteries conveys. The "Homeric Hymn to Demeter," attributed by the ancients to Homer and dating from a time before writing, is the myth's cultic version. This segment describes the founding of the Eleusinian Mysteries.

> She [Demeter] went to the kings who administer the laws ... and showed them the celebration of holy rites and explained to all ... the awful mysteries not to be transgressed, violated or divulged, because the tongue is restrained by reverence for the gods. Whoever on this earth has seen these is blessed, but he who has no part in the holy rites has another lot as he wastes away in dank darkness.[237]

In the *Triptolemos*, the playwright Sophocles includes the following line in reference to the Eleusinian Mysteries. "Thrice blessed are those among men who, after beholding these rites, go down to Hades. Only for them is there life; all the rest will suffer an evil lot."[238] The phrase indicates a formula that would have been immediately understood by his audience.

Finally, Plutarch, the philosopher, biographer, and high priest of Apollon at Delphi wrote in his essay, "On the Soul," that the soul's state at death is the same as during the great initiations. It is clear he is referencing the Eleusinian Mysteries.

> Then [at the point of death] it [the soul] suffers something like those who participate in the great initiations suffer. Hence even the word 'dying' [teleutan] is like the word to be initiated [teleisthai], and the act of dying is like the act of being initiated. First of all, there are wanderings and wearisome rushings about and certain journeys fearful and unending (atelestoi) through the darkness and then before the very end (telos) all the terrors—fright and trembling and sweating and amazement. But then one encounters an extraordinary light, and pure regions and meadows offer welcome, with voices and dances and majesties of sacred sounds and holy sights; in which now the completely

---

237. Athanassakis, trans., "Homeric Hymn to Demeter," 1–15.
238. Sophokles, "Sophokles. Fragments," 837.

initiated one (tanteles memyemenos), becoming free and set loose, enjoys the *rites, crowned and consorts with pure and holy men.*[239]

The essential claim of the Eleusinian Mysteries is that the process of being initiated dramatically changes your experience after death. While I am focused here on the Eleusinian Mysteries, the Orphic and Dionysiac Mysteries make explicit that this change is not just about death, it is also about rebirth.[240] Reincarnation is explicitly part of the belief structures in a good portion of Hellenic traditions.

MY THEORY ABOUT THE MYSTERIES

The fundamental claim in the Eleusinian along with the Orphic and Dionysiac Mysteries is that the initiates' experience after death is changed. They are blessed. In Hellenic thought, the baneful thing about mortality is not the actual dying—it is the forgetting. Our natural dying process includes "drinking from the river Lethe," which is where we get the word "lethal." When we go through this process, we forget everything we know. We forget our relationships. We forget our sense of self. When Odysseus manages to conjure Tiresias, Achilles, and others from the Underworld, he temporarily restores their memories and they become themselves once more. Without their memories, they are just shades—not full humans.[241]

From the perspective of reincarnation, the problem with being mortal is we live short lives, die, and return without memories—starting over again and again. Each incarnation, we have to relearn almost everything. This makes our progress slow. It skews our perspectives about what is important. It keeps us chained on a wheel that just keeps turning and turning, with only a tiny window of opportunity to try to gain some excellence. This, not death itself, is the great burden of mortality.

I believe, functionally, the Eleusinian, Orphic, and Dionysiac Mysteries were the ritual equivalent of practices in the *Tibetan Book of the Dead*. They did something to enable at least some continuity of consciousness across the bridges of death and rebirth. The Orphic texts include instructions, often about

239. Plutarch, *Moralia*.

240. Cole, "Landscapes of Dionysos and Elysian Fields," 193–217.

241. Homer, *Odyssey*.

not drinking the first water you come to in the other place, but instead giving a passphrase to the beings you meet there.[242] My composite reconstruction of the formula is, "I am a child of Earth and starry Heaven, but my race is of Heaven alone. Give to me the waters of Mnemosyne, which are mine to drink by right."

The initiates may have learned or experienced certain things preparing them to navigate the process of death, including avoiding pitfalls that make them lose their memory. They were taken under the protection of certain Theoi who would assist them in their death process. It is possible initiation conveyed some identifying mark on their immortal aspects. I think they were being trained in how to die.

A Call to Action

I want us to rebirth practices preparing us to control our dying and our reincarnations that don't require people to withdraw into monastic life. I think it is possible and worth our effort.

If there are things that could radically change our dangerous collective trajectory, we shouldn't spend all our energy wondering if they are windmills—we should go for it. To me, pursuing the rebirth of the mysteries is justified by the transformative potential in their claims. The cost of failure is seeming foolish or wasting time, whereas success liberates humans from the burdens of mortality. If we could rebirth an intervention in which large numbers of humans could stop forgetting across incarnations but could pick up close to where they left off in their growth; if we could collectively begin to see what life looks like across a longer-term trajectory and stop grasping at short-term wins while sacrificing the long-term health of ourselves, our relationships, and our planet—this is what real spiritual revolution looks like.

I have not yet figured it out but have a three-pronged strategy for working on it, generally matching my strategies for rebirthing ancient Greek religion.

Rebuild Relationships

All these rites require working with some Great Ones. The initiates of the Eleusinian Mysteries experience the intercession of Demeter and Persephone. The Mysteries of Dionysus and the Orphic Mysteries have the intercession

---

242. Edmonds, *"Orphic" Gold Tablets and Greek Religion.*

of Dionysus. The difference between the Hellenic mysteries and the practices in the *Tibetan Book of the Dead* is that the Hellenic Mysteries include divine intercession.

Reconnecting Lines of Power

By lines of power, I mean *dynamis*, or energetic power. When Alaric destroyed the Sanctuary at Eleusis, it is not that the cult's dynamism was naturally expended. It was ruptured through violence. There are equivalents of live electrical lines lying around in the other planes. If you can figure out how to fashion a dongle, so to speak, you can plug in and get the energy flowing again into this world. In and of itself, that is an act of service. Some of our social imbalances come from the fact that some types of energy don't have as many ways to flow into (or out of) our world at the moment. This process is more art than science—you can often access these lines of power by using symbolism, myth, story, and the arts.

Reverse Engineering Tech

We can build new tech by reverse engineering ancient techniques. Start with the ancient tech's function, break it down, analyze it, figure out how it works in the system, and then experiment. It doesn't matter if it looks anything like what was done in the ancient days if it works. Sometimes tapping into some symbology manages to reconnect lines of power that can then be linked into the new tech. For the mysteries, we need to study things like near-death experience literature and other manuals and teachings on dying like the *Tibetan Book of the Dead*, as well as the Mystery Cults.

A Closer Look at the Eleusinian Mysteries

The Eleusinian Mysteries are the oldest Mystery Cult. The oaths of secrecy make rebirthing any of them challenging. Let's look at the Eleusinian Mysteries as a case study.

The Mythology

Here is a dramatic retelling of the *Homeric Hymn to Demeter*.[243] This mythic version is hyperlocal to Eleusis. It names cult places and outlines the beginning of

---

243.   Athanassakis, "Homeric Hymn to Demeter."

the Eleusinian Mysteries. Persephone is never mentioned by name; she is only called Kore. This is an incredibly abbreviated version of this hymn.

Kore is out on the Rharian plains picking flowers with the daughters of the Ocean. It was a beautiful day when suddenly, near the Kephisos river, under a fig tree, She sees the most beautiful flower She's ever seen in Her life! (Note: sacred geography.) She runs to it, She picks it, and suddenly ... the Earth opens, and up comes Hades in His chariot. He grabs Her. She screams. And back down into the Underworld He goes, taking Kore with Him.

Demeter hears Her daughter screaming and comes tearing down in a panic to the Rharian plains where She last saw Her. "Where is my daughter? Where is my daughter? I can't feel Her presence anywhere on the Earth!"

She runs into Hekate, the goddess of all things liminal.

Hekate says, "I heard Her, but I didn't see who took Her. Let's go see Helios, god of the sun. He sees all."

With all swiftness, they go to consult Helios, who says, "I am Helios, god of the sun. I see all. It was Hades. Zeus gave your daughter to Him to be His bride. Now ... I know You're upset, but truly, I swear, He will make an excellent husband. They are actually a really good match."

Demeter is utterly outraged: "How dare He?! How dare They?! How dare all of You?! I am not setting one foot in Olympus until I get my daughter back!"

Demeter goes back to the Rharian plain wearing the disguise of an old mortal woman. She's both grieving and furious. She comes to Eleusis and sinks down weeping on a stone by the road (the Agelastos Petra, the mirthless rock. Note: sacred geography).

The daughters of King Kelios and Queen Metaneira come down from the palace to get water from the Kallichoron Well. (Note: sacred geography.) They pass by Demeter and see Her weeping. Kind and concerned, they ask if She is well. Demeter gives them some nonsense story about pirates. The young daughters tell Demeter She would make a great nurse for their infant brother and bring Her to the palace.

Demeter walks into the palace and Queen Metaneira looks up and perceives divine radiance but is confused because her eyes tell her it is just an old woman. Even though she is queen, the sense of divinity causes her to jump up and offer Demeter her chair. Demeter declines and orders a low stool with a ram's skin on it. (This references a ritual action that is part of the Lesser Mysteries.)

Demeter sits down but is mournful. The servant, Iambe, makes her laugh—some people think by being bawdy, but that isn't clear from the hymn. What is clear—Iambe is hilarious.

Queen Metaneira offers Demeter wine. Demeter proclaims that wine is inappropriate and gives instructions about how to make the kykeon from barley mixed with water and pennyroyal. (This clearly references cultic activity.)

Demeter becomes the nurse for the infant, Demophoon. Queen Metaneira thinks, "My little son is doing so well with this new nurse, almost like he's a little god! I'm suspicious. I think I'll spy on her." At night, Demeter anoints the baby with ambrosia and then puts him in the fire to burn the mortality out of him. (The use of fire in this context is important cultic information.) Metaneira freaks out and interrupts the process. Demeter throws off Her mortal disguise, calls Metaneira an idiot and proclaims She would have made Demophoon a god. She commands that Eleusis build Her a temple to live in, which becomes the Anaktaron—the most ancient part of the temple of the Mysteries that is the holiest of the holies.

Demeter goes to Her temple proclaiming She will not allow anything to grow until Kore is returned to Her and slams the door. Famine begins. A year goes by. People are dying. A diplomatic delegation is sent from Olympus. The delegation fails. Another diplomatic delegation is sent from Olympus. The delegation fails.

"My rage is implacable!" screams Demeter.

Hermes returns to Olympus and says, "Hey uh, Zeus ... yeah ... um ... Her rage is implacable. She is seriously going to kill them all."

Zeus folds and sends Hermes to go to Hades and bring Kore back. (Note the important role of Hermes, who is the psychopompe—the guide of souls to and from the Land of the Dead.)

Meanwhile in the Underworld, Hades realizes Kore will have to return to the Upperworld. He "tricks" Her into eating three pomegranate seeds, guaranteeing She will have to come back to Him.

Hermes brings Kore back to Eleusis where She is reunited with Her mother. Demeter asks Kore if she ate anything. Revealing the three seeds, Demeter tells Her daughter She will have to return to Hades for one third of each year. Demeter suddenly makes the Earth fruitful and ends the famine.

Demeter then says, "Now, eponymous ancestors of the priestly families, come and I shall teach you the awful Mysteries not to be transgressed, violated, or divulged, because the tongue is restrained by reverence for the Gods. Whoever on this Earth has seen—and note, I did say 'seen'—these is blessed, but he who has no part in the holy rites has another lot as he wastes away in dank darkness."

The Evidence

No one revealed the secrets of the Eleusinian Mysteries—an offense punishable by death. Here's what we do have. There are a bunch of references in ancient literature that talk around the Mysteries, making references and allusions. With thirty thousand people a year being initiated and Eleusis being close to Athens, when Athenian playwrights made references to the Eleusinian Mysteries, a significant portion of their audience were initiates.[244] The playwrights would not have put anything contradicting the Mysteries into their plays. In fact, there might well be references an initiate would understand with greater depth, while still skirting the potential execution-invoking revelations.

We have a host of what I call negative evidence in which we are reading between the lines—but the evidence does give us lines to read between. Similarly, we have art that would not have revealed the Eleusinian Mysteries but wouldn't depict incorrect information.

Perhaps most importantly, we have the sanctuary's archaeological remains. Melded with the *Homeric Hymn to Demeter*, this tells us a lot about the rite's sacred geography. In the archaeological evidence, we have inscriptions including laws and votives.[245]

The evidence from the Christian Fathers is so unreliable, I think it can be discarded. We know none were initiates and they have strongly polemical reasons for claiming to "reveal the secrets of the Mysteries."

---

244.   Kerenyi, *Eleusis*.
245.   Mylonas, *Eleusis and the Eleusinian Mysteries*.

Structure of the Cult

The basic structure of the cult itself gives two important pieces of information. First, the priesthoods are lineage based, which was uncommon. This indicates a mode of transfer of knowledge, skill, and possibly power down the generations. Secondly, initiation was widely available through society.

Priestly Families

The priests of the Eleusinian Mysteries came from two ancient families, the Eumolpids and the Kerykes, dating back to at least the early Bronze Age and possibly even into the late Neolithic.[246] This implies the archaic knowledge about how to initiate people as well as particular sacred contacts were passed along from the cult's founding.

The Hierophant and the Priestess of Demeter and Kore were the two highest-ranking positions and were members of the Eumolpid family. The tarot card bears little resemblance to the High Priest of the Mysteries. *Hierophant* means "the one who shows the holy things or makes them appear." This emphasis on "sight" as the dominant sense is important.

The second priestly family was the Kerykes. This family traced its lineage back to Hermes. The second-highest priest at Eleusis was the Daduchos. He carried the two torches that were symbols of the Eleusinian Mysteries and reference both Hekate and Hermes. The role of the Daduchos was as the guide who led the initiates through the ritual, like a psychopompe. His role is sometimes translated as "the herald." This priest bears the symbols of the two liminal deities. The Keryx, who made the announcements beginning the Mysteries, and the priest who conducted sacrifices were members of the Kerykes family.

A group of priestesses, Hierophantids, could be drawn from either family. Finally, any member of either family could serve as a *mystagogos*, which means "leader of the initiates." Each initiate needed a sponsor who taught and helped them prepare. Each *mystagogos* could sponsor numerous people a year.

Eligibility for Initiation

The Mysteries were open to adult men and women and were broadly available and inclusive. Initiation into the Mysteries was available to slaves and free

---

246. Mylonas, *Eleusis and the Eleusinian Mysteries*.

people and to Greeks and non-Greeks, so long as the non-Greeks understood the language. Initiation was closed to those who were guilty of capital crimes. All initiates had to go through a significant regimen of ritual purification.

The Lesser Mysteries

Preliminary and preparatory rites took place around February. The Lesser Mysteries would have included any content that needed to be "taught" to the candidates for initiation. The Lesser Mysteries were held at Agra, which is a suburb of Athens on the banks of the river Ilissos. Any Eumolpid or Kerykes could be a *mystagogos* and sponsor the would-be initiates in these preparatory rites.[247] Most rites in the Lesser Mysteries were about ritual purification. The initiates bathed in the Ilissos, which was quite cold that time of year.[248]

Mythologically, the Lesser Mysteries were created to allow Herakles to be initiated into the Eleusinian Mysteries. Those who committed capital crimes were not permitted to initiate. However, there were circumstances in which one may have killed but were still eligible. Killing another human always creates very intense *miasma*—spiritual pollution. Those who had this deeper form of pollution required special purification, including those who had killed in war, by accident, when they were not in a mental state of culpability (as when Herakles killed His family in a state of madness), or in a justifiable homicide. Whatever the cause, taking human life requires intense purification.

In the Lesser Mysteries, those who had deep spiritual pollution went through a special rite in which the Daduchos slaughtered a white ram. The fleece was placed on a low stool, like the chair brought to Demeter in the myth. A cloth was hung over their head, causing some sensory deprivation and creating an opportunity for a shift in consciousness. A priestess stood behind the penitent and held a winnowing basket or fan over the initiate's head. This is an implement used to separate grain from chaff. It is possible, but not clear, that the priestess sprinkles barley over the initiate's head that is then gathered and burned. This parallels a ritual action performed to consecrate animal sacrifices.[249]

---

247.   Kerenyi, *Eleusis*.

248.   Mylonas, *Eleusis and the Eleusinian Mysteries*.

249.   Mylonas, *Eleusis and the Eleusinian Mysteries*.

The Greater Mysteries

The Greater Mysteries were held in September. Before the beginning of the Mysteries, a priestly delegation from Eleusis brought the *hiera*, the sacred objects, to Athens, where they stayed in a temple called the City Eleusinion, located at the northern base of the Acropolis. The Temple of Hekate holds the boundary between the Eleusinion and the Agora.[250]

On the first day, the Hierokeryx announced the celebration of the Mysteries, available to anyone free from *miasma* and who understood Greek. The aspiring initiates were inspected for fitness and then entered the Eleusinion after washing their hands. Presumably they were given instruction preparing them for the initiatory process. They would have been psychologically preparing themselves for the past seven months.[251]

Day number two: "To the sea, oh *mystai!*" *Mystai* means "initiates" and this was the ritualized "cry" as they went down to the sea. This was a day of intense purification. The sea is immaculate and deeply cleansing on all levels of being. Not only did the initiates bathe in the sea, but each had a piglet for an expiatory piglet sacrifice. Each took their piglet into the sea with them and then personally sacrificed it.[252] Anything that could be infecting a person would be absorbed by the piglet and destroyed on the fire with it.

The third day included sacrifices, but these were not expiatory. The general demeanor was solemn.

Day four was the Epidauria. Mythologically, when Asklepios was still a mortal physician living in Epidauros, He was coming to be initiated at Eleusis but was late. The Epidauria repeats the purification rituals. This indicates the essential importance of this ritual purification to undergoing initiation.[253]

Day five is Pompe Day! This was the day of a fabulous procession going for fourteen miles to Eleusis. All the initiates gathered in the Keramikos and walked "The Sacred Way" connecting Athens to Eleusis. A figure of the god Iacchos was at the procession's front. He embodied the Eleusinian cry of enthusiasm, which is, "Iacchos, Iacchos, Iacchos!" Iacchos looks like the Daduchos, herald of the *mystai*. During the procession, the initiates carried branches of myrtle

---

250.   Mylonas, *Eleusis and the Eleusinian Mysteries.*

251.   Mylonas, *Eleusis and the Eleusinian Mysteries.*

252.   Mylonas, *Eleusis and the Eleusinian Mysteries.*

253.   Mylonas, *Eleusis and the Eleusinian Mysteries.*

that had strands of wool and wore wreaths of myrtle. Myrtle is an important funerary plant. The priestesses carried the *hiera*, those unknown sacred items, in special baskets on their heads. Whatever the *hiera* are, they had to fit in those baskets and be light enough for women to carry for fourteen miles. The initiates were now fasting. It is not clear how complete their fasting was—we don't know if they drank water. However, they were fasting and walking fourteen miles. They arrived by torchlight at night.[254]

Days six and seven were the core of the Mysteries. The initiates were still fasting. We know there were dances at the Kallichoron Well, which literally means "the Well of Beautiful Dances." The *telete*, which is the actual initiation, happened at night in the sanctuary's inner part. At some point, the initiates drank the *kykeon*.[255]

The eighth day was called the Plemochoai, which are libations for the dead. It is named for a particular vessel used in these libations. Each initiate placed one vessel in the east and one in the west and then turned them over. There was feasting and celebrating. On the ninth day, the initiates dispersed.[256]

The Core of the Eleusinian Mysteries

The core of the Mysteries is called the *telete*. We know it was not about agriculture, but about death and dying. The fundamental claim of the Mysteries was that it altered the fate of the initiates after death, freeing them from the fear of death.

Sacred Geography

During the rite, the initiates were moving through sacred geography. At Eleusis, there were three places recognized as entrances to the Underworld. There is the Ploutonian Cave, which you encountered earlier. The Kallichoron Well, the Well of Beautiful Dances, was supposed to be an entrance to Hades and is really close to the Ploutonian Cave. Finally, out on the Rharian plain near the banks of the Kephisos under a fig tree, there was a third place considered to be a portal into Hades.

---

254. Mylonas, *Eleusis and the Eleusinian Mysteries*.
255. Mylonas, *Eleusis and the Eleusinian Mysteries*.
256. Mylonas, *Eleusis and the Eleusinian Mysteries*.

Right between the Kallichoron Well and the cave is the Agelastos Petra, the mirthless stone, where Demeter sank down weeping. There are other stories about it related to journeys to the Underworld. When Theseus decided he was going to Hades on an ill-advised and ill-fated scheme, part of his preparation for going to the Underworld with the intention of returning was sitting on the Agelastos Petra.[257] It is in the initiatory sanctuary.

Finally, there is the Anaktaron—the holiest of holies. It is a small building, the oldest version dating back to Mycenaean times. It stayed in the same place, even as the temple, later called the Telesterion, was built around it to accommodate more people. The Anaktaron is where Demeter physically lived for a time. It is imbued with Her power. At the initiation's height, the initiates were inside the Telesterion and the Hierophant's chair was right beside the Anaktaron's door.[258] We know there was a great sacred fire in the Telesterion, likely in the Anaktaron itself. The Hierophant's chair had a thick stone covering and roof—probably to protect him from the heat. The roof had an opening and there were tales of the sacred fire being seen from a distance on the day of the *telete*.[259]

The initiates were moving through this sacred landscape during the initiation, led by the Daduchos. The Divine Presence was immediate and visceral.

The Condition of Initiates

The initiates had been fasting and had walked fourteen miles. They were probably kept awake and were sleep deprived. All of this can lead to altered states of consciousness. During the *telete* they experienced some sensory deprivation. There is debate about whether they were blindfolded, but the rites were certainly at night with minimal light. While the Daduchos carried torches, which are a symbol of the Mysteries, he may have been the only one.

At some point in the rite, the initiates drank the *kykeon*. There were special vessels for the *kykeon* portions, indicating a controlled dosage.[260] The barley water mixed with pennyroyal was carried from Athens and would have fermented. The active ingredient of pennyroyal, an abortifacient, is soluble in alcohol. This would have packed quite a punch for people who were already

257.   Kerenyi, *Eleusis*.

258.   Mylonas, *Eleusis and the Eleusinian Mysteries*.

259.   Kerenyi, *Eleusis*.

260.   Kerenyi, *Eleusis*.

in a physically weakened state. I originally thought it might actually induce a full near-death experience. While possible, I now suspect that theory is too extreme, but it would definitely have a powerful effect.

Ancient Comments

There is an ancient formula saying the Mysteries consisted of three things: things done or enacted, things shown or made to appear, and things spoken.[261] Aristotle says the Mysteries do not strictly impart knowledge, but rather cause an experience in the soul.[262] The poet Pindar says the initiate "knows" death.[263] As we saw earlier, Plutarch discusses a movement from terror into joy and wonder.[264]

Things Done

Ritual dances were important. The Kallichoron well's name indicates ritual dancing. We know Diagoras of Melos was prosecuted for "dancing out" the Mysteries outside its ritual context.[265] Ritual dancing might have moved people into a deeper altered state. Another possibility is the initiates, in moving through the sacred landscape, participated in a drama surrounding the abduction of Persephone and Her mother's search.[266]

Things Beheld

The core of the Mysteries involved beholding or seeing. Even in the Hymn, Demeter says those who have "seen" these rites will be blessed. We know there were sacred objects only the Hierophant (and possibly the priestesses) could handle. We know they were small enough to be put into special baskets that could be carried for long distances on the heads of the priestesses. Whatever these items were, they were unspeakably ancient and were probably considered to have been directly given by the Goddess.[267]

In addition to the *hiera*, the testimony about the Mysteries makes clear there was *phasmata*—the appearance of spirit beings—associated with them.

---

261. Mylonas, *Eleusis and the Eleusinian Mysteries.*
262. Burkert, *Ancient Mystery Cults.*
263. Mylonas, *Eleusis and the Eleusinian Mysteries.*
264. Plutarch, *Moralia.*
265. Kerenyi, *Eleusis.*
266. Petridou, "'Blessed Is He, Who Has Seen,'" 309–41.
267. Mylonas, *Eleusis and the Eleusinian Mysteries.*

It is likely that the height of the Mysteries involved an epiphany of Kore. In a second century CE papyrus, Herakles says to "Lock up Eleusis and the sacred fire."[268] He has no need of initiation because He already beheld Kore. There is a similar reference in Euripides. A great gong, like those used in the theater to portray thunder, may have been in the Telesterion. The sound of this gong was jarring. At an important moment in "Oedipus at Kolonos," which includes Eleusinian allusions, a great gong is rung and Persephone appears from the underworld, only seen by Oedipus, at the moment of his *apotheosis*.[269]

Fire is important. Herakles specifically mentions the Sacred Fire when saying He had already seen Persephone, which may indicate an epiphany comes from interacting with the Sacred Fire.[270] Demeter placed the infant, Demophoon, into the fire to burn the mortality out of him and would have made him a god. There is another interesting bit of testimony about the Brahman Zarmaros. Zarmaros came from India to be initiated into the Eleusinian Mysteries. At the end of the Mysteries when asked what he thought, he basically said something to the effect of, "You think that is a big deal, watch this," and self-immolated.[271] This story was told by Greeks so it has a Greek perspective, but what it reveals about the Mysteries is the Hellenic understanding of this Indian custom. In the Greek understanding of Hindu culture, self-immolation was a way to immediately become a god through fire. This story conveys that the Eleusinian Mysteries were doing something with a similar end through less drastic means, but not as effectively or efficiently as self-immolation. Proclus, the last major Pagan philosopher writing after the sanctuary of Eleusis had been destroyed, said he believed the result of the Mysteries was that they could make you like a god.[272] Plato in both the *Symposium* and the *Phaedrus* used Eleusinian language comparing the philosopher who glimpsed the Forms as similar to an initiate of the Mysteries.

---

268.   Ensdiø, "To Lock Up Eleusis."

269.   Sophocles, "Oedipus at Colonus," 77–155.

270.   Ensdiø, "To Lock Up Eleusis."

271.   Kerenyi, *Eleusis*.

272.   Van den Berg, "'Becoming Like God' According to Proclus' Interpretation of the Timaeus," 189–202.

Hekate and the Empousa

We know Hekate is important to the Mysteries. She is mentioned in the Hymn and is often understood as helping Persephone. She is frequently depicted with two torches, the symbol of the Mysteries carried by the Daduchos. Her temple is at the City Eleusinion's edge.

Hekate is the goddess of all things liminal—the in-between spaces, like doorways and crossroads and all in-between states of being. Death isn't a liminal state. The process of dying is liminal.

In ancient Hellenic religion, Hekate is always a beautiful maiden. However, a class of beings called *empousai* are in Her retinue. An *empousa* is a frightening shape-shifting female being. In *Frogs*, Aristophanes makes numerous references to the Eleusinian Mysteries. Dionysus and his slave Xanthias are journeying to the Underworld. Early in their journey, they are confronted by an *empousa*, who may have been Hekate Herself. The encounter severely rattles Dionysus.[273]

This scene is reminiscent of the journey to the underworld in the *Aneid*.[274] In the early part of the journey, Aeneas is confronted by a group of terrifying female spirits and draws his sword. There is a lost poem about Herakles's journey to the Underworld in which He is confronted early in the voyage by a gorgon. Hermes restrains Herakles from attacking.[275] In all these instances there is, early in the journey to the Underworld, a confrontation with a frightening female figure, and the correct response is to refrain from attacking and control your fear. This seems important.

Near–Death Experiences

Near-death experiences (NDE) are one of the handful of extraordinary spiritual experiences (ESE) that appear across cultures and have a fairly standard phenomenological description.[276] These experiences occur even when the culture has no framework providing expectations or meaning for the experiences. The extraordinary spiritual experiences include near-death experience, out-of-body experience, visitation from the dead, past-life memories, being "hag ridden"

---

273.   Brown, "Dionysus and the Mysteries," 41–50.

274.   Virgil, *Aneid*.

275.   Brown, "Dionysus and the Mysteries," 41–50.

276.   Hufford, "Healing Power of Extraordinary Spiritual Experiences," 137–56.

(experience of a malevolent presence coupled with sleep paralysis), and the unitive mystical experience.

The common components of a near-death experience include a loud or upsetting noise, often on the way out of the body; entering the darkness; spiritual contacts (ancestors, deities, etc.); seeing the light; and entering the light.[277] I think the Eleusinian Mysteries may have given people some framework and practice about how to navigate these situations. Certain pieces of what we know about the Mysteries map well onto this framework. Initiates begin in the dark and they move into the light of the Sacred Fire of Eleusis at the end. There is good reason to suspect a jarring gong was used. Reading Plutarch, I think it is possible the initiates would have been confronted by frightening *phasmata*, like the *empousa,* and would encounter another *phasmata* that was the epiphany of Persephone. This experience with Persephone would mark them in a specific way.[278] When dying, their prior experiences with the Mysteries would function as training so they would know what to do and not be afraid. Something in their subtle physiology was probably changed in a way that assisted them in death.

Prepare for Dying

When we look at near-death experiences and the information we have from sources like the *Tibetan Book of the Dead*, some aspects of the dying process are common and some are malleable. For example, divine contacts are there, but who shows up seems to be culturally specific. In our culture, we expect and experience ancestors. In Hindu culture, they see Hindu deities. Christians often see Jesus. Hindus don't see Jesus and Christians don't see Durga. Our prior relationships may determine who shows up for us when we die and whether we have certain kinds of intercession. I think it is likely initiation left a "sign" on the immortal part of the initiate, meaning they would experience a different path based on divine intercession. In order to rebirth this kind of practice, rebuilding the divine relationships is essential.

Another lesson from our sources is our emotional state when we are going through the death process is supremely important. Confusion is a real risk. The sooner we realize we are dead, the better, because there are a lot of choices

---

277.   Blackmore, *Dying to Live.*

278.   Ustinova, *Caves and the Ancient Greek Mind.*

that come quickly. So, preparation in the stages of dying and becoming familiar with them is important, as is not being afraid.

I suspect the upsetting noise attested to in the literature has to do with getting outside your body on the level of the etheric (sticky) body because I, personally, have experienced it in an out-of-body experience. It seems as though the key to dealing with it is to know what is happening and not to be afraid.

The general lesson seems to be, if you hear something scary, don't panic. If you see something scary, like an *empousa* or the wrathful deities in the *Tibetan Book of the Dead*—don't panic. They are part of the process. You say with confidence you are an initiate and don't react to them. The faster you realize you are dead, the better. There are choices. Ask for help and say you are an initiate. Say you want to maintain your memories. Don't be afraid. You are a child of Earth and starry Heaven, but your race is of Heaven alone.

I am hopeful we can find a way to rebirth something that serves the same purpose as the Mysteries—namely, effective death training coupled with building strong relationships with compassionate beings who will help us maintain continuity of consciousness across death and rebirth. This is a worthy initiative.

Exercise
SOME INITIAL STEPS IN REBIRTHING THE MYSTERIES

Rebirthing the Mysteries will require the Theoi to help us do so, but there are some initial steps we can take.

1. Strive to build relationships with the Great Ones associated with the Mysteries with the intention of rebirthing them. The main deities are Demeter, Persephone, Hades, and Dionysus.

2. Develop, share, and use intensive purification rituals. I have shared a substitute for the piglet expiatory sacrifice. Developing a purification rite for those who have killed, such as what is found in the Lesser Mysteries, would be a powerful contribution. Working on deep purification indicates serious intention to the Great Ones.

3. Undertaking intensive study of NDEs and manuals like the *Tibetan Book of the Dead*, as well as what we know about the Mysteries, while praying to the Great Ones of the Mysteries and asking for guidance.

4. The Mysteries were a complex of rites that happened over days and included advanced training. Hold that scheme in mind and consider ways to think about constituent parts, like levels of training, purification rites, rites to strengthen the relationship with the Great Ones of the Mysteries prior to the initiation itself, ways to give thanks, and so on. A contribution of any piece is worthy.

5. Experiment with developing rituals following the pattern of the dying experience while receiving guidance from the Great Ones. In the rites, using some imagery from the ancient cults will help. Use omens and other methods to verify you are understanding the guidance correctly.

6. Build a community of others who are trying to do this rebirthing so we can share our progress, experiments, and findings.

A Final Thought

I got the following insight while communing with Apollon. When the great heroes go off to the Underworld to accomplish a quest, Persephone is always there. They never show up and then find it is one of Her "Olympus" months. Persephone is always in the Underworld. She is also always on Olympus. But She is also sometimes here. Like us. And if we can live in that realization—that we, too, are always in Hades and we are always on Olympus and we are sometimes here—then we will have transcended our mortality.

CHAPTER THIRTEEN

HEROES, THE HEROIC PATH, AND *APOTHEOSIS*

Ancient Greece was a land full of heroes. Heroes are important to modern practitioners for two reasons. First, heroes are intercessory. They can be called upon to aid us if we build relationships with them. Second, hero lore and cult give us knowledge about how to walk a heroic path and hold open to us the possibility of *apotheosis,* which is the process of becoming one of the Theoi.

What Is a Hero?

Hero is a Greek word referring to a deceased person who exhibited some excellence (*areté*) to the edge of human capacity, was of benefit to the world beyond their near and dear during life and continues to be of benefit in this way after death. No one is appropriately called a hero while alive.[279] This is quite different from how we colloquially use "hero" in English. Throughout this chapter, I am using the Hellenic understanding.

Being a hero does not imply perfection. In fact, heroes often have deep personal flaws.[280] However, in some important domain, they were evolved to the limit of human capacity. There were many heroes in ancient Greece. Moral perfection is not a prerequisite for being a hero.

---

279. Nagy, *Ancient Greek Hero in 24 Hours.*
280. Nagy, *Ancient Greek Hero in 24 Hours.*

Being a "saint" indicates a type of moral or spiritual development up to the edge of human capacity. All saints are heroes, but not all heroes are saints. Becoming a hero is not an impossible aspiration.

In addition to having achieved excellence in some domain, the hero was concerned with and of benefit to the broader community—not just intimates. There is a broader focus of attention and care than experienced by "normal" people. This scope is possible for most of us. If we focus our development on an area of excellence and use that emerging excellence to care for those beyond our near and dear, then we are beginning to walk a heroic path. After death, heroes continue being intercessory beyond functioning as personal ancestors— either sharing their particular excellence with living humans regardless of blood connection, or as protectors of all inhabitants of particular places.[281] In Modern Pagan parlance, a hero is one of the Mighty Dead. In some cases, a hero goes on to become a god through *apotheosis*.

HERO CULTS

To be effectively intercessory, heroes need to be "fed." Ancient hero cults had sacred places—often including the hero's corpse as a link—in which regular rites were performed to keep the relationship with the hero open and the hero's intercessory powers strong.[282] A typical hero cult included a garden around a grave.[283] Libations and sacrifices were regularly offered. Often these were poured into a pit—a *bothros*.[284] Usually there were specific festivals for the hero. It was common to pray and make offerings when calling upon the hero for help.

All this activity kept the relationship with the hero harmonious and strong. It enabled them to act. From the perspective of contemporary occult philosophy, human beings build the bridges of power, enabling those who do not normally reside in our physical reality to act locally here. Our energy and attention build that bridge. In ancient practice, when a person who led a heroic life died, the people watched for omens or consulted an oracle to determine if

---

281.   Nagy, *Ancient Greek Hero in 24 Hours*.

282.   Rice and Stambaugh, *Sources for the Study of Greek Religion*.

283.   Nagy, *Ancient Greek Hero in 24 Hours*.

284.   Nagy, *Ancient Greek Hero in 24 Hours*.

the deceased could be the object of a hero cult.[285] If the answer was yes, then heroic rites were created to feed the new hero, enabling them to remain in relationship with the living and strengthening their power to help.

From the perspective of contemporary practitioners, while there are a few especially big ancient heroes who continue to have some power, most would need to be fed regularly in order to function again in an intercessory manner. However, human beings did not cease living heroic lives. There are some ancient beings who can be fruitfully worked with and rebuilding the connection is worthwhile; however, there are contemporary heroes who may be more appropriate intercessors for our lives, if we can strengthen their connection and power to act. Often the "founder"—*archegetes* in Greek—is a potential heroic figure. Remember, a hero is not necessarily a saint. We call on them for a particular reason.

In the United States, our best bet for a national hero is our *archegetes*, George Washington. George Washington—a slaveholder—is far from perfect. His true excellence was that his practical wisdom and commitment to democracy allowed him to walk away from extraordinary power in a time when there was no model for his behavior. He could have been king. He chose to be a regular citizen.

George Washington might be the first modern hero and may have relevance beyond the United States. The great heroic challenge from the beginning of modernity through now is not the accumulation of power—it is self-restraint in relation to power through the use of wisdom. We are constantly confronted by circumstances in which we have the power to do things that may serve our immediate self-interest or might even appear as though they will bring great good, but which we ought not to do. When we observe so many of our desperate contemporary struggles—the climate crisis, artificial intelligence and data ethics, germ line genetic editing, many of our political and economic situations—the great heroic challenge is to restrain the unfettered use of our power.

The ancient hero cults left us clues about how to strengthen the capacity for intercession of ancestors who meet the Hellenic definition of a hero—those in life who achieved excellence in some arena at the level of human capacity,

---

285. Edmunds, "Religiosity of Alexander," 363–91.

who were beneficent beyond their near and dear, and for whom we have indications they are willing to be intercessory in this way now that they are dead.

If you or your community wanted to begin working with a being you believe might qualify as a hero in this sense, first consult omens and oracles to see if the being is willing to serve and to sharpen your understanding of the hero's agenda. Relics are useful, but not necessary. Using images or icons of the hero and regularly making offerings, prayers, and other forms of attention is critical. If you are striving to create a more permanent relationship as a collective with one of the Mighty Dead, choosing festival dates in which the hero is the center of attention is useful.

Heroes, being former mortals, require more "feeding" than the Theoi in order to remain in relationship with living humans. If any are going to truly function at the level of a hero for long, it will require a group. For this reason, I suggest tapping into heroes who are already recognized by the culture in which you are embedded. Create some structure around events and activities that already exist, focusing them to actually feed the hero. Then build a practice of calling on them to commune and ask for assistance.

Later in this chapter, I share information on various Hellenic heroes that serve as models of various types and are amenable to working with contemporary practitioners. We should look within our current context as well.

Exercise
Establishing a Relationship with a Hero
This working will help you build a relationship with a being who is intercessory.

What You'll Need
Research resources and offerings.

Directions
This is a project that will take some time and effort. Give yourself at least a month.

Step 1: Choose the hero to build a relationship with. Think of someone from the last several hundred years who has qualities you deeply admire and meets the following three criteria:

- Exhibited some excellence up to the level of human capacity that is also relevant to your agenda.
- Lived in such a way to be of benefit to more than their near and dear.
- Is dead.

Step 2: Learn as much as you can, reading biographies and so on, and take time "speaking" to the being, letting them know you want to be in relationship with them.

Step 3: Watch for omens and use provoked omens to assess willingness.

Step 4: Begin making offerings while always checking with omens or provoked omens. Experiment with what is better received than others. You may want to get some iconography that evokes the being.

Step 5: Identify a date from the biography that seems to be a "special" date and make it a festival. It can be a birthday, death date, or the date of some particularly significant accomplishment. Throw a party for the being. Invite friends and say it is in the being's honor and tell stories.

Step 6: As you understand the hero's agenda, do things to honor them and begin calling on them as an intercessor. Give thanks when you see intercessory behavior.

Step 7: If it seems the hero is responsive and wants to be in relationship with us, if you have like-minded others, share what you are doing.

HEROIC CHARACTERISTICS IN ANCIENT GREECE

You have to die to become a hero. While living, a hero is "unseasonal."[286] The ancient Greek words for "conclusion," "ultimate purpose," "perfection," "death," and "initiate of the Mysteries" are all closely related. Hera is the goddess of the natural cycles of time, but a hero is only "on time" in death. Therefore, there is frequent antagonism between Hera and heroes, even though the very word *hero* is related to Her. As a contemporary practitioner on an initiatory path, my understanding of initiation is that it accelerates the natural processes of spiritual evolution and, therefore, is "unnatural." This acceleration is part of the heroic path. Those walking a heroic path are out of sync with their culture. There is always ambivalence about heroes, even when they are lauded as great benefactors.

---

286.   Nagy, *Ancient Greek Hero in 24 Hours.*

One way heroes don't fit their culture is that they are extreme.[287] In myth, heroes are extreme in their good and their bad. Their concerns reflect a larger and more abstract scope than "normal" human cares, meaning they are concerned with issues beyond those affecting themselves and their near and dear. Heroes, being at the limit of human capacity in some domain, have more power than a "normal" person. Any increase in power comes with greater potential to cause harm as well as benefit to others.

A frequent pattern in heroic myth is related to the harm caused by a hero, the tragedy coming from that harm, and the necessity of purifying the *miasma* resulting from the harm.[288] As a reminder, *miasma* is spiritual pollution coming from being out of right relationship. Clearing *miasma* always requires intentional intervention to cleanse it so healing can commence. *Miasma* can be caused either by *hamartia* or by *hubris*. *Hamartia* is the "tragic mistake." Human beings, including heroes, are not omniscient. Our knowledge is limited, but we have to rely on what knowledge we have and our intentions to guide our decisions and actions. The tragedy of the human condition is that this means there are times in which, with the best of intentions, we cause harm, resulting in *miasma*. Heroes, operating with more power and a bigger scope, can cause even greater harm. The other cause of *miasma* is *hubris*, which is corruption of character through the lack of virtue. This is more "blameworthy," but with work, character can be improved. Purifying *miasma* so healing can take place is important heroic work and is often the motivation for heroic deeds, like the Labors of Herakles, which were undertaken to purify the *miasma* from killing His family.[289] The purified hero can bring purification of *miasma* to the community through the rites of a hero cult.[290]

Areté and the Hero

As a reminder, *areté* is a Greek word meaning both "excellence" and "virtue." Such virtues include what we typically think of as the moral virtues, as well as other forms of excellence. A hero has developed at least one area of excellence to the limit of human capacity. *Areté* is not innate; it can be developed. Personal

---

287.   Nagy, *Ancient Greek Hero in 24 Hours.*

288.   Nagy, *Ancient Greek Hero in 24 Hours.*

289.   Stafford, *Herakles.*

290.   Nagy, *Ancient Greek Hero in 24 Hours.*

character is constituted from the virtues we have developed and those that are underdeveloped. Excellence is not a "fixed" quality one has or lacks. Aristotle's *Nicomachaean Ethics* is a profound text providing a method for systematically developing the virtues and will be covered in more depth in chapter 14.[291] For the purposes of leading a heroic life, it is important to understand that excellence is developed through intentional cultivation. This requires creating habits supporting the excellence and developing friendships that encourage and inspire the quest for excellence. Developing the excellence of a particular domain up to the level of human capacity requires choosing a focus and including practices to cultivate the moral virtues that are most important for that domain.

The foundational moral virtues include those listed below.

- Moderation: Right relationship to pleasure.
- Courage: Right relationship to fear.
- Sincerity (Confidence): Right relationship to recognizing one's own merit.
- Gentleness: Right relationship to anger.
- Generosity: Right relationship to resources.

Some intellectual excellences follow.

- Prudence: The moral virtues tell you the goal, but practical wisdom tells you how to achieve it.
- Temperance: When your mind tells you something is bad, you can resist it.
- Philia: The love that is friendship, which is both the medium for development of virtues and a virtue itself.
- Contemplation: Any activity in which we are engaged in deep, reflective thought.

The specialization in which you are striving to develop excellence will require special emphasis on some of the moral and intellectual virtues. For example, if striving to develop excellence as a Warrior or Protector, excellence

---

291.   Aristotle, *Nicomachaean Ethics*.

in courage and gentleness are essential. If one is on a quest to become an excellent visionary, truthfulness and confidence are essential.

Divine Antagonism

In myth and cult, heroes face antagonism by at least one of the Theoi—typically by the god the hero most closely resembles. The *agon*, which is a contest or a struggle, is central to the Greek idea of accelerated growth and is where we get the words *protagonist* and *antagonist* to describe the struggle's two sides.[292] In the worthy struggle, having the right type of antagonist forces the protagonist to stretch their limits. Functionally, the divine antagonist acts as an initiator—driving the hero through ordeals and challenges to become more and more like the God. The hero functionally mediates the God's power into the world. Sometimes the God acts in the role of a mentor. Frequently the hero has a type of attraction to the God who is instrumental in their death—but it is important to recall, the would-be hero only truly becomes a hero in the moment of death. Having developed some capacity in life to the point where no more improvement is possible in human form, in death the hero becomes something greater than human. Some examples of this pattern are Herakles, whose very name means "the Glory of Hera"; Achilles and Apollon; and Odysseus's relationship to both Poseidon and Athena.

Initiation through Combat

Heroic initiation through combat is historically the most common way in which people became heroes, but the way in which warfare worked in ancient Greece is so radically different than modern warfare that it needs some context. Additionally, there may be ways to work with Ares in a contemporary fashion that don't require violence.

The mode of initiation for Ares is the warrior's mortal combat and the "excellence" achieved is in transcending your mortal instincts. In order for the combat to count toward developing *areté* allowing the warrior to become something more than human, there are a number of prerequisites. First, the combatants must participate by choice. If any party is participating against their will, then the combat cannot function in this sacred way. Second, the foes must be roughly evenly matched. The antagonists must be able to push each

---

292.   Nagy, *Ancient Greek Hero in 24 Hours.*

other past their current limits. This cannot work if they are not evenly matched in all ways, including their weaponry. Asymmetry disrupts the pattern. The combat must be intimate. The combatants must be fully, immediately present to each other. They cannot be shooting at each other from a distance, for example. During the combat, they must have full and present consciousness about the fact they are hazarding their mortal lives, and they must face death in such a way that overcomes every mortal instinct of self-preservation. To die heroically in battle, they must be fully stabilized in and identified with the immortal aspect of their being at the moment of death. In this way, Ares, historically, is the great initiator.

Modern warfare, with its emphasis on technology, asymmetry, fighting at a distance, and frequently including compulsion to participate is unrecognizable from this perspective. There is no glory for Ares in it. Romanticized versions that emphasize the role of a warrior as protecting something precious is also, frankly, insufficient for it to be part of the Glory of Ares. For Ares, this initiation is about the contest between warriors striving to overcome mortal instinct.

Ares does not require violence so much as practices allowing us to face death in ways that overcome the mortal instincts for self-preservation by identifying with and being stabilized in the part of us that is immortal at the moment of our death. We can develop profitable new ways of working with Ares, who has "initiated" more heroes than any other.

Beneficence

Humans are social creatures and it is completely natural for us to work for the benefit of others with whom we are in close relationships. It is also natural for us to benefit those we think of as similar to us in some way. A hero has a broader scope of concern. The deeds of the hero expressing their *areté* benefit a broad community and express a motivation—assumed in heroic cult—that the individual desires to be of benefit after death to those with whom they had no personal connection in life.[293]

If striving to live heroically, we should cultivate our sense of purpose and our motivation to be of benefit. Choosing a motto or developing personal statements of purpose that can be regularly repeated helps build our motivation and

---

293. Nagy, *Ancient Greek Hero in 24 Hours.*

strengthen our beneficence. Similarly, we can intentionally develop big-picture perspectives to complement our intimate perspectives, especially when engaging in self-reflection.

Apotheosis

Apotheosis means "to become a god." There are numerous instances in which a hero became one of the Theoi.[294] In all the examples of which I am aware, the additional ingredient is what we might call "grace." One of the Great Ones who has intimate love for the hero intervenes directly on the hero's behalf.

An example is the hero Herakles. In the iconography and stories, Herakles is accompanied by Athena in His labors. There are many instances in art in which Herakles and Athena are shown as companions, often relaxing together.[295] The iconography of the *apotheosis* of Herakles depicts His ascendance as a wedding—with Herakles in the role of bride. Athena is shown driving the chariot to Olympus with Herakles as Her passenger. Sometimes She is shown gripping Herakles by the wrist and taking Him before the throne of Zeus. These are both part of the wedding ceremony of taking the bride from her father's house to the groom's household.[296]

A more traditionally gendered approach is when Dionysus causes Ariadne to "fall asleep"—a sleep from which She never awakens in mortal form. He takes Her as His bride and makes Her one of the Theoi. In this case, Ariadne's excellence is in the perfection of Her love—originally given to Theseus and then to Dionysus.[297] Ganymede was taken by Zeus in a similar fashion and made the cupbearer of Olympus.[298]

Dionysus and Asklepios are interesting cases because both were born mortal but became prominent gods. The myth of Dionysus, son of Zeus and Semele, includes a gruesome death and then rebirth as one of the Theoi. Asklepios, mortal son of Apollon and Koronis, perfected healing to the point

---

294. Petrovic, "Deification—Gods or Men?"

295. Deacy, "Herakles and His 'Girl,'" 37–50.

296. Cameron, "Athena and Herakles a Divine Couple."

297. Otto, "Ariadne," 181–88.

298. Kinsey, ed., *Heroes and Heroines of Greece and Rome*.

where he could raise the dead. He was killed by Zeus but was then turned into one of the Theoi.[299]

From the perspective of a contemporary practitioner, this indicates that mortals have the capacity to become something else, and there is a role for the pursuit of excellence and a role for the grace of the Theoi. It also clearly indicates that the Theoi can and do build very personal relationships with some humans.

The Metaphor of Apprenticeship

One type of relationship a hero can have with the Theoi is akin to an apprenticeship. The heroic myths and cults show us that the divine "antagonist" of a hero is the one who is most like the hero, and the hero is learning to master certain forms of excellence related to the God's domains. That hero is learning to be like the God while doing Their work in the world. The aim, ultimately, is to be able to do this beyond death and possibly become one of the Theoi, often then joining the "retinue" of a particular Great One.

An apprenticeship is a mutual relationship, predicated upon an understanding that the apprentice is learning how to gain full expertise in a domain through direct work under the master craftsperson's supervision. An apprentice learns through doing, but the work is scaffolded. The master also takes some measure of responsibility for the apprentice's care. The mutual goal is that the apprentice will eventually become the master's peer.

This is the type of relationship at least some Great Ones want to have with us and it is how I understand my own relationship with Apollon. Of course, it is not something we can demand. An apprenticeship is a model of mutuality and there is a whole host of responsibilities coming with it on both sides—and these responsibilities can be felt as limitations. For example, there are certain types of "warrior" work I cannot do—not because they are inherently bad, but because they are incompatible with my apprenticeship with Apollon.

I think this is a path that may be open to more of us than we realize. Even if you are using the idea of apprenticeship as a metaphor rather than building that actual type of relationship with one of the Theoi, asking yourself whether any of the Great Ones are models of what you would like to be and then

---

299. Stafford, *Herakles*.

approaching your development as though you are an apprentice would help provide structure for growth.

LIVING LIFE AS A HEROIC SONG

Ancient Greek culture is song culture, and in song culture the song itself is a type of reality.[300] There are elements common in hero song that give guidance to those striving to live a heroic life—but choosing to live your life as a heroic song is, in itself, a powerful practice. The truth revealed in this approach is that human beings do not live their lives exclusively within the flow of linear time. We construct our sense of ourselves and the life we are living through the creative act of stories we tell ourselves about who and what we are, the world we are living in, and our place in it. This is not solipsism where an individual creates their world fully free from external reality, but it does call into focus the incredible power we have to shape our individual and collective reality based on the creative act of storytelling. Whenever we pay attention to a moment, let others slip from memory, make connections, and construct meaning—which most of us do unconsciously and without intention all the time—we are creating ourselves and our lives. I invite everyone to intentionally live their life as a heroic song. Claim your power and be your own bard.

Sacred Journey

A frequent theme in heroic song is the *theoria*, which is a sacred journey. Joseph Campbell's masterpiece, *Hero with a Thousand Faces,* is particularly focused on the hero's journey and is worth reading.[301] A *theoria* is a quest and it is a pilgrimage to the sacred. In song culture, the time of the song itself is more real than our regular experience of time because a song is taking us into immortal time. So, the hero, in going on a *theoria*—a sacred journey—is stepping into time that is more real than natural time.[302] This practice includes experiencing your life as a sacred journey. This can take many forms beyond what we often think of as heroic. Socrates described his life's work of philosophizing as a *theoria*.[303] That is how he understood his life—as a sacred journey seeking Truth.

300.   Nagy, *Ancient Greek Hero in 24 Hours.*

301.   Campbell, *Hero with a Thousand Faces.*

302.   Nagy, *Ancient Greek Hero in 24 Hours.*

303.   Plato, "Apology."

After his death, he was revered as an intercessory hero for those who commit their lives to loving wisdom.

Many religions have the idea of pilgrimage as a form of sacred journeying. When I visit Greece, I undertake my journey as a pilgrimage. In shifting my perception, my expectations, and the way in which I engage with the entire process to make the experience a sacred journey, I have types of experiences that are radically different from experiences of normal life. However, one does not have to go to a distant location; it is largely a matter of perspective in which you intentionally shift into a sacred mind frame and focus on your very life being a journey. The processes of your life touch the sacred, and you reflect on your personal story and sing yourself the heroic song of who and what you are.

Into the Eschatia

During a *theoria*, the hero goes into the *eschatia*—the furthermost reaches. Outside the boundaries of the *polis*—outside human society—there are heroes and monsters. The main difference between them is whether they are motivated to be of benefit to others. In stepping into the *eschatia*—in whatever form that may take—the would-be hero goes outside the norms of their society.[304] A hero unmakes the compulsive parts of their socialization and then chooses what to take back on. To use a contemporary esoteric interpretation, when a hero is in the *eschatia*, they have the ability to move between various levels of consciousness and operate at will in different aspects of reality beyond the range of what can be accomplished if one stays within the strictures of everyday society.

The Ordeals

The growth heroes experience is catalyzed by facing a number of ordeals, often accompanied by divine guidance. These ordeals force the hero to stretch, and they function as initiatory challenges.[305] For contemporary people, living your life as a heroic song allows you to give sacred context to the challenges you face and crystalize the lessons you learn. If you approach life in this manner, it is important to discern between stretches leading to growth and those leading to debilitating injury. Similarly, it is important to determine what is an initiatory ordeal and what is a distraction. In crystalizing lessons, if a particular theme

---

304. Ensdiø, "To Lock Up Eleusis."

305. Nagy, *Ancient Greek Hero in 24 Hours*.

keeps emerging as an ordeal, then the work requires you to pay attention and dig deeper. Finally—as a warning—be careful about making other living beings into monsters in your song.

Katharsis

Returning to the concept of *miasma* in heroic song, the word *katharsis* / catharsis means "to cleanse *miasma*." Heroic *katharsis* cleanses the *miasma* from their society. Heroes give this benefit to those beyond their near and dear. Currently, the Light of our world is obscured due to overwhelming *miasma* that functions like smog. A person striving to walk a heroic path—seeking to increase the potency of their actions by developing excellence and then focusing on cleansing their own *miasma*—sets up resonance that benefits the whole system.

Exercise
WRITE A CHAPTER IN YOUR HEROIC SONG
Your purpose here is to reflect on how this study is part of your sacred journey and experience viewing your life as a heroic song.

What You'll Need
A journal and pen or a computer.

Directions
Write your story about how you came to read this book as it relates to your *theoria*—the sacred quest of your life. What is the larger picture in terms of what prompted you to read it? What are the roots of this part of your journey and what meaning does it have for you? Have you faced ordeals that forced you to grow in this process? What lessons have you learned from the ordeals? How does it fit into your larger narrative about who and what you are? Where is this part of your quest leading you? This is your heroic story—don't be afraid to go big in your thinking.

ILLUSTRATIVE HEROES

There are many ancient Greek heroes. Heroes have stories concerning their excellence and they must have a presence in cult in which they are intercessory. I selected these heroes to demonstrate the wide range of heroic *areté*.

Herakles

Herakles is the most ancient Hellenic hero and serves as a prototype—His *areté* being strength and endurance. I think He is actually a Neolithic hero. The earthly sites mentioned in His core myth are located on the Argolid plain on the Peloponnesus—which is sacred to Hera. The cities associated with Herakles are the oldest Mycenean settlements. His main weapon is a club. His myth includes persecution by His divine antagonist, Hera, even though His name means "the Glory of Hera," and He is the hero of Her territory. He commits terrible atrocities and then must undertake great heroic deeds of strength in penance. He is accompanied and guided by Athena, who is often a companion of heroes. He travels outside of mortal realms—both to the underworld and to Isle of the Hesperides. His death is by burning, and, as discussed in the chapter on the Mysteries, death by fire often indicates the mortal aspect's destruction and the freeing of the immortal.[306]

Achilles and Patroklos

Achilles and Patroklos—whose hero song is Homer's *Iliad*, greatest of all hero songs in the Hellenic tradition—have two forms of excellence developed to the limit of human capacity. They are both great warriors, Achilles being the greatest warrior who ever lived. Equally important, they embody a certain type of love—the love of being full, equal companions. Certainly, by the time of classical Greece, it was assumed this deep love had an erotic component, but (unlike Ganymede) *eros* is not the primary aspect of that relationship. Instead, it was the deep soul connection where they were described as a single soul sharing two bodies. Together, they shared a grave and a cult. Their main divine antagonist is Apollon, who is the deity they are most like. They were both gifted healers, were depicted singing and playing the *kithara* (Apollon's sacred instrument), and were trained by Chiron, who was Apollon's foster son.[307]

Odysseus

Odysseus, hero of the other Homeric epic and a main character in the *Iliad* as well, most closely resembles Athena, being described as *polymetis* (possessing

---

306. Stafford, *Herakles*.
307. Nagy, *Ancient Greek Hero in 24 Hours*.

many types of thinking or cunning), which is also a common epithet for Athena. He is the ultimate journeyer and, as such, is like Athena and Poseidon. Odysseus demonstrates excellence as the *kubernetes*, which is a ship's steersman, but also is the leader of a society. This is where we get the word *gubernator* (governor) and the "ship of state" metaphor. Odysseus is a trickster and, like Herakles, visits lands outside of normal mortal reality. Even though the term *shamanism* is problematic since it is rooted in a particular set of Boreal cultures, this human capacity to travel outside of "normal" reality is an excellence of this hero.[308]

Asklepios

Asklepios, as mentioned, became such a gifted healer He brought a mortal back to life. His *areté* is absolute mastery over a particular domain of practice—medicine. He was killed by one of Zeus's thunderbolts and then resurrected as one of the Theoi. Again, note that Asklepios was destroyed by being burned. Asklepios had many cult sites and was always worshipped with His divine father, Apollon, and often with Artemis as well.

Ariadne

Ariadne's heroic excellence is that she knew how to allow herself to be loved.[309] The idea that truly allowing oneself to be fully seen and to be the beloved as an act of heroism is a powerful lesson.

---

308.   Nagy, *Ancient Greek Hero in 24 Hours.*
309.   Otto, "Ariadne."

CHAPTER FOURTEEN
PHILOSOPHY AS A SACRED PRACTICE AND PATH

The practice of philosophy can be exhilarating, but most modern people don't experience it this way. Philosophy needs rehabilitation and to be reestablished as a sacred quest for wisdom. If we encounter philosophy at all, it is usually as an academic discipline in college. While I greatly respect my colleagues in philosophy departments, the current academic approach is out of sync with how it was practiced in ancient Greece (and Rome). We lost its essence.

The first clue is encoded in the name *philosophia*.[310] This is a compound word consisting of *philia* (love) and *sophia* (wisdom). Philosophy is literally the practice of loving wisdom. In Greek, there are several words that can be translated as "love." *Philia* is not an abstract kind of love. It is the deeply intimate, personal, affectionate love we have for our dearest friends and family. *Philia* mixed with *eros* is romantic love. Practicing philosophy is developing this type of love with wisdom. How philosophy is usually taught now is dry and only appeals to a narrow range of human capacity rather than engaging people's full humanity. Ancient Greek philosophers strove to live as intimate lovers of wisdom.

Most contemporary philosophical discussions are primarily descriptive rather than focusing on practice. I am grateful for the wealth of philosophical texts we have—both preserved ancient texts and all written since.

---

310. Divey, ed., *Divry's Modern English-Greek and Greek-English Desk Dictionary*.

Yet, I often find the way these texts are approached to be lacking. I understand philosophical texts to be maps to certain kinds of cognitive experiences. Philosophers are exploring the true nature of reality using human mental capacities as the tools of exploration. While they are sharing their findings in their writings, philosophers are also leaving maps others can follow to have the same experiences.

I find the way philosophy is most often discussed is like describing and comparing maps, but not actually using them. It is as if a group of people deeply knew all the extant maps of Paris. They could compare the maps of different eras. They could debate the quality of different mapmakers and investigate the reasons certain items were included or excluded. This is interesting but is fundamentally different than using the map to navigate Paris. When studying a philosophical text, I invite you to use it as a map and have the experience. This is in the spirit of ancient Greek philosophy.

Finally, I am concerned that we think of philosophy as being the domain of elite experts. Calling oneself a "philosopher" these days smacks of unbalanced pride. This is a far cry from the situation in ancient Greece. While there were some extraordinary ancient Hellenic intellects who were philosophers, the path to living as a lover of wisdom was not confined to experts. I want us to rehabilitate philosophy so it is not intimidating. Few have a mind as sharp as Aristotle—the founder of logic—but any of us can live as a lover of wisdom, should we choose to do so.

WHAT IS ANCIENT GREEK PHILOSOPHY?

Philosophy is a systematic exploration of the nature of reality using reason as the tool of investigation. There are two fundamental and interrelated questions foundational to Hellenic philosophy. The first: What is the true nature of reality? The second: What does this mean for living a good human life?

Trying to answer these two questions is a quest for *sophia*. The motivation for this quest must be love. The philosopher's quest is to actively live as a lover of wisdom. Philosophy is a sacred way of life.

The Birth of Philosophy

Historically, philosophy arises in two cultures simultaneously and independently: Greece and India.[311] The paths of these cultures intersect early in the develop-

---

311.   Seaford, *Origins of Philosophy in Ancient Greece and India.*

ment of philosophy with the campaigns of Alexander the Great, Aristotle's pupil, and mutually influenced each other for some time.

The initial discoveries leading to philosophy's birth in Greece will sound similar to those who are versed in Indian philosophy. Greek philosophy was born in Ionia, the part of ancient Greece that is now in Turkey. Intellectuals there were carefully observing the world. While on the surface, the world seems stable, upon closer observation, they realized everything is in a constant state of flux, yet, there seems to be some type of continuity or stability behind appearances. These early philosophers developed a strong distrust of appearances and began using reason as the tool for exploration.

Because Greek philosophers always wanted to know the implications of all discoveries for leading a good human life, ethics are at the core of Hellenic philosophy. From early on, we see all the branches of philosophy in nascent form—metaphysics, logic, epistemology, empiricism, political philosophy, aesthetics, and so on. In all, there is a strong drive to figure out the nature of the Good.[312]

Eudaimonia

An important term used in ancient Greek ethics is *eudaimonic ethics*. *Eudaimonia* is another composite word that is revealing. Often translated as "happiness," *eudaimonia* is made up of *eu* (good) and *daimon*. *Daimon* is a category word, often translated as "spirit," that can refer to any class of beings who do not primarily exist in a physical body. It can refer to the Theoi, to heroes, to nature spirits of different types, to ancestors, or to those aspects of ourselves that are not in our bodies—including our highest spiritual selves. *Eudaimonia* is calling us to live as good spirits. If we live in ways that attend to feeding, developing, and nurturing our spiritual nature, we will be fundamentally happy.

Approaching Philosophical Texts

While we have a large number of ancient philosophical texts, it is a fraction of what we know existed. Our views can be skewed based on what survived. For example, we have Plato's dialogues. They are profound and are also striking pieces of artistic literature. His dialogues were intended for the public. We do not have his lectures for his special students—but we know they existed. On the

---

312.   Copleston, *History of Philosophy*.

other hand, when considering Plato's most important student, Aristotle, we only have the lectures intended for his students and do not have his dialogues, even though we know they existed. We should hesitate to draw firm conclusions comparing the two men because we are not comparing similar sources.

I encourage trying to read the original texts rather than relying heavily on secondary sources. Try to follow the map left by the original author. The sources we still possess have influenced thinkers after them, many of whom approach the ancient philosophers from a monotheistic position. While there is nothing wrong with that and it has led to some important developments, if you want to allow the full range of possibilities in the text to open in front of you, experiencing the original source directly can be powerful.

LIGHTNING TOUR OF HELLENIC PHILOSOPHY

Entire libraries could be filled with books about ancient Greek philosophy. My intention here is to give you a quick summary to help you walk a sacred path in living as a friend of Wisdom. To do that, it helps to get a general sense of philosophy's development in Greece. In the history of Hellenic philosophy, Socrates is the turning point. Everything changes with him.

Pre-Socratics

As mentioned, philosophy was born in Ionia when a group of thinkers began investigating what lay behind the world of appearances. They are called Pre-Socratics. The early atomists proposed what Modern Pagans would recognize as the elements in their search for the stability lying behind the flux of the manifest world.

The Atomists

Thales of Miletus—active in the early sixth century BCE—is considered the first philosopher. He concluded that water is the primary element and was also first to detect a unity in difference. Following him were other important Pre-Socratics including Anaximenes, Anaximander, and Heraclitus, who proposed other elements as the primary. The four major elements—earth, air, fire, and water—were theorized during the Pre-Socratic period. Later, Aristotle added the fifth element of ether to the initial four.[313]

---

313. Copleston, *History of Philosophy*.

The main importance of early Pre-Socratic atomists is that they were beginning to use ways of knowing that are neither sensory nor sensory correlative. In modern occult parlance, the "astral" senses are still sensory correlative. What the philosophers were using is beyond the astral senses—they were beginning to explore reality using abstract reason alone.

Parmenides

A particularly important Pre-Socratic philosopher is Parmenides who was based in Elea, which is now in Italy. Parmenides was a great mystic and a monist. He believed everything in reality is ultimately one great divine being and our sense of separation is fundamentally rooted in illusion.[314] When Parmenides was an old man, he visited Athens and spoke with a young Socrates. This encounter, imaginatively told by Plato in *Parmenides*, was formative for Socrates.[315]

Pythagoras

Pythagoras of Samos, who founded his own school in what is now Italy, was also active before Socrates. We do not have any writings from Pythagoras, but there are extant texts by later Pythagoreans and biographies of Pythagoras. Pythagoras seems to have been strongly influenced by the Orphic Mysteries. His school embraced a conception of the human soul similar to Orphism, including believing in reincarnation. The Pythagoreans believed all of reality is, in some way, divine mathematics. Additionally, Pythagoreans emphasized the value of community and set up communal living for their initiates. Socrates and Plato seem to have been influenced by Pythagorean thought.[316]

The Sophists

The Sophists arose in response to the birth of democracy in ancient Athens, which then rapidly spread to other cities.[317] The Sophists were teachers of rhetoric. Ancient Greek democracy was direct democracy. All citizen males voted on almost everything important to the city. Prior to democracy, affairs of state were decided by those who were in the ruling classes and were socialized from

---

314.   Copleston, *History of Philosophy*.
315.   Plato, *Plato's Parmenides*.
316.   Copleston, *History of Philosophy*.
317.   Copleston, *History of Philosophy*.

a young age into the responsibilities of governance. With democracy, all that changed. Suddenly, if you wanted to get anything done, you had to persuade massive numbers of people. Additionally, juries for trials consisted of dozens of people for minor infractions up to five hundred for a capital crime. Being able to speak persuasively was an essential life skill.

The Sophists stepped into this gap. While these teachers had a powerful presence in Athens as the first and largest democracy, they also traveled and taught in other cities. As such, they often functioned as diplomats. Because their clients could be people on any side of any issue, these rhetoric teachers tended to be relativists. They often embodied the idea that everyone is entitled to their own opinion and advocated for a type of statecraft rooted in pragmatism and compromise.[318]

Socrates

Socrates, a citizen of Athens who worked as a manual laborer and had a lifelong fascination with philosophy as a quest for wisdom, was absolutely opposed to the Sophists' pragmatic relativism. Socrates believed *no one* was entitled to their own opinion. It is the duty of each of us, as humans, to move from opinion to knowledge. Socrates was skeptical about most claims to knowledge and began asking, "How do we know what we know?" With this development, Socrates turned from looking outward to looking inward, focusing attention on questions like, "What is the nature of reason?" In order to pursue this quest, Socrates created a method called dialectic, which is a form of rigorous conversation in which carefully asking and answering questions—especially clarifying and challenging assumptions and definitions—allows people to explore the nature of reality together. Throughout his life, Socrates was primarily interested in trying to understand the nature of "the Good."[319] We do not have any writings from Socrates himself. The writings about him by his contemporaries include the dialogues of Plato in which Socrates is often a character, the writings of his student Xenophon, and the brutal lampooning of Socrates by the comic playwright Aristophanes.

---

318. Copleston, *History of Philosophy*.
319. Copleston, *History of Philosophy*.

In 399 BCE at approximately the age of 71, Socrates was executed in Athens. His student, Plato, recounts his trial in the *Apology*—an *apology* literally means "an argument in defense of something." Given the trial was witnessed by many hundreds of people who were still alive at the time Plato was writing, I think it is probably true to historical reality. Socrates seems to have intentionally martyred himself for the chance to publicly critique the corruption of his own society.[320]

Plato

Plato is the most important student of Socrates, and soon after the death of his mentor, he founded a philosophical school in Athens—the Academy—to carry on the work for which Socrates had recently been executed.[321] In no small measure, the *Apology* is also Plato's defense speech. Plato's work and the work of his Academy built on the foundation laid by Socrates, but Plato was a powerfully original philosopher in his own right. Given we have no texts by Socrates, it is difficult to ascertain which ideas were Plato's original contributions, but Aristotle tells us the Doctrine of the Forms is original to Plato. It is likely Plato was a mystic and may have been working backward from a unitive mystical experience to try to understand it.

The theory of the Forms or Divine Ideas/Ideals is that there are divine archetypes that are immortal, eternal, and never changing, that never fully manifest but are the source of all transient things in the world. Plato makes a causal claim that the things in the world have their source in these Divine Ideas or Forms. So, for example, when we perceive a song, it is a manifestation of Music. Music is only manifest in instances—a song, a performance, and so forth—but we can still talk about Music. We can explore what Music itself is. But Music, as a whole, is never fully manifest. It is eternal, and things that are musical can only exist because Music exists. Music itself is a Form or a Divine Idea. It is abstract, but it is real and, in a fundamental way, is more real than any particular manifestation.

Plato also continued to develop theories about the nature of the soul and knowledge that seem to originate in Socrates but are certainly carried to new

320. Plato, "Apology."
321. Copleston, *History of Philosophy*.

heights. Additionally, he speculated on the appropriate nature of human society through texts like *The Republic* and *The Laws*.

Plato's dialogues are incredible pieces of theatrical art. I recommend reading Platonic dialogues and trying to follow the maps laid out by this extraordinary philosopher. Even where I disagree with his conclusions, I can attest that the process of allowing yourself to be influenced by the experience strengthens your capacity to be dynamic in your higher mind.

Aristotle

Aristotle never knew Socrates, but he joined Plato's Academy as a young man and remained, studying and teaching under Plato, for twenty years until Plato's death. It is clear from Aristotle's writings, he had the deepest regard for his teacher throughout his life, although he disagreed with him on certain topics, including the Divine Ideas. After Plato's death, Aristotle was invited by King Philip of Macedonia to his court to teach his son, Alexander (who became Alexander the Great), and Alexander's cohort. When Alexander became king after Philip's assassination, he helped Aristotle return to Athens and found his own school, the Lyceum.[322]

Aristotle had one of the keenest, most precise intellects that has ever been in human form. He is the founder of logic.[323] I don't always agree with him—I think some of his arguments are rooted in the prejudices of his day and they grate on my contemporary sensibilities—but the structure of his argumentation is beautiful. He was interested in everything, and many branches of philosophy, in addition to logic, are founded by him. His texts address metaphysics, natural philosophy (essentially science), aesthetics, ethics, political philosophy, and literary criticism—he was a stunning polymath.

Aristotle was far more interested in the immanent than the transcendent. His true focus was on understanding the manifested world we live in and how to improve it and ourselves. He was driven by the quest for Truth but was also quite pragmatic. Aristotle focused attention on *areté*—excellence—how individuals can become deeply good humans and how human society can be

---

322. Copleston, *History of Philosophy*.
323. Copleston, *History of Philosophy*.

arranged and managed to encourage human flourishing. Aristotle is deep. Aristotle can be tough, but Aristotle always keeps it real.

Stoicism

Another ancient Greek philosophical school that arose after Socrates is Stoicism. Stoicism flourished in the Roman Empire but was born in Athens and inspired by Socrates. When Zeno of Citium came to Athens, he asked around to find the person whose lifestyle most closely resembled Socrates and became the student of Crates the Cynic. The Cynics—most famously Diogenes of Sinope—were known for their theory that human downfall comes from thinking we are above nature. The way human cultures force us to live outside our true nature results in our moral corruption. Animals never live outside their nature and are never morally corrupt.[324]

Upon Crates's death, Zeno started his own school that met in the Stoa Poikile—a building in the Athenian Agora—hence the "Stoics." Zeno—and later Cleanthes, Chryssipus, and the great Stoics of Rome (Seneca, Epictetus, and Marcus Aurelius)—diverged from the Cynics. The Stoics did not see human culture as inherently corrupting. When they analyzed human nature, they, in agreement with Aristotle, concluded that human beings are always social; we arrange ourselves in groups because that is our nature. We, therefore, owe duty to each other. The Stoics also agreed with the Platonic and Aristotelian schools that the capacity for reason is the fundamental differentiation between humans and animals. Therefore, it is our duty to act for the good of others using our reason.[325]

Metaphysically, the Stoics believed in a material monism, hearkening back to Pre-Socratics like Heraclitus. They believed everything is essentially One— Divine Fire. They also believed that since everything is truly one great Divine Being, everything is happening according to Providence—everything is fated, meaning "destined" rather than the more common understanding of *moira*. For a Stoic, the big issue is how they respond to their fate. As Seneca says, "The willing soul Fate leads, but the unwilling drags along."[326] Whether or not you

---

324. Irvine, *Guide to the Good Life*.
325. Irvine, *Guide to the Good Life*.
326. Seneca, "On Obedience to the Universal Will," 29.

agree with their fatalistic metaphysics, the Stoics developed powerful tech-niques for cultivating tranquility in this turbulent world, enabling you to do your duty. Specifics are shared later in this chapter.

Neoplatonism

There are other ancient Hellenic philosophical schools to explore—I men-tioned the Cynics, there are also the Skeptics and the Epicureans—but I find the Platonic, Aristotelian, and Stoic schools to be the most useful in practice, especially in their synthesis, added together with a healthy dose of mysticism, which is Neoplatonism. The father of Neoplatonism is Plotinus who was living in Rome and writing in Greek in the third century CE. After Plotinus, Iambli-chus brought theurgy (spiritual alchemy) into the mix. Proclus, the last great Pagan philosopher of Greece and Rome, headed the Neoplatonic school in Athens.[327]

In Neoplatonism, the best of all three main schools of philosophy was melded. Plotinus is indisputably one of the world's great mystics. We know he was both following Plato and having unitive mystical experiences. Plotinus takes other philosophers, especially Aristotle, very seriously. Aristotle's critique of the Divine Ideas was addressed by Plotinus and other Neoplatonists through the doctrine of emanation.

Exercise
ACTIVE IMAGINATION OF EMANATION

Using active imagination to experience emanation is a form of contem-plation that causes you to operate in the aspect of self that is not sensory correlative. It is a meditative technique that takes you beyond the astral. Repetition strengthens your capacity to act in this aspect of self.

What You'll Need

A recording device. A quiet place where you can listen undisturbed.

---

327. Copleston, *History of Philosophy.*

Directions

Record yourself reading the text slowly, as a pathworking. Close your eyes and listen to the recording, using your active imagination to try to experience the ideas.

Close your eyes and take a deep breath. Feel all your stress drop away and be fully present, relaxed, and engaged. Open yourself to experience.

Now, imagine all things are ultimately One. Plotinus calls this "the One," but that is a misnomer because the All is transcendent, beyond time, beyond space, and beyond attributes—because as soon as we say it *is* something, that implies it cannot *not* be that thing and is, therefore, limited. We are talking about something without limits—it is everything and nothing.

This is what the world's mystics keep trying to describe. They say it is "ineffable," "unspeakable," and then try to speak about it for hundreds of pages. The "unspeakable" nature of the mystical unitive experience violates the fundamental categories upon which language is built. There are no attributes. It is really hard to say anything without attributes. The experience is outside of time and outside of space—the two Kantian categories that are supposed to frame all human thought—but the unitive mystical experience is an exception. All language is rooted in time and space. All verbs imply actions, which imply time; all nouns imply space. All language presupposes a subject and an object—a speaker and that which is spoken about. In a unitive mystical experience, there is no distinction between subject and object. In fact, as soon as you realize you are having the experience, it is over. You have reentered separation and the time stream.

Lock into your understanding that the Source is outside of time and space, has no attributes, and there is no distinction between subject and object. The One, this unitive source, can have no self-knowledge because to do so requires a division between the subject (the one apprehending) and the object of apprehension (the One). Now, in your imagination, follow the path down.

Some potentiality in the One causes it to have this self-contemplation; it has a thought about itself, making the level contemplating the One the next level of being, called the *Nous* or Divine Mind. This is the initial emanation. Imagine yourself as that first level of emanation, contemplating the One.

As the Divine Mind is contemplating the One, it is having thoughts, and those thoughts are the third level. Imagine you are the Divine Mind, and in your contemplation of the One, you have a thought—one of the Platonic Ideas, perhaps the Idea of the Good. Move your imagination into the transcendent Idea of the Good. From that place, you have thoughts about the nature of the Good and you think of some type of goodness, which creates the next level. And so, the many things of the world are created. Each level contemplates the level above, and the thoughts arising from this contemplation become the next emanation until potency runs out in the physical. Everything is ultimately thought, and all levels of reality are also participating up the chain to the One. Because of this, any of us, through using reason and contemplation, can return to the source through philosophical contemplation. You have just completed a form of Neoplatonic contemplation.

You can also do this in reverse, starting with some goodness you see in the world, contemplating what it reveals about the Good, and climbing into the Ideas. Contemplate what the source of the Good would be, and then allow yourself to sit in receptive contemplation until all differentiation falls away and you enter the One. Neoplatonism makes the love of wisdom a pathway to mystical union with the Source of All.

Now, become aware once more of your body. Shift your attention back into this time and place. Move slightly, and when you are ready to fully return, open your eyes.

Implications of the Neoplatonic View of Reality

The Neoplatonic diagnosis for the challenges we face are useful. In this emanatory scheme, we exist on all levels of reality from the One all the way down to our densest form. The problem is, the lower levels—like those in the physical world—are not perfect. This is not because there is an evil force in the world corrupting us. It is because of copy degradation. Since each level is created by the beings of the level above contemplating the level one more above them, they are not getting the entire picture and distortion begins to creep in. By the time the creative energy runs out in dense matter, we are dealing with the copy of a copy of a copy of a copy and so forth. Distortions need to be corrected through philosophical contemplation.

Because we are most immediately aware of that part of ourselves living in the body, that is the part we tend to think of as "us." Furthermore, the higher aspects of our nature—the parts that are one with divine reason—have to be intentionally exercised. We are often not active in our higher spiritual natures. Neoplatonism advises processes of character development and philosophical contemplation to help purify and strengthen the fitness of our higher nature. Exercises using your philosophical contemplative imagination are critical for spiritual refinement.

THE CHARIOT AND THE TURNING POINT

An incredibly powerful philosophical and spiritual image is the chariot as described in Plato's *Phaedrus* and immortalized in the tarot.[328] The chariot portrays the multiple parts of a human soul. It includes a dark horse, a white horse, and the charioteer. This all refers to the nonphysical spiritual parts of a human being. None of these parts of the soul are bad. They are all necessary, and a well-functioning human being will have strength in all and be well-coordinated.

The dark horse is the soul's appetitive functions. It is the part closest to the body and includes our desires and aversions. The dark horse is not bad. You need the dark horse to be strong.

The white horse is the part of the soul that includes the noble emotions and dynamism. It is the part of our soul that can be courageous, spirited, generous, and tender. This horse also needs to be strong.

Finally, the charioteer is our reason—our highest self. Our reason is sourced in Divine Reason. The charioteer gets the horses to cooperate and steers them together.

You really see how this works when you understand the "turning point." This refers to critical liminal moments in which there are actions that fundamentally alter the course. This image is from ancient Greek chariot racing and was certainly in Plato's mind when he described the soul as the Chariot.

Ancient Greek chariot racing was among the oldest and most important parts of sacred games, including festivals like the Olympics or funeral games honoring a hero. In the race, the chariot rushes down a line until it comes to a point—typically the grave of a sacred hero. At this "turning point," the charioteer must

---

328.   Plato, "Phaedrus," 405–579.

guide the horses through a dangerous and daring maneuver, making a hairpin turn around the "point." To do this, the charioteer must precisely and dynamically let out the reins of one of the horses while simultaneously reining in the other horse tightly.[329] If we think of the chariot at the turning point as referencing the soul, the charioteer—the reason and highest aspect of spirit—has to be dynamically sensitive to and in control of all aspects of the self to keep everything moving together toward desired ends. Neither horse can be ignored and both have to be encouraged to perform at their top capacity, led by the charioteer. This analogy can be a useful tool when engaging in self-reflection.

VIRTUE AND SPIRITUAL SELF-CULTIVATION

Living as a lover of wisdom requires us to constantly be on a journey of spiritual evolution. Aristotle's *Nicomachaean Ethics* is a manual for how to do this.[330] As discussed, the Greek word *areté* (virtue) is the set of excellences expressing our rarified human nature. The process of intentionally cultivating *areté* purifies the self while awakening and strengthening our focus in the immortal part of our being. In other words, developing *areté* strengthens our identification with our *daimon*—our spirit—and leads to *eudaimonia*, leading the life of a good spirit, which is happiness.

Aristotle makes a distinction between moral excellences about our character and intellectual excellences. Once we develop moral virtues, we will have a disposition to act in a morally excellent way—a courageous person's default is to act courageously; they no longer have to consciously decide to be courageous. Virtues are developed through habit. We become what we do over and over again.[331]

Intellectual virtues require the intentional use of reason each time they are used. While the moral virtues set the defaults of your moral character, developing intellectual virtues is about increasing capacities—developing them requires instruction or intentional learning. Capacity is built by practice and must be maintained by practice.[332]

---

329.   Nagy, *Ancient Greek Hero in 24 Hours*.

330.   Aristotle, *Nicomachaean Ethics*.

331.   Aristotle.

332.   Aristotle.

Virtues are expressed in and developed through actions. It is less that the person is courageous but rather that their behavior is consistently courageous. Humans are social by nature and living as a good spirit means putting our excellences to good use in the world. Right action is doing the right thing in the right way at the right time and in the right place. This means making the morally correct decision is context specific (right time, right place) and asserts that it is not just action toward the morally right end, but that the manner in which the action is taken is also morally relevant.[333]

To be virtuous, an action must have three binding conditions. First, when acting, you have to act from knowledge—it can't be accidental. If you drop money on the ground and someone else picks it up, that is not a generous act. Second, the virtuous act must be chosen for its own sake. If you give money and your motivation is that it will increase your social status, that is not a truly generous act, even if it is a huge amount of money. Finally, for an act to be truly virtuous, it must come from a fixed disposition rather than arising from a whim. It is the default setting. While you are in the process of cultivating a more virtuous default through habit, the act may not yet be firmly fixed in your disposition, but with continued practice, it will be.

The moral virtues can be discovered along the "virtuous mean" in which they are in right relationship to some quality. For example, courage is the right relationship to fear. With too much fear, you act in a cowardly manner, but if you are in a dangerous situation and don't have enough fear, you can behave recklessly, which is not the excellence of courage. The virtue of courage is the divine mean in which right relationship to fear is correctly embodied. This is similar for other moral virtues.

What Are the Specific Moral Virtues?

As discussed in the last chapter, depending on the type of hero you are striving to be, different virtues may be emphasized. It is useful to look at various lists of virtues and choose the two to three that are immediate priorities for your development. From an Aristotelian perspective, these are the most important moral virtues.[334] You may identify others.

---

333.   Aristotle.
334.   Aristotle.

DEFICIENCY	VIRTUE	EXCESS
Fearfulness	Courage	Overconfidence/Rashness
Insensibility to Pleasure	Moderation	Profligacy
Meanness	Generosity	Prodigality
Paltriness	Magnificence	Vulgarity
Undue Humility	Confidence/Pride	Overestimation of One's Ability or Merit
Small Souled/Petty	Magnanimity/*Megalopsyche* (to Be Big Souled)	Vanity
Aorgesia (Not Moved by Righteous Anger)	Gentleness	Irascibility
Quarrelsomeness	Friendliness/Agreeableness	Obsequiousness
Self-Deprecation	Sincerity/Truthfulness	Boastfulness
Boorishness	Wittiness	Buffoonery
Taking Too Little Good/Too Much Bad	Justice	Taking Too Much Good/Too Little Bad
Shamelessness	Modesty	Shyness

Exercise
IDENTIFYING PRIORITY VIRTUES FOR YOUR DEVELOPMENT
This exercise will help you focus on developmental goals for your self-cultivation.

What You'll Need
A journal, pen, and timer.

Directions
Thinking back to your contemplations about what kind of heroic path you feel drawn to pursue, what are two to three essential virtues related to that path? Write each on a separate document. For each virtue, set a timer for ten minutes and journal using the following prompts.

1. Why is this virtue important to you?
2. When have you demonstrated a deficiency of the virtue?
3. When have you demonstrated an excess of the virtue?
4. Do you tend more toward excess or deficiency?

Developing the Moral Virtues
The way to develop the moral virtues is to create habits enacting them repeatedly until they become your "default." We become what we do over and over again. There are a number of practical recommendations to bring this about.

To develop a virtue—let's use "generosity" as an example—incorporate easy-to-accomplish actions into your daily life that build your habit of generosity. For example, buy a colleague a cup of coffee. Constant repetition is what is important. From the perspective of developing a habit of generosity, it is better to buy someone a cup of coffee every week for a year than to give a much larger single donation. Incorporate these practices into your daily life in an organic way so you will reliably do them. Good intentions without action have no value in this type of work. Strategically developing triggers for behavior will help.

Think broadly about your virtue. There are many forms of generosity, including adopting generous interpretations of the intention of others. Maybe you choose certain physical signs that mean you are annoyed with someone as a habit trigger. "When I feel my jaw clench while interacting with another person, I will ..." and then you choose the action allowing you to practice your virtue. Perhaps your practice is, "I will count to twenty and then try to think of three reasons why the person undertaking the annoying behavior might be doing it. I will then choose the most generous interpretation."

It is also possible to be generous with one's attention. You could develop a habit allowing you to practice generosity through giving attention. Maybe your trigger is, "When I am in a conversation with another person (trigger), I will turn off my phone, make eye contact, and give my conversation partner my undivided attention (habitual behavior)." Or, "When I leave a building, I will greet the first person I see and wish them a blessed day." These are examples of developing habits and using triggers to activate the habitual actions that build virtue.

Exercise
Planning Your Virtuous Habits
This exercise will help you transform your theoretical understanding into practical knowledge for self-cultivation.

What You'll Need
A journal, pen, and timer.

Directions
For each virtue from the last exercise, set a timer for ten minutes and respond to the following prompts:

1. Thinking broadly, make a list of ways in which your virtue can be expressed.
2. List three actions you can take regularly that express your virtue.
3. For each of your actions, identify a triger for the action you want to take.

Practice your habits for three months and then take some time to review the impact of your practice on your character. Make a note in your calendar to assess your progress three months from now.

The Intellectual Virtues

The intellectual virtues intentionally use reason and must be learned and practiced—they will atrophy if not regularly used. These are the charioteer's excellences. Aristotle names five different intellectual virtues: prudence, temperance, skill/art, friendship, and wisdom.

Prudence

Prudence is practical wisdom and gets inadequate attention within spiritual circles. Lofty ideals may direct you toward what you think should happen, but prudence allows you to manifest them. People with prudence have good, reliable judgment. Most of us are uneven in relation to prudence. We may be excellent in certain domains and lack excellence in others. Honest self-assessment is essential. Look at yourself as though you were observing a dear friend—try to get a bit of distance but approach yourself with both honesty and love.

Exercise
IMPROVE PRUDENCE
Self-assessment for self-cultivation.

What You'll Need
A journal, pen, and timer.

Directions
Set a timer for ten minutes and answer the following prompts.

1. List the major domains of your life (e.g., health, personal finance, business networking).
2. For each domain, answer the following:
   - How good is your judgment?
   - Do your strategies work? Why or why not?
   - What themes do you see?

Once you have identified areas of weakness through this exercise, begin to study them. Read what you can and, if you know someone who is really strong in an area of your weakness, approach them as a mentor.

Temperance

Temperance is related to willpower. Temperance is expressed when the mind determines you should refrain from something and then you are able to follow the mind's dictates. When you decide you should do something and are able to follow through, that is also temperance. Temperance enables the horses to take direction from the charioteer.

The following are practical ways to increase your temperance.

- Build in a ritual pause between when you are about to do something and when you actually act. For example, building a ritual pause before you eat ice cream—like singing happy birthday three times to yourself—will often give enough space for the charioteer to assert itself.
- Undertake periodic "training periods" through voluntary deprivations.
- Establish ritualized patterns, like daily prayers.

Skill and Art

Learning or improving any skill or art strengthens the intellectual virtues. It requires you to engage the mind's evaluative abilities to track your progress, and you are exercising your ability to connect new knowledge to existing knowledge.

Friendship

Friendship, *philia*, is the most important virtue according to Aristotle. No one would choose to be without friends even if they could have all other good things.[335] Friendship is both an excellence in and of itself and it is within the context of friendship that many other virtues are developed and exercised.

The highest type of friendship is the "virtuous friendship." Affection is an aspect of this type of friendship, but it is more than just an affectionate relationship. In a virtuous friendship, you practice the virtues with each other—friends help make each other more excellent. They inspire and assist each other in becoming better people. In this type of friendship, because your highest wish is for your friend's highest good, a true friend will tell you when you are straying from your own best nature and call you back to it with love and honesty.

---

335.   Aristotle.

The people in your life are the single most important part of your environment and shape what you do over and over again. It is important to build virtuous relationships with people who make you better and to avoid friendships that make you worse. You can have compassion for people, but you must also guard your own character from the influence of negative relationships.

Making regular time to have substantive engagement with friends is one of the best things we can do for our happiness and soul-development. At a minimum, make time to see each other in person, turn off phones, and have a real conversation.

Wisdom

Wisdom requires shifting attention into the immortal part of self and contemplating the nature of reality from that position. Ancient Hellenic contemplative practices are different than mindfulness meditation. They are more directed. One form is focused study of something that challenges your higher mind. This can involve studying a text or a topic. It is possible to move outside of time and space through absorption during deep study.

Another popular ancient Greek method is to engage in focused and deep conversation exploring ideas with at least one interlocuter. This is what Socratic dialectic is about, but it doesn't have to be formally structured. There is great value in discussing ideas with others.

For those who lack interested conversational partners, a time-tested method is writing essays. The word *essay* itself means "to try out." Great essayists like Plutarch or Montaigne were engaged in a form of contemplation occurring through the process of their writing. They were thinking deeply and exploring as they were in the process of literary creation. It requires becoming active and focused in the rational and immortal aspect of self.

The Neoplatonic form of contemplation shared earlier is a form of contemplation. Repeated use of such contemplative methods strengthens wisdom.

STOIC TRANQUILITY TRAINING PRACTICES

Stoic tranquility practices are useful for helping you maintain your spiritual center. Although Stoicism began in Greece, the Roman Stoics—especially Seneca, Epictetus, and Marcus Aurelius—are the most helpful.

As mentioned, the Stoics believe that everything that happens is ultimately part of the divine plan and is destined. Fate is expressed through the true nature of all beings. Humans are social by nature and have a naturally prosocial orientation. As part of our divine nature, we owe duty to each other and the world. Because all things are ultimately predestined, what matters is not the outcome of our actions, but how we respond to our destiny.

While I am not a fatalist, I understand we are embedded within systems constraining our power and that we rarely have total control over our contexts—yet we still have duty. The Stoics created a host of pragmatic techniques for developing and maintaining tranquility because they enable someone to stay active and be of service in a turbulent and troubling world.

When we are in the grips of overpowering emotions, we can't access our reason—the Charioteer is offline. This is especially dangerous in the midst of a crisis when we need to make good decisions quickly. If we don't train in tranquility, we are likely to be at our weakest in the circumstances demanding the most of us.

Life includes suffering, and emotions like the fear of suffering cause additional suffering. One common reason people betray their character and undermine their virtue is fear of suffering. The stronger our training in maintaining tranquility in the midst of challenging circumstances, the less likely it will be that we betray ourselves.

Our current historical moment is filled with turbulent circumstances that cause suffering and demand massive societal change: e.g., the climate catastrophe, political and civil strife, surveillance capitalism, and the attention economy. Additionally, human beings have negativity bias. Anything evoking negative emotions—especially anger and fear—has a greater impact on us than something evoking positive emotions. While this is rooted in a survival instinct that gets us to pay sufficient attention to danger, it is a vulnerability that allows our minds to get hacked and trains us in habits of anger and rage, impacting our character.

Managing Negative Emotions

Seneca's essay "On Anger" teaches how to manage anger in a way that can promote tranquility and can be adapted to any negative or troubling emotion.[336] He challenges Aristotle's notion that the virtue of gentleness can include

---

336.   Seneca, "On Anger."

appropriate or righteous anger. Seneca believes anger can never be virtuous. He asserts that anger always causes harm to the one experiencing it, so it cannot be virtuous. In the grips of anger no one can access reason, so it cannot effectively motivate anyone working for justice. Anger may give you the illusion it is motivating you to combat injustice, but the real motivation arises from some other virtue, like care. Perhaps the biggest reason to control anger is that it is a type of fire that will naturally spin and increase. It can be extremely difficult to stop once it begins.

Exercise
EXPLORING ANGER

Generate a deeper understanding of your relationship to anger. This exercise can be used for other troubling emotions as well.

What You'll Need

Journal and pen.

Directions

Find a quiet place where you can work uninterrupted.

1. Make a list of things that tend to make you angry.
2. Think of three times you were angry. Does the pattern of your anger tend to follow a particular course? Describe it.
3. Remember a time you were angry and try to remember it in your body. Note in as much detail as you can the way anger affects your body. Do you clench your jaw? Does your voice get faster or louder?
4. Are there any physical warning signs you notice that are a prelude to anger? Do you feel tightness in your gut?
5. Are there circumstances that make it more likely you will get angry? For example, if you are hungry or in crowds? These are factors that lower your coping capacity.

Create a Stoic Anger Management Strategy

Understanding the way your anger works allows you to design a personal strategy. Avoid triggers that are avoidable. You minimize contextual situations that lower your capacity for equanimity. If triggers are unavoidable, plan your encounters with them when your environment is conducive to having maximum capacity—like being well rested and hydrated, having even blood sugar, being in a quiet environment, and being at your strongest point in the day.

Using Body Cues to Manage Your Anger

Be attentive to your bodily warning signs indicating you are getting angry. Note the signs and make your body do the opposite. For example, if you naturally start talking more rapidly and loudly when getting upset, force yourself to slow down and lower your volume. If you tend to start clenching your fists, force yourself to relax your hands. If you start to fidget in agitation, force yourself to be still. Forcing the opposite physical reaction helps dissipate the building anger.

Separating Triggers and Interpretation of Triggers

Another practice involves making a strong division in your thinking between the factors triggering anger and your interpretation of the triggers. Once you separate the interpretation from the trigger, you can then ask if there are additional interpretations that *could* be the case.

For example, imagine you are driving and someone cuts you off. It is logical to experience negative emotion in response to danger. However, rather than attributing additional intention, build in a pause. Objectively, you don't know why the other driver cut you off. Imagine your most generous interpretation. Maybe they got a scary call from the hospital and are rushing to be with a loved one. This could be true—you don't know it isn't. Imagine if this new interpretation were true. How would you feel about the incident then? What is being strengthened in your own character and mind? Choose the interpretation that is most generous and best for your own character.

Pausing to Manage Difficult Emotions

Building in a pause before action enables us to dissipate anger. Under the influence of anger, it is natural to act before our reason has a chance to weigh in. Methods like forcing yourself to silently count to twenty before speaking or acting, walking around the block, saying an affirmation a specified number of times—all these little rituals rupture the fire of anger and give our charioteer a chance to intervene. Once your charioteer is back online, remind yourself of your ideals and the virtues you are striving to embody.

Refraining from Action

Finally, the Stoics recommend you make a commitment to refrain from action when angry. If you act, you will be in danger of betraying your ideals and making unwise decisions. If you are experiencing "righteous anger," focus on your commitment to justice to identify your particular duty. Try to quell the anger before acting—but if it won't pass, ask a trusted loved one to do your duty in your stead.

The strategy and exercises discussed in this section can be used with any difficult emotion. If there is another that is more troublesome for you, go back and reread this section and exercises substituting the name of your troublesome emotion.

Negative Imagining

There are many sources of suffering. It is undeniable that painful, bad things happen and they hurt. Our interpretation of painful things often adds additional harm. Even though we know pain is part of life, we are often shocked and unprepared when bad things happen. The shock itself is an added dose of suffering. Additionally, humans suffer from "hedonic adaptation," which means when something good happens, we get used to it, take it for granted, and stop experiencing the good from it. The technique of negative imagining helps.[337]

In negative imagining, you think about something upsetting or scary to you and then you imagine it happening as vividly as you can. It is advised that at some point you imagine your own death and the death of loved ones. This process has many benefits. There are practical things you can do to prepare for certain circumstances. It can lead to mindful examination of how you spend your time—the ultimate scarce and valued resource for mortal beings. It can help you prevent regrets. You can plan to mitigate various risks.

Another benefit is that in imagining suffering, when the events happen, we have already experienced pieces of it. This titrates the suffering and lessens its impact. When we think about losing what is precious to us, it helps us return to appreciating what we have. It is a powerful antidote to hedonic adaptation.

---

337.   Irvine, *Guide to the Good Life.*

Exercise
NEGATIVE IMAGINING
Experience this Stoic tranquility training technique and build resilience to suffering.

What You'll Need
A quiet place to think. Optional: Journal and pen.

Directions
Imagine that in the next couple of weeks, you receive a scary, potentially life-threatening medical diagnosis. Try to feel the emotions as strongly as possible. Imagine what you would do. What would likely happen? What is the worst-case scenario? Who would you call on to help you and what would that look like for them? What would your choices be? Would you make different life decisions than you are currently making if you knew you were going to get the diagnosis? What would you regret? What are some things you can do, practically, right now to mitigate danger or regrets?

Practicing Hardship

Stoics advise periodically practicing hardships in which we voluntarily undertake some deprivation and discomfort or choose to forgo some pleasures for specified periods of time. A common form is fasting, but there are many options. It can be undertaking uncomfortable physical rigors or exposing oneself to the elements more than normal. It can be willingly forgoing some pleasure or convenience, like not watching television for a month or walking to work. If you are planning any physical form of practicing hardship, work with your healthcare team to ensure you can do so safely. The point is to train, not to injure.

By practicing hardship, we gain confidence we can manage hard times. This increases our courage. This practice helps develop the virtue of temperance, increasing our willpower. It also increases our appreciation for what we have.

Gratitude Practice

The benefits of a gratitude practice are well documented in current psychological studies and were also known to the Stoics. Intentionally calling to mind those things for which we are grateful and reminding ourselves of what is wonderful in life is a powerful way to develop and maintain tranquility. Gratitude practice is especially powerful if paired with practicing hardship.

In *Meditations*, Marcus Aurelius begins his work by naming every person who has influenced him in a good way and specifying what he got from their example and instruction.[338] A gratitude journal or practice of posting about something you are grateful for every day helps you maintain a positive outlook on life.

Embrace Constraints

We are embedded within systems that include constraints; having total control over external circumstances is highly unlikely. The true locus of control is our own character. From a Stoic perspective, we use our logic to determine the best course of action that is rooted in our values, our sense of duty to others, and our ideal character. Once you have done so, follow that conclusion, acting according to your duty, and then let go of the outcome.

Rather than focusing on external results, reframe your goals to be internal; your goal is to best perform your duty. This moves your goals into the realm over which you have control. For example, one of my goals is, "I will do my best to defend the integrity of our democracy." I try to maintain focus on fulfilling my duty rather than focusing on outcomes because my control is limited—but I can fulfill my duty with integrity.

End-of-Day Review

An end-of-day review is recommended by many traditions. Make the process simple enough so you do it. Seneca asked himself three questions every day.[339]

1. What bad habit have I cured today?
2. What failing have I resisted?
3. Where can I improve?

The main benefit is forcing yourself to reflect on your day. Having a record of your growth is also useful. The questions you ask yourself need to be part of your plan. Some questions I have asked myself include the following: What

338. Aurelius, *Meditations*.
339. Seneca, *Delphi Complete Works of Seneca the Younger*.

did I do to develop virtue/excellence today? For what am I grateful? What did I do to be of service today? What did I learn today? Where did I struggle today?

Just remember, if you resist doing it because it is too complicated, simplify.

Exercise
DAILY REVIEW
Reflection for self-cultivation.

What You'll Need
Journal and pen.

Directions
For the next six months, at the day's end, ask yourself these questions.

1. What did I do to develop virtue/excellence today?
2. What did I learn?
3. How can I improve?
4. What is one thing today for which I am grateful?

Exercise
MAKE A PLAN FOR SELF-CULTIVATION
The ancient lovers of wisdom left us a trove of treasures we can use to improve ourselves. I suggest making a reasonable plan that doesn't take on too much all at once and stick to it for six months to a year.

1. Choose two or three virtues to focus on for six months to a year.
2. Create habits and triggers for each.
3. Identify your most troublesome emotion and then use Stoic practices to work toward more tranquility.
4. Choose a text that will stretch you and study it as a contemplative exercise.
5. Adopt a daily review practice.

CHAPTER FIFTEEN
ANCIENT GREEK MAGIC

As both a Pagan whose primary sacred relationships come from ancient Greece and a witch, magic is an important part of my practice. There are entire books on ancient Greek and Hellenistic magic. This chapter grounds the topic by discussing the basics and shares some adaptations for contemporary purposes.

Scholarly works on ancient Greek magic spend tremendous effort trying to define magic in the ancient world. Those discussions are not helpful for practitioners. My current practical definition of magic is "practices or ways of working that bring about change through the intentional and skilled use of forms of causation different than those used or observed in everyday life." This is predicated on a magical worldview that assumes individuals and reality exist on many levels of being and that we can become skilled and conscious actors in all aspects of reality.

Culture and capacity can change. Some things that are currently "magical" could become part of everyday reality. Other capacities, if they cease to have a place in culture, may recede until only specialized magical practitioners can use them. This definition includes a much broader range of activity than ancient Greeks would recognize as magic. It includes many practices in ancient civic religion, personal religion, and the Mysteries covered in previous chapters. Certain capacities, like understanding omens, used to be common but receded until only specialized practitioners, like magicians, develop them now. It is my hope that someday many practices involving building relationships with the Theoi and spirits will be part of common experience again and no longer "magical" per se.

Types of Magic

There are three ancient Greek words translated as "magic": *mageia, pharmakon,* and *goetia.*[340] All three were distinct areas of specialized practice performed by paid experts on behalf of individuals. The experts and their practices were outside of civic, household, or Mystery Religions and had a morally ambiguous reputation. Magic rites were conducted in privacy if not secrecy. Finally, magic was frequently used and part of common life, even if morally ambiguous.

The first kind of magic is where we get the word *magic*—derived from *mageia*—and a practitioner is a *magos*. Present throughout Greece by at least the fifth century BCE, *mageia* was believed to come from Persia, giving the flavor of dangerous exoticism. *Magoi* were itinerant specialists hired for ritual healing, cursing, blessing, and divination. Sometimes their methods included a type of private initiation claiming similarity to Mystery initiations.[341] From the perspective of contemporary magicians, *mageia* has a flavor similar to Ceremonial Magic.

Pharmakon worked with *materia*, especially plants. Typically, the product was a potion that was created and used within a ritual context. This form of magic is particularly related to the goddess Hekate and the great witches of Greek lore like Circe and Medea. While the mythological and dramatic sources emphasize poisons, *pharmakon* includes healing potions, love potions, and alchemical practices using *materia* in the search for transcendence. In fact, Empedocles, the Pre-Socratic philosopher who first postulated the four elements, practiced and taught *pharmakon*, approaching his philosophical work through the mindset of magic. He believed that through his practice he had transcended the limitations of mortality.[342] As in modern witchcraft, a potion gains its potency not only from the material ingredients, but also because of the way those ingredients are interacted with, like using incantations.[343]

---

340. Graf, *Magic in the Ancient World.*
341. Graf, *Magic in the Ancient World.*
342. Graf, *Magic in the Ancient World.*
343. Edmonds, *Drawing Down the Moon.*

Goetia refers to practices modern practitioners would label "shamanic." The *goes*—a word related to the verb *lament*—works in an ecstatic trance to summon the dead for consultation or intervention.[344]

ANCIENT SOURCES

We know about ancient Greek magic from a number of sources. First, there is literature, including the epics, plays, and histories. It is important to remember that dramas are dramatic. Epics must be epic. Material in them cannot be unrecognizable from the standpoint of real magical practice but will be larger than life. There are treatises and laws against magic, including those by Plato.[345] This antagonism toward magic and magicians is not precisely because of magic itself but reflects the prevalence of curse work. Other philosophical treatises, like those by Theophrastus (Father of Botany) give valuable information that would now be considered "magic."[346]

The high number of curses cast yields its own source of evidence. Archaeologists recovered an extraordinary number of curse tablets, figurines used in cursing, and other relevant objects.[347] We also have surviving protective amulets, some of which are inscribed with spells.[348] Evidence of magic survives in art. In particular, the *iynx/iunx,* an important implement of erotic and attraction magic, is in some images of Aphrodite.[349] This kind of material evidence helps us understand how people actually practiced.

Finally, we are blessed to have the *Papyri Graecae Magicae* (PGM), also known as the *Greek Magical Papyri*. This collection of ancient liturgy and spells is from the Hellenistic through the Roman era. It is highly syncretic and mostly produced in Graeco-Roman Egypt. The study of the *PGM* could fill numerous volumes. In this chapter, I stick to more strictly Hellenic sources, but I encourage anyone interested to explore the *PGM*. I use the translation by Betz.[350]

---

344.   Graf, *Magic in the Ancient World*.

345.   Faraone, "Agonistic Context of Early Greek Binding Spells," 3–32.

346.   Scarborough, "Pharmacology of Sacred Plants, Herbs, and Roots."

347.   Faraone, "Agonistic Context of Early Greek Binding Spells," 3–32.

348.   Kotansky, "Incantations and Prayers for Salvation on Inscribed Greek Amulets," 107–37.

349.   Edmonds, *Drawing Down the Moon*.

350.   Betz, ed., *Greek Magical Papyri in Translation*.

THE MAGICIAN

It was common for all individuals to have a close relationship with one of the Theoi, but for magicians, this closeness was particularly rich and deep. In chapter 2, we discussed the implicit theology of *onómata barbariká*, in which ancient Greek magicians would call the Theoi by their "non-Greek names," and how this conveyed a quest to know the nature of the Great One with whom they were closest beyond the limitation of cultural knowledge. Many rites or experiences by which one became a magician presuppose intimacy with divine beings. That close relationship with the divine manifests in the magician as more than human efficacy and knowledge. Becoming a magician was about acquiring specific knowledge and involved receiving teachings and empowerment directly from divine beings. The training of a magician is an initiation through which the magician is granted *charisma*, which is a Greek word meaning "favor or gift from a divine being."

Magic rites use Mystery and initiatory language. Fellow magicians are "fellow initiates" while nonmagicians are "uninitiated." Through this intimacy with a deity, the magician perceives differently than other mortals and is able to act with skill and power that are closed to most. In performing magic, the magician calls to the Great One using keys and signs, demonstrating this hard-won personal knowledge that transcends cultural teachings. When a magician makes a request, it is on the basis of intimate relationship.[351]

FORMS OF MAGIC AND MAGICAL STRATEGY

All types of magical acts discussed below can be used individually for a single purpose or as part of a larger strategy. The basic ancient Greek method for dealing with situations when things go wrong, be it at an individual or a societal level, is the strategy of healing.

1. Recognize the *miasma*. Realize things are not as they should be—that they are not in alignment with *themis*—and that right relationship is violated.

2. Look for the *miasma*'s causes by consulting oracles, using divination, and looking for omens.

---

351. Graf, *Magic in the Ancient World*.

3. Figure out what needs to be done to remove the causes with the same divinatory methods.

4. Remove the cause. Traditional methods include forcing it into an image and then carrying it out of the community through *apompe* and burying it. Bind the malefic if it cannot be removed.

5. Attend to wounded relationships if there are beings who have been offended or hurt. This is a restorative justice approach with the spirit world, the natural world, and other humans.

6. Strengthen the beneficial. This can include rituals for positive and protective deities, including creating or feeding vessels for Them so They can interact with the community. It is also the purpose of many amulets.

Removing Bane through Apompe

If you have identified there is a source of *miasma* or some other bane, like a plague, it is important to remediate or remove the *miasma's* source. If the *miasma's* cause is ruptured relationship, it is essential to do what is necessary to heal the relationship. Sometimes, a power needs to be removed. Sometimes an actual item is polluted and must be removed. Other times, the cause of *miasma* is more abstract and has to be forced into a form. The method for doing this is to force the bane into a representation, like a poppet or figurine. For example, the ancient Greek symbol for plagues is a mouse. A mouse figurine can be ritually made to represent the plague the community is facing. The representation is then put into a box.

Once the bane is linked to a physical object, it is ritually carried outside whatever boundary is relevant: the household, the city, and so on. This is called *apompe*, which is a reverse procession. *Apompe* is a solemn ritual and should be done on foot. Outside the boundary, bury the item in a box in a secret place. If the image has a face, be sure it is buried facedown with the head facing away from the boundary. Another option is to ask a river to take the item holding the bane. Be sure to ask the river, check the omens, and make sure the item won't poison the water. Ideally, carry the item over running water on your way beyond the boundary.

Binding or Restraining Magic

Often you cannot remove a problematic element but have to bind its power. Binding spells (*katadesmos*; in Latin, *defixio*) were common forms of magic. These spells were usually cast by a magician on behalf of a customer. Mostly they were about trying to weaken a competitor and aimed at binding their power to hurt the person paying the magician. Extreme competitiveness was a feature of ancient Greek culture, creating a lot of high-stakes situations that were anxiety provoking. This was especially true in highly litigious Athens where the courts were regularly weaponized. These spells "bind up" some capacity of the target, like binding the tongue of a rival in politics so they couldn't find the right words when speaking.[352]

Surviving binding spells show intense rivalries between businesses, in courtships and athletic contests, between citizens vying for influence, and in households. Such spells seem to have been booming business, as was the process of removing such bindings or protecting against them. Believing in this type of magic was not considered irrational. Reasoned opposition, such as Plato's, was not about its irrationality or lack of efficacy, but its detrimental effect on society.

The basic form of *katadesmos* is a binding formula that is both spoken and written. A chthonic deity is invoked (most often Hermes the Restrainer or Hekate). The tablet with the curse is read aloud, rolled, pierced with a nail, and then deposited in some opening to the Underworld like a grave, well, or crossroads. Sometimes the tablet is accompanied by a symbolically manipulated figure. Most surviving curse tablets are on lead—a common material for letter writing. Other materials could be used, including pot shards (*ostraka*) or wax. If papyrus was used, it hasn't survived. Retrograde writing (writing backward) was common. Sometimes the nail used was taken from a sunken ship. In general, the more symbolism one piles up in a magical act, the stronger the magic.[353]

There are a few common formulas for binding. One is for the magician to assert causal authority with "I bind." "I bind X's hands, tongue, feet." Sometimes it is more passive, like, "May X's hands, tongue, and feet be bound." A deity can be invoked, given an argument as to why they should care, and then asked to

---

352.   Faraone, "Agonistic Context of Early Greek Binding Spells."
353.   Faraone, "Agonistic Context of Early Greek Binding Spells."

intervene. "Hermes the Restrainer! May X be unsuccessful in Y." Sometimes the target is "assigned" to a particular deity to deal with, which mimics legal formulas. "Hermes the Restrainer, I assign X to you for your judgment." Sympathetic analogy can be used, like, "As a corpse is silent and lifeless, may X be silent, useless, and unable to move against me." This type is often accompanied by poppets that are bound and silenced with nails or pins.[354]

The process of magically writing the spell down makes it more permanent and effective; it gives it form. The piercing is a way of "nailing down" and restraining. A curse could be bound with a string and knotted 365 times for each day of the year.[355]

Placing the item where Underworld spirits can receive it is necessary for the spell's efficacy. The grave of one of the untimely dead was seen as particularly efficacious.[356]

While we consider most binding spells to be baneful magic, there are situations in which restraining someone might be ethical, like restraining someone's anger or ability to act if they are likely to harm themselves or others. While sometimes binding is a preemptive strike against a rival, it can also be about taking away someone's ability to cause harm. This may cause some harm in return but might still be the right ethical call. Magic is often the defense of last resort for those denied formal power.

Binding Magic for the Public Good

Katadesmos could be used for the public good. A large public statue of Ares in chains had a binding spell associated with it and was intended to bind the warlike power of an enemy that threatened to invade.[357] As a modern adaptation, if there is an organization causing harm in the community, many have logos and mascots with eyes and mouths that can be bound using the traditional formulas and practices to restrain them from harm.

---

354. Faraone, "Agonistic Context of Early Greek Binding Spells."

355. Edmonds, *Drawing Down the Moon*.

356. Edmonds, *Drawing Down the Moon*.

357. Faraone, "Agonistic Context of Early Greek Binding Spells."

Exercise
BINDING SPELL FOR SITUATIONS OF DOMESTIC VIOLENCE

This spell is to bind the ability of an abuser to cause harm.

What You'll Need

Aluminum foil (in place of lead sheets), a sharpie, and a nail. A place to bury it and a shovel.

Directions

Call into your mind the person you are trying to protect and how much you want to protect them. Let the power of that desire build and then see the person who is hurting them. Have your piece of foil in front of you with your marker. Say, "Hermes Kátochos, Restrainer! I call to you!"

Begin your spell, writing your words retrograde (backward from right to left so it is a mirror image) as you speak the words while also seeing and feeling the power of your intention.

> Hermes Kátochos, I assign [abuser] to you for your judgment! Bind [abuser's] hands and feet, take away [abuser's] power to inflict harm. Bind [abuser's] tongue so it can do no harm. May [abuser's] words and power fail when trying to control or harm [victim] in any aspect of life. [Abuser] is silent and unable to move against [victim] or anyone else. Bind [abuser's] power down, nail down [abuser's] influence, rend the veil of [abuser's] glamour so all see [abuser] in a true light.

Read it aloud one more time and then begin folding the foil, saying "I nail [abuser's] power down!" repeatedly as you do so. When it is small but still thin enough, you can put the nail through. Continue the chant while piercing the foil through with the nail and seeing the abuser's power being bound. At the end, proclaim, "[Abuser's] power is bound!" Take the nailed foil and bury it somewhere it will never be found, ideally in a graveyard or down a well, but anyplace that is not your home will do. Thank Hermes Kátochos.

Justice Spells

Binding spells are preventative, but justice spells are about either punishment or rectifying harm done. The petitioner, who must be identified, is bringing their case to some group of Great Ones and asking for justice. It is common to appeal to the Underworld Court, which includes Hades, Persephone, and the Erinyes, or to appeal to solar deities, since They see all.[358]

The structure matches the formula for petitioning a royal figure. The spell calls on particular deities using Their honorifics and epithets referring to Their role in upholding justice or meting out punishment. It expresses supplication and makes the case for how justice has been violated and why the desired outcome is appropriate. The deities are entreated to have mercy on the petitioner. The case is given over to the Gods with the understanding that They will do what is truly right. Sometimes the accused is "assigned to" or "consecrated to" the deity. It is not uncommon for the spell to include exculpatory language in which the petitioner asks to be protected from contagion that might arise from contact with the culprit, since sometimes this cannot be avoided. Disease was believed to be a common punishment.[359] Justice spells can also be used when you do not know the perpetrator.

I have used justice spells in instances where I believed there were bad actors at work, but where I also recognized I did not have all the information. Sometimes I combine a judicial spell with a binding spell when I believe an individual or group is engaged in ongoing harm to innocents. I petition for the target to be held accountable for past harm and restrained from committing future harm.

Exercise
JUSTICE SPELL FOR AN UNKNOWN PERPETRATOR

A spell calling the Underworld Court to ask for justice against an unknown perpetrator.

What You'll Need

An offering.

---

358.   Versnel, "Beyond Cursing," 60–106.

359.   Versnel, "Beyond Cursing," 60–106.

Directions

Pray to Hades and Persephone.

> *Hades Aidoneus and Persephone Despoina, blessed king and queen of the Underworld, renowned for your justice and mercy, I, [Petitioner], call to the Underworld Court! A grievous harm has been done. [In a sentence, name the harm.] It is my place to call to you because [explain your standing, for example that you are the victim or your relation to the victim]. I do not know who the perpetrator is. I call for justice and assign the perpetrator to you for your judgment. Dread holy ones, hold the perpetrator to account and prevent the perpetrator from harming others. I honor you and your wisdom. Please accept this offering as an expression of my gratitude.*

Give the offering.

Attracting Spells

Erotic spells were the most common attracting magic but would be considered baneful now. *Agogai* are rituals designed to lead a desired person to one's bed, compelling them into sexual surrender by creating obsession. Desperate and dangerous women using magic to lure sexy men was a literary trope—and projection. Surviving evidence suggests most people casting erotic magic were men trying to ensorcell young women. This probably has to do with how structured courtship was, making it difficult to get young women alone.[360]

Agogai spells can take many forms. They can rely on an intermediary spirit sent to torment the target until she comes to the man calling her. Some use sympathetic magic with fire to make someone burn with lust. Various potions and oils, if you can manage to get the target to drink or touch them, will create a bond compelling them to come to the person casting the spell.

---

360.   Edmonds, *Drawing Down the Moon.*

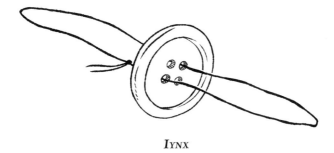

IYNX

Using an *iynx,* or sometimes a *rhombus* or *strophalos,* is interesting because it can be adapted for more benefic purposes. The *iynx* is like a button whirligig toy that makes a whirring noise. A *rhombus* is a bullroarer and a *strophalos* is a whirling disc or wheel that is sacred to Hekate. Named for the wryneck bird, as you spin the *iynx,* you speak the spell of attraction. Its spinning creates repetition, increasing the power of the spoken spell. The *iynx* is a common motif in jewelry and erotic art. It functions like a prayer wheel or fretting spell, increasing the thought form's power. The sound it emits while spinning is important to the magic. The philosopher and magician Proclus was adept at using the *iynx.* It is associated with Aphrodite but is also sacred to Hekate, as are the *rhombus* and *strophalos.* Any of these can be used in any attracting/increasing spell.[361]

Exercise
A SPELL OF INCREASE USING AN IYNX
This is a spell for increase.

What You'll Need
A 5-by-5-inch piece of cardboard, scissors, pen, a 3-foot piece of string (any kind).

Directions
Identify something you want to increase in your life. Trace a circle on a piece of cardboard as large as a water glass, and then cut it out. Poke two holes in the circle large enough for a string to easily go through. Cut a three-foot piece of string and string it through, tying the ends together. On each

361. Edmonds, *Drawing Down the Moon.*

side of the cardboard, write your intention in the formula "[your intention], come to me!" For example, "Wealth, come to me!" Put as much power into it as you can and charge it with intention. You can decorate it if you like. Pull the string so the disc is in the middle. Hold one side still while you swing the other end in a circular motion, winding it up, while you repeat your incantation. Once your string is as twisted as it can be, hold both ends of the string tightly and move your hands in and out while saying your incantation. With each turn, see your incantation written on the wheel passing through all the realms and drawing your target to you.

Variation: Iynx Spell for the Public Good

Follow the instructions for the previous spell, but instead of calling to something for yourself, think of an intention of what you want to increase in your community or society. Create a statement that is also a command for what you want. For example, "Kindness increase!"

Protection Amulets

Protection magic can stand on its own or be incorporated into other activities. Amulets were commonly used to strengthen and protect patients undergoing medical treatment. Disease was understood to result from *miasma*, so protecting oneself from *miasma* was important—especially when vulnerable. *Miasma*, being spiritual pollution, might not be the immediate fault of the person afflicted but can be in the environment. Regular purification and cleansing are essential, but amulets help manage life in a world impacted by *miasma*.

The Greek words for amulets include *periammon*, which means "something that is tied on," and *phylakterion*, which means "something that protects" and is where we get the English word *phylactery*. Amulets do not have power alone but require appropriate incantations.[362] You must tell the amulet its job. This is similar to how contemporary witches work. A particular stone may have characteristic potencies, but if you don't tell it what you want it to do, it is not a spell—it is just a rock.

Amulets could be made of plants, stones, or metals and could come in many forms—often a ring. They were typically inscribed. They could be pro-

---

362. Kotansky, "Incantations and Prayers for Salvation on Inscribed Greek Amulets."

grammed for many purposes in addition to protection, like bringing victory or to draw blessings. The use of amulets as part of larger magical strategies is a useful model.

Objects left in particular locations can function as amulets for those pieces of Earth. Often you can find statues or art depicting Athena in one of Her guises, including Themis, in civic buildings. If you begin treating them as sacred representations and vessels for Athena as the protector of Democracy, they will start functioning in this way. I also find working with public statues as though they are large amulets tied to their location works well, For example, I ask the lions on bridges to protect the bridge. Pay attention to your public statuary. Another type of vessel is the *baityloi*, which are protective stones traditionally taken from a local river and dedicated to Apollon Alexikakos, the averter of evil. Place them outside of important buildings as ward stones.

Exercise
PROTECTION AMULET
A spell to create an amulet that will provide personal protection.

What You'll Need
A piece of jewelry you will wear every day—rings are ideal. The design should resonate as "protection" to you. Gorgons and snakes are traditional, but you may want a protective stone, like carnelian. Water with sea salt dissolved, frankincense or a bay leaf, and a safe vessel for burning. If choosing frankincense, you will need charcoal.

Directions
Purify the jewelry by immersing it quickly in sea salt water and then pass it through smoke of frankincense or bay leaf. Think of the power of the guardian and choose an appropriate name. Hold the jewelry and speak to it.

> *[Name], [Name], I name you [Name],*
> *Guardian of my body,*
> *Guarantor of my safety,*
> *When there is danger, you will warn me and direct me away.*

If I am threatened, you will frighten the aggressor until they retreat.

I will hear your warning and will listen.

[Name], [Name], I name you [Name].

Put on your new amulet and periodically speak to it by name.

CONCLUSION

My friends, we have reached the end of this stage of our *theoria* in our heroic song. I invite you to gaze backward over our time together and think again on Mnemosyne—Holy Mother Memory. Think back to when you first began reading these pages and your progress through them. Did you experience anything that felt more like remembering than learning? Did you ever feel like you were reading something you have always known, but didn't realize it until that moment? If you did have this experience, I encourage you to revisit it in your mind as viscerally as you can and pay attention to the sensations so you will recognize this phenomenon in the future. That is the gift of Divine Memory. It is wisdom that is always available to us, but we are not trained to recognize it.

Throughout our time together, you have been drinking the healing Waters of Mnemosyne, calling to the immortal parts of self—the parts that are an aspect of the Source of All—and strengthening their link to the part of you that is currently in incarnation. It is my hope that you are both in stronger relationships with the Theoi and that you have called your Self back to yourself and re-membered. I am hopeful that your imagination of what could be—of alternatives to the way we are living now—has deepened.

I am grateful for our fellowship, for the chance to introduce you to the Theoi as I know Them, and to share the foundations of ancient

Greek religion for Modern Pagans. I hope you will continue to participate in rebirthing and re-membering these sacred traditions and building the beloved community rooted in *philia* and the pursuit of *areté*. Together, through continuing to drink the Waters of Mnemosyne, we can bring more divine Light down, allowing us to better align what is with what should be.

For the next steps in your journey, I suggest deepening your practice and building your relationships as described in the book. Know it takes time to build strong relationships. I encourage you to read ancient sources in translation. Even if you read some before in a different context, reread them with your new perspective.

RECOMMENDED ANCIENT TEXTS FOR NEXT STEPS

Start with what interests you the most. The texts I recommend have numerous translations and are often available from your public library. Ask a librarian for help if you cannot find what you want.

HYMNS

- *The Homeric Hymns*
- *The Orphic Hymns*
- Any hymn by Pindar

EPICS

- *Iliad* by Homer
- *Odyssey* by Homer

PLAYS

- Anything by Aeschylus
- Anything by Sophocles
- Anything by Euripides
- Anything by Aristophanes

HISTORIES

- *Histories* by Herodotus
- *Description of Greece* by Pausanias
- *Lives* or *Parallel Lives* by Plutarch (same thing with different variations on the translated title)

PHILOSOPHY

- *Nicomachean Ethics* by Aristotle
- Anything by Plato

GLOSSARY OF GREEK WORDS

Acropolis: Upper city, typically an ancient citadel given to the Theoi.

Adyton: The inner sanctum in a temple, typically restricted access.

Agathos: Morally good and kind. Agathos Daimon is the "good spirit."

Agogai: A spell of attraction, usually erotic attraction.

Agon: Competition. From which we get *protagonist* and *antagonist*.

Alsos: Sacred grove.

Amphidromia: Ritual in which a newborn is welcomed into the *oikos*.

Anabasis: Ascent. Going up.

Anaktaron: Holiest of the Holies in Eleusis. The temple's portion where Demeter lived when She was on Earth.

Apompe: Ritual procession out of the community. Used in removing an influence from the community.

Apotheosis: The act and process of a human becoming one of the Theoi.

Archegetes: The Founder. A type of hero.

Areté: Virtue and excellence. The rarified essence of a living being in its perfect state.

Aulos: Double-reed instrument sacred to Dionysus—ancestor of the oboe and bassoon.

Bothros: A pit in which offerings to chthonic beings are thrown or poured.

Cella: Main room of a temple where the God's sacred statue is located.

Charis: Grace. Favor. The Charites are the goddesses who are the Graces. Charisma is a gift of grace given by the Theoi.

Chresmologues: The people who recorded the oracles and the recordings of oracular utterances.

Chthonios/Chthonic: Of Earth and Underworld.

Cosmopolis: The view that the world is a polis and one is a citizen of the world.

Daimon: Any of the spirits that do not primarily exist in physical bodies, usually other than the Theoi. This can include the immortal parts of ourselves that are not bound by body.

Daphne: Bay laurel tree or leaves and also the nymph, beloved by Apollon, who is the bay laurel.

Deipnon: Evening supper on the dark of the moon left at the crossroads in honor of Hekate. Historically, it would have been a feast for those under Her care who were on the margins of society.

Dekate: The tenth part, or a tithe, given to the Theoi in thanks for the accomplishment of a venture.

Dodeka Theoi: The twelve gods we call the Olympians.

Dynamis: Potency of active energy from which we get *dynamism*.

Ekstasis: A state of consciousness in which you stand outside yourself. From which we get *ecstasy*.

Empousa: A class of terrifying female beings in Hekate's retinue.

Epheboi: Young men serving their mandatory military service and training to become full citizens.

Epiphaneia (Eng. epiphany): An intervention in which one of the Theoi makes Themselves directly known in this world.

Eschatia: The furthermost reaches. The wilderness beyond human civilization.

Eudaimonia: Often translated as "happiness," it is the state of being a "good/blessed spirit." Eudaimonic ethics are centered on the idea that what is ethical is that which allows us to live as good spirits.

Goes: A practitioner of *Goetia* who is able to work directly with the spirits of the dead.

Goetia: A branch of magic we would recognize as "shamanic" in nature and involves working directly with the spirit world, especially the ancestors.

Hagnos: Both ritual and moral purity.

Hamartia: The tragic mistake. Part of the human condition.

Hellene/Hellas: Greek/Greece.

Heptascopy: Divining truth from investigating the liver of a sacrificial animal.

Hestiatorion: A dining hall in sanctuaries where participants would share a sacred meal with each other and the Theoi.

Hiera: The sacred. The sacred objects carried by priestesses back and forth between Eleusis and Athens for the Mysteries.

Hiera rezein: To do the sacred things. The ritual complex called sacrifice.

Holokauston: To burn an offering totally without the sacrificed offering being part of a shared meal.

Horos/horoi: Boundary stone/stones.

Hubris: Flaw of character for which one bears moral culpability.

Iynx/iunx: Object like a button whirligig used in erotic magic and spells of increase.

Kadiskos: Sacred jar that becomes a vessel for Zeus Kteios (of the storeroom) to bless the prosperity of the *oikos.*

Kalos: Good and beautiful, both aesthetically and morally.

Katabasis: To descend or turn inward.

Katadesmos: Magical binding or restraining.

Katoptromancy: Scrying into mirrors.

Khora: The countryside and villages associated with a particular community.

Kithara: A seven-stringed instrument in the lyre family used by professional musicians and sacred to Apollon.

Kledon: Overheard speech that has symbolic meaning revealing truth.

Kleromancy: Divination through lots, dice, or knucklebones.

Kohes: Libations poured to the ancestors.

Kouros: Statues of young men often in honor of Apollon, who is the patron of young men.

Kubernetes: The sailor who steers the ship. This becomes a synonym for a political leader and is the source from which we get governor and the metaphor "the ship of state."

Kykeon: Potion, in particular the potion used in the Eleusinian Mysteries.

Mageia: A type of magic Greeks considered to have origins in Persia. Its flavor is similar to Ceremonial Magic.

Magos/magoi: A magician or magicians, properly a practitioner of *mageia*.

Mantis: A religious specialist who is possessed by a god, usually Apollon, to speak oracles.

Megalopsyche: The excellence/virtue of being big souled. Rising above petty things.

Miasma: Spiritual pollution.

Mnemosyne: Memory and the goddess of memory who is mother of the Muses.

Moira: Fate, but not predestination. It is the underlying structure of reality.

Moiragetes: Leader of the Fates. A title given to Apollon and to Zeus and indicates total understanding of the underlying structure of reality and the ability to advise based on that understanding.

Mystagogos: Leader of initiates in the Mysteries. This position functions as a sponsor who is responsible for the would-be initiates and their preparation.

Mystai: Mystery initiates.

Mysteria: The Mysteries. A specialized form of Greek religion that is initiatory.

Naiskos: A shrine.

Naos: A temple.

Noumenia: The first day of the month. The morning after the dark of the moon.

Oikos: The household. This is the base unit of Greek society.

Ologymos: Ululation. The ritual cry of women at the moment a sacrificial animal is slain.

Omphalos: Naval, specifically the naval stone marking the center of all things. This is a cult symbol of Apollon and is present in His oracular temples—the most important being in Delphi.

Oneiromancy: Divination through dreams.

Onómata barbariká: The "barbarous names" which means the names of the Theoi in any non-Greek language.

Opisthodomos: The back room in a temple, often where sacred items are stored.

Paian: A type of hymn sung to Apollon and later to Asklepios as well. It is related to Their role as healers.

Parthenos: Virgin, but it can also mean a female who holds her own sovereignty apart from men. Artemis and Athena usually have this title, but sometimes Aphrodite does as well. It is different from *kore*, which means a young woman or maiden who is before marriageable age.

Pelanos: A barley cake that is a ritual offering. In some cults, the temple sold the pelanos as an entry fee.

Periammon: An amulet.

Peribolos: Boundary wall.

Pharmakon: A type of magic using *materia*, like potions.

Phasmata: The appearance of a spirit.

Phiale: A flat bowl with a raised omphalos in the center used for libations.

Philia: The love that is friendship, which includes personal affection.

Philosophia: Philosophy, the love of wisdom.

Phratry: The fraternity. A social organization that is larger than the *oikos* in which members shared various civic duties and held sacrifice rituals together.

Phylakterion: A protection amulet.

Polis: The society of which one is a member. In ancient Greece, this would be the city-state.

Polymetis: Many intelligences; also indicates cunningness. Frequent descriptor of Athena and Odysseus.

Pompe: Ritual procession.

Pronaos: The porch of a temple.

Propylaea: Monumental gateway to the sacred precinct.

Prytaneion: Building containing the city's sacred hearth.

Psychopompe: Guide of the dead. Literally, "soul procession."

Pythia: The *mantis* of Apollon at Delphi related to Pytho, which means "to rot."

Rhombus: A type of bullroarer used in some rituals and also in increase magic.

Rhyton: A ceremonial drinking vessel shaped like a horn and usually includes an animal's head motif that is used for libations.

Schole: Leisure time, meaning the time set apart from all duties of life. It is only with sufficient schole that we can devote ourselves to the development of *areté*.

Sophia: Wisdom.

Strophalos: A whirling disc or wheel used in some rituals and also in increase magic. Sacred to Hekate.

Techne: Technology. Physical, practical things created by humans out of raw materials.

Teleisthai: "To be initiated" into the Mysteries.

Telete: The actual Mystery initiation.

Teleutan: Dying.

Telos: The end. The true purpose.

Temenos: The sacred precinct.

Themistes: The way things should be.

Theoi: The Gods.

Theophaneia (Eng. theophany): The direct appearance of one of the Theoi.

Theoria: A sacred journey.

Theoxenia: Hospitality for the Gods. It is a ritual meal in which the Gods are invited as guests.

Thuein: "To make smoke." A name for ritual sacrifice to the Gods.

WORKS CITED

Aeschylus. "The Eumenides." In *The Orestes Plays of Aeschylus*, translated by Paul Roche, 155–202. New York: New American Library, 1962.

Alexiou, Margaret. *The Ritual Lament in Greek Tradition, Second Edition*. Edited by Dimitrios Yatromanolakis and Panagiotis Roilos. New York: Rowman & Littlefield, 2002. http://nrs.harvard.edu/urn -3:hul.ebook:CHS_AlexiouM.Ritual_Lament_in_Greek_Tradition .2002.

Andronicos, Manolis. *Delphi*. Athens, Greece: Ekdotike Athenon S.A., 1983.

Anghelina, Catalin. "The Homeric Gates of Horn and Ivory." *Museum Helveticum* 67, no. 2 (2010): 65–72.

Aristotle. *Nicomachaean Ethics*. Translated by H. Rackham. Loeb Classical Library. Cambridge, MA: Harvard University Press, 1934.

———. "On Divination in Sleep." In *The Complete Works of Aristotle: The Revised Oxford Translation*, edited by Barnes, Jonathan, translated by Beare, J.I., 1:736–39. Princeton, NJ: Princeton University Press, 1984.

———. "On Dreams." In *The Complete Works of Aristotle: The Revised Oxford Translation*, edited by Barnes, Jonathan, translated by Bear, J.I., 1:729–35. Princeton, NJ: Princeton University Press, 1984.

―――. *Politics*. Translated by H. Rackham. Loeb Classical Library. Cambridge, MA: Harvard University Press, 1944.

Arrian. *The Campaigns of Alexander*. Translated by Aubrey de Selincourt. New York: Penguin Books, 2003.

Athanassakis, Apostolos N., trans. "Homeric Hymn to Apollon." In *The Homeric Hymns*, 15–47. Baltimore, MD: The Johns Hopkins University Press, 1976.

―――. "Homeric Hymn to Athena." In *The Homeric Hymns*, 66. Baltimore, MD: The Johns Hopkins University Press, 1976.

―――. "Homeric Hymn to Demeter." In *The Homeric Hymns*, 1–15. Baltimore, MD: The Johns Hopkins University Press, 1976.

Atsma, Aaron J. "The Theoi Project." Accessed November 5, 2023. https://www.theoi.com.

Aurelius, Marcus. *Meditations: A New Translation (Modern Library)*. Modern Library, 2002.

Betz, Hans Dieter, ed. *The Greek Magical Papyri in Translation: Including the Demotic Spells, Second Edition*. Chicago: University of Chicago Press, 1992.

Blackmore, Susan. *Dying to Live: Near-Death Experiences*. New York: Prometheus Books, 1993.

Boer, Jelle De, J. R. Hale, and J. Chanton. "New Evidence for the Geological Origins of the Ancient Delphic Oracle." *Geology* 29, no. 8 (2001): 707–10.

Boer, J. Z. De, and J. R. Hale. "The Geological Origins of the Oracle at Delphi, Greece." In *The Archaelogy of Catastrophes,* edited by W. J. McGuire, D. R. Griffiths, and P. L. Hancock, 399–412. London: The Geological Society, 2000.

Brown, Christopher G. "Dionysus and the Mysteries: Aristophanes, Frogs 285ff." *The Classical Quarterly* 41, no. 1 (1991): 41–50.

Burkert, Walter. *Ancient Mystery Cults*. Cambridge, MA: Harvard University Press, 1987.

―――. *Greek Religion*. Cambridge, MA: Harvard University Press, 1985.

Cameron, Alexander Scott. "Athena and Herakles a Divine Couple? The Use of Ancient Sexual Artistic Conventions in Context." University of California Irvine, 2018.

Campbell, Joseph. *The Hero with a Thousand Faces*. New York: Pantheon Books, 1949.

Central Intelligence Agency. "Greece." *CIA World Fact Book* (blog). Accessed November 3, 2023. https://www.cia.gov/the-world-factbook/countries/greece/.

Cole, Sudan G. "Landscapes of Dionysos and Elysian Fields." In *Greek Mysteries: The Archaeology and Ritual of Ancient Greek Secret Cults*, edited by Cosmopoulos, Michael B., 193–217. New York: Routledge, 2003.

Cole, Susan Guettel. *Landscapes, Gender, and Ritual Space: The Ancient Greek Experience*. Berkeley, CA: University of California Press, 2004.

Connely, Joan Breton. *Portrait of a Priestess: Women and Ritual in Ancient Greece*. Princeton, NJ: Princeton University Press, 2007.

Copleston, Frederick S. J. *A History of Philosophy: Volume I: Greece and Rome*. Vol. 1. 9 vols. New York: Image Books, 1993.

Cox, Cheryl Anne. *Household Interests: Property, Marriage Strategies, and Family Dynamics in Ancient Athens*. Princeton, NJ: Princeton University Press, 1998.

D'Aulaire, Ingri, and Edgar Parin D'Aulaire. *D'Aulaires' Book of Greek Myths*. Garden City, NY: DoubleDay & Company, 1962.

Deacy, Susan. "Gods—Olympian or Chthonian?" In *The Oxford Handbook of Ancient Greek Religion*, edited by Esther Eidinow and Julia Kindt, 356–67. Oxford: Oxford University Press, 2015.

———. "Herakles and His 'Girl': Athena, Heroism and Beyond." In *Herakles and Hercules: Exploring a Graeco-Roman Divinity*, edited by Louis Rawlings and Hugh Bowden, 37–50. Swansea, Wales: The Classical Press of Wales, 2005.

Dickie, Matthew W. *Magic and Magicians in the Greco-Roman World*. New York: Routledge, 2001.

Dillon, Matthew. "Households, Families, and Women." In *The Oxford Handbook of Ancient Greek Religion*, edited by Esther Eidinow and Julia Kindt, 241–55. Oxford: Oxford University Press, 2015.

Divey, George C., ed. *Divry's Modern English-Greek and Greek-English Desk Dictionary*. New York: D.C. Divry, 1976.

Edelstein, Ludwig. *Ancient Medicine: Selected Papers of Ludwig Edelstein*. Edited by Temkin, Owsei and Temkin, C. Lilian. Translated by Temkin, C. Lilian. Baltimore: Johns Hopkins University Press, 1967.

Edmonds, Radcliffe G. III. *Drawing Down the Moon: Magic in the Ancient Greco -Roman World*. Princeton, NJ: Princeton University Press, 2019.

———. *The "Orphic" Gold Tablets and Greek Religion: Further Along the Path*. Cambridge: Cambridge University Press, 2011.

Edmunds, Lowell. "The Religiosity of Alexander." *Greek and Roman Byzantine Studies* 12, no. 3 (1971): 363–91.

Ensdiø, Dag Øistein. "To Lock Up Eleusis: A Question of Liminal Space." *Numen* 47, no. 4 (2000): 351–86.

Evans, Nancy A. "Sanctuaries, Sacrifices, and the Eleusinian Mysteries." *Numen: International Review for the History of Religions* 49, no. 3 (2002): 227–54.

Faraone, Christopher A. "The Agonistic Context of Early Greek Binding Spells." In *Magick Hiera: Ancient Greek Magic and Religion*, edited by Christopher A. Faraone and Dirk Obbink, 3–32. New York: Oxford University Press, 1991.

Feen, Richard Harrow. "Keeping the Balance: Ancient Greek Philosophical Concerns with Population and Environment." *Population and Environment* 17, no. 6 (1996): 447–58.

Flower, Michael Attyah. *The Seer in Ancient Greece*. Berkeley, CA: University of California Press, 2008.

Fontenrose, Joseph. *The Delphic Oracle: Its Operations and Response*. Berkeley, CA: University of California Press, 1978.

———. *The Delphic Oracle: Its Operations and Response*. Berkeley, CA: University of California Press, 1978.

Galen. *Galen: On Food and Diet*. Translated by Mark Grant. London: Routledge, 2000.

Gawlinski, Laura. "The Athenian Calendar of Sacrifices: A New Fragment from the Athenian Agora." *Hesperia: The Journal of the American School of Classical Studies at Athens* 76, no. 1 (3007): 37–55.

Graf, Fitz. *Apollo*. New York: Routledge, 2009.

———. "Healing." In *The Oxford Handbook of Ancient Greek Religion*, edited by Esther Eidinow and Julia Kindt, 505–18. Oxford: Oxford University Press, 2015.

———. *Magic in the Ancient World*. Translated by Franklin Philip. Cambridge, MA: Harvard University Press, 1997.

Haarman, Harald. *Roots of Ancient Greek Civilization: The Influence of Old Europe*. Jefferson, N.C: McFarland, 2014.

Håland, Evy Johanne. "Water Sources and the Sacred in Modern and Ancient Greece and Beyond." *Water History* 1 (2009): 83–108.

Hamilton, Mary. *Incubation: Or, the Cure of Disease in Pagan Temples and Christian Churches*. London: W.C. Henderson & Son, St. Andrews, 1906.

Herodotus. *The Histories*. Translated by Aubrey de Sélincourt. New York: Penguin Books, 1954.

———. *The Histories*. Translated by Robin Waterfield. New York: Oxford University Press, 1998.

———. *The Histories*. Translated by Tom Holland. New York: Viking, 2014.

Herodotus and Aubrey De Sélincourt. *Herodotus: The Histories*. History.English, 599 pages. [Harmondsworth, Middlesex]: Penguin Books, 1955. catalog. hathitrust.org/Record/102105186.

Hitch, Sarah, and Rutherford, Ian, eds. *Animal Sacrifice in the Ancient Greek World*. Cambridge: Cambridge University Press, 2017.

Homer. *The Iliad of Homer,*. Translated by Richmond Lattimore. Chicago: Chicago University Press, 1951.

———. *The Odyssey*. Translated by Wilson, Emily. New York: W. W. Norton, 2018.

Hufford, David J. "The Healing Power of Extraordinary Spiritual Experiences." *Journal of Near- Death Studies* 32, no. 3 (2014): 137–56.

Humphreys, S.C. *The Family, Women and Death: Comparative Studies: Second Edition*. Ann Arbor, Michigan: The University of Michigan Press, 1993.

"Idiot." In *Oxford English Dictionary*, n.d. https://doi.org/10.1093/OED /6390117550.

Instone, Stephen. *Greek Personal Religion: A Reader*. Oxford: Aris and Phillips, 2009.

Irvine, William B. *A Guide to the Good Life: The Ancient Art of Stoic Joy*. New York: Oxford University Press, 20009.

Johnston, Sarah Iles. *Ancient Greek Divination*. Oxford: Wiley-Blackwell, 2008.

———. *Hekate Soteira*. Atlanta: Scholars Press, 1990.

———. "Oracles and Divination." In *The Oxford Handbook of Ancient Greek Religion*, edited by Eidinow, Esther and Kindt, Julia, 477–89. Oxford: Oxford University Press, 2015.

Kearns, Emily. *Ancient Greek Religion: A Sourcebook*. Malden, MA: Wiley -Blackwell, 2010.

———. "The Nature of Heroines." In *The Sacred and the Feminine in Ancient Greece*, edited by Blundell, Sue and Williamson, Margaret, 96–110. New York: Routledge, 1998.

Kennedy, John F. "President John F. Kennedy's Inaugural Address," 1961. https://www.archives.gov/milestone-documents/president-john -f-kennedys-inaugural-address.

Kerenyi, Carl. *Eleusis: Archetypal Image of Mother and Daughter*. Translated by Manheim, Ralph. Princeton, NJ: Princeton University Press, 1967.

Kinsey, Brian, ed. *Heroes and Heroines of Greece and Rome*. New York: Marshall Cavendish Reference, 2012.

Kotansky, Roy. "Incantations and Prayers for Salvation on Inscribed Greek Amulets." In *Magick Hiera: Ancient Greek Magic and Religion*, edited by Faraone, Christopher A. and Dirk Obbink, 107–37. New York: Oxford University Press, 1991.

Larson, Jennifer. *Understanding Greek Religion*. New York: Routledge, 2016.

Lipsey, Roger. *Have You Been to Delphi? Tales of the Ancient Oracle for Modern Minds*. Albany NY: State University of New York Press, 2001.

Morris, Ian, and Barry B. Powell. *The Greeks: History, Culture, and Society*. Upper Saddle River, NJ: Pearson Prentice Hall, 2006.

Mylonas, George E. *Eleusis and the Eleusinian Mysteries*. Princeton, NJ: Princeton University Press, 1961.

Nagy, Gregory. *The Ancient Greek Hero in 24 Hours*. Cambridge, MA: The Belknap Press of Harvard University Press, 2013.

Naiden, Fred. "Sacrifice." In *The Oxford Handbook of Ancient Greek Religion*, edited by Esther Eidinow and Julia Kindt, 463–75. Oxford: Oxford University Press, 2015.

Naiden, F. S. *Smoke Signals for the Gods: Ancient Greek Sacrifice from the Archaic through the Roman Periods*. Oxford: Oxford University Press, 2013.

———. "The Fallacy of the Willing Victim." *The Journal of Hellenic Studies* 127 (2007): 61–73.

National Greek Tourism Organisation. "Islands." *Visit Greece* (blog). Accessed November 2, 2023. https://www.visitgreece.gr/islands/.

Otto, Walter F. "Ariadne," 181–88. Dallas: Spring Publications, 1965.

Ovid. *The Metamorphoses*. Translated by Horace Gregory. New York: Viking Press, 1958.

Panopoulos, Christos Pandion, Panagiotopoulous, Panagiotis, and Armyras, Erymanthos. *Hellenic Polytheism: Household Worship*. Translated by Madytinos and Madytinou. Athens, Greece: Labrys Polytheistic Community, 2014.

Parke, H. W. *Greek Oracles*. London: Hutchinson University Library, 1967.

Parke, H. W, and D. E. W. Wormell. *The Delphic Oracle*. Oxford: Basil Blackwell, 1956.

Pausanius. *Guide to Greece: Volume 1 Central Greece*. Translated by Peter Levi. New York: Penguin Books, 1971.

———. *Pausanias Descriptions of Greece, with an English Translation by W. H. S. Jones*. Edited by Richard Ernest Wycherley. Translated by William Henry Samuel Jones. London: Heinemann, 1918.

Pedley, John. *Sanctuaries and the Sacred in the Ancient Greek World*. Cambridge: Cambridge University Press, 2005.

Petridou, Georgia. "'Blessed Is He, Who Has Seen': The Power of Ritual Viewing and Fraing in Eleusis." *Helios* 40, no. 1–2 (2013): 309–41. https://doi.org/10.1353/hel.2013.0015.

Petrovic, Ivana. "Deification—Gods or Men?"." In *The Oxford Handbook of Ancient Greek Religion*, 429–43. Oxford: Oxford University Press, 2015.

Petsas, Photios M. *Delphi: Monuments and Museum*. Athens, Greece: Krene Editions, 2013.

Pitruzzella, Salvo. "Drama and Healing in Ancient Greece: Demeter and Ask-leios." *Dramatherapy* 33, no. 2 (2011): 74–86.

Plato. "Apology." In *Euthypho, Apology, Crito, Phaedo, Phaedrus*, translated by Harold North Fowler. Loeb Classical Library. Cambridge, MA: Harvard University Press, 1934.

———. "Phaedo." In *Plato: Euthyphro, Apology, Crito, Phaedo*, translated by Harold North Fowler, 193–403. Cambridge, MA: Harvard University Press, 1914.

———. "Phaedrus." In *Euthypho, Apology, Crito, Phaedo, Phaedrus*, translated by Harold North Fowler, 405–579. Loeb Classical Library. Cambridge, MA: Harvard University Press, 1934.

———. *Plato's Parmenides, Revised Edition*. Translated by R. E. Allen. New Haven, CT: Yale University Press, 1997.

———. "The Laws." In *The Works of Plato*, translated by B. Jowett, 400–482. New York: Tudor Publishing Company, n.d.

Platt, Verity. "Epiphany." In *The Oxford Handbook of Ancient Greek Religion*, edited by Esther Eidinow and Julia Kindt, 492–504. Oxford: Oxford University Press, 2015.

Plutarch. *Moralia*. Translated by Gregorius N. Bernadakis. Leipzig: Teubner, 1895.

———. "The Oracles at Delphi No Longer Given In Verse." In *Moralia V*, translated by Frank Cole Babbitt, 255–345. Loeb Classical Library. Cambridge, MA: Harvard University Press, 1936.

Plutarch and Frank Cole Babbitt. "The Obsolescence of Oracles." In *Moralia V*, 348–501. Loeb Classical Library. Cambridge, MA: Harvard University Press, 1936.

Pollan, Michael. *How to Change Your Mind: What the New Science of Psychedelics Teaches Us About Consciousness, Dying, Addiction, Depression, and Transcendence*. New York: Penguin Books, 2018.

Pomeroy, Sarah B. *Xenophon Oeconomicus: A Social and Historical Commentary*. Oxford: Clarendon Press, 1994.

Rice, David G., and John E. Stambaugh. "Sacrifices and Festivals." In *Sources for the Study of Greek Religion: Corrected Version.* The Society for Biblical Literature, 2009.

———. *Sources for the Study of Greek Religion.* Society for Biblical Literature, 2009.

"Sacrifice." In *Merriam-Webster.Com Dictionary.* Accessed November 7, 2023. https://www.merriam-webster.com/dictionary/sacrifice.

Scarborough, John. "The Pharmacology of Sacred Plants, Herbs, and Roots." In *Magick Hiera: Ancient Greek Magic and Religion,* edited by Christopher A. Faraone and Dirk Obbink, 138–74. New York: Oxford University Press, 1991.

Scott, Michael. *Delphi and Olympia: The Spatial Politics of Panhellenism in the Archaic and Classical Periods.* New York: Cambridge University Press, 2010.

Seaford, Richard. *The Origins of Philosophy in Ancient Greece and India: A Historical Comparison.* New York: Cambridge University Press, 2020.

Seneca, Lucius Annaeus. *Delphi Complete Works of Seneca the Younger,* n.d.

———. "On Anger." In *Seneca the Younger: Complete Works,* translated by Aubrey Stewart. Delphi Classics, 2014.

———. "On Obedience to the Universal Will." In *Epistles / Seneca; with an English Translation,* translated by Richard M. Gummere, 29. Cambridge, MA: Harvard University Press, 1996.

Sofroniew, Alexandra. *Household Gods: Private Devotion in Ancient Greece and Rome.* Los Angeles: The J. Paul Getty Museum, 2015.

Sophocles. "Oedipus at Colonus." In *Sophocles I,* edited by David Grene and Richmond Lattimore, translated by Robert Fitzgerald, 77–155. Chicago: University of Chicago Press, 1954.

Sophokles. "Sophokles. Fragments." In *Fragments Vol 3,* translated by Alfred Alfred Chilton Pearson, fr. 837. Cambridge: Cambridge University Press, 1917.

Sourvinou-Inwood, Christiane. "Early Sanctuaries, the Eighth Century and Ritual Space: Fragments of a Discourse." In *Greek Sanctuaries: New Approaches,* edited by Nanno Marinatos and Robin Hagg, 1–17. London: Routledge, 1993.

Stafford, Emma. *Herakles*. New York: Routledge, 2012.

Stoneman, Richard. *The Ancient Oracles: Making the Gods Speak*. New Haven, CT: Yale University Press, 2011.

Tomilson, R. A. *Epidauros*. Austin: University of Texas Press, 1983.

Ustinova, Yulia. *Caves and the Ancient Greek Mind: Descending Underground in the Search for Ultimate Truth*. Oxford: Oxford University Press, 2009.

Ustura, Nilgün. *Pergamon Asklepion: Under the Light of Ancient Age Medicine*. Istanbul: Duru Basim Yayin Reklamctltk ve Gida San. Tic. Ltd. Şti, 2007.

Van den Berg, Robbert. "'Becoming Like God' According to Proclus' Interpretation of the Timaeus, The Eleusinian Mysteries, and the Chaldaean Oracles." *Bulletin of the Institute of Classical Studies* 46, no. S78 (2003): 189–202.

Versnel, Hendrik S. "Prayers and Curses." In *The Oxford Handbook of Ancient Greek Religion*. Edited by Esther Eidinow and Julia Kindt. Oxford: Oxford University Press, 2015.

Versnel, H. S. "Beyond Cursing: The Appeal to Justice in Judicial Prayers." In *Magick Hiera: Ancient Greek Magic and Religion*, edited by Faraone, Christopher A. and Dirk Obbink, 60–106. New York: Oxford University Press, 1991.

Virgil. *The Aneid*. Translated by Robert Fitzgerald. New York: Vintage Books, 1980.

Vlassopoulos, Kostas. "Religion in Communities." In *The Oxford Handbook of Ancient Greek Religion*. Edited by Esther Eidinow and Julia Kindt. Oxford: Oxford University Press, 2015.

INDEX